THE OMEGA SEED

Paolo Soleri

THE OMEGA SEED

An Eschatological Hypothesis

ANCHOR BOOKS
Anchor Press/Doubleday
Garden City, New York
1981

The Anchor edition is the first publication of *The Omega Seed*.
It is published simultaneously in hard and paper covers.
Anchor Books edition: 1981

ISBN: 0-385-15889-0
Library of Congress Catalog Card Number 80-2753
Printed in the United States of America

Contents

(media), but only pure spirit (message). Neither space, time, mass, nor energy will impede its being since they will have been consumed in the process of creating it.

REVELATION, INVENTION, CREATION

2. AN ESCHATOLOGICAL HYPOTHESIS

LOGOS AS THE OMEGA SEED

DIAGRAMS

3. SPACE AND MAN

THE URBAN EFFECT AS THE GENESIS OF THE DIVINE

MASS TRANSIT–MASS DELUSION

the fracture of the bridge channeling matter into spirit. Ultimately, it consigns consciousness to the protoconsciousness
of a computerized will.

4. RELATIVE POVERTY AND FRUGALITY

ARCOSANTI AS INTENT

ARCOMEDIA

5. SACRED SPACES

ARCHITECTURE AS INFORMATION

TALL BUILDINGS AND GIGANTISM

ECOLOGY AS THEOLOGY

6. THE TECHNOLOGICAL FRANKENSTEIN AND THE (DELPHIC) ORACLE

The "technology" which constructs organisms (biotechnology) is a complexification thrust. The technology produced by the mind of man is a simplication thrust. The second is either subservient to the first or its nemesis. Since in the absence of technology the evolution of consciousness would be subject to limitations inherent in the flesh which reflect upon the mind, the denouement rests on handling the oracular (mob-oriented) pronouncements of the technological Frankenstein in ways which "force" (with its help) the spirit from matter.

THE MEDIOCRITY OF INTOLERANCE

It is paradoxical that a certain dosage of wisdom is necessary to become wise, the paradox of youth having to go about knowing. It is misleading and cruel on the part of the "teacher" to consign the world to the student on the terms that we are all created equal, that we are all innately good, that we are all creative. The consequence of such bland innocence is mediocrity and intolerance. When experience is a dirty word, the password becomes: "Do your own thing, the sooner the better."

A BETTER QUALITY OF WRONGNESS?

Feasibility and desirability are often incompatible. A technocratic society has an irresistible penchant toward feasibility which always couples with the market feasibility, "Will it sell? We'll see to it that it does." The ethos of such society becomes dangerously mediocre, and mediocrity wears poorly with evolution. A better quality of wrongness is the passport to obsolescence and death.

NOMINAL FREEDOM, CONTEXTUAL COERCION

PREFUTURE AND ITS PERILS (OVERSIMPLIFICATION)

Preface
Paolo Soleri and Christian Faith

JOHN B. COBB, JR.

"For I reckon that the sufferings we now endure bear no comparison with the splendour, as yet unrevealed, which is in store for us. For the created universe waits with eager expectation for God's sons to be revealed. It was made the victim of frustration, not by its own choice, but because of him who made it so; yet always there was hope, because the universe itself is to be freed from the shackles of mortality and enter upon the liberty and splendour of the children of God. Up to the present, we know, the whole created universe groans in all its parts as if in the pangs of childbirth. Not only so, but even we, to whom the Spirit is given as firstfruits of the harvest to come, are groaning inwardly while we wait for God to make us his sons and set our whole body free. For we have been saved, though only in hope. Now to see is no longer to hope: why should a man endure and wait for what he already sees? But if we hope for something we do not yet see, then, in waiting for it, we show our endurance." (Romans 8:18–25, The New English Bible)

There are important differences between this ancient vision of Paul of Tarsus and the contemporary vision of Paolo Soleri. In Paul the accent falls on expectant waiting for what the supernatural God will do. In Soleri the accent falls on our responsibility to share in the creation of the Omega God. Paul hopes for the imminent coming of the anticipated consummation. Soleri sees it in the remote future. Paul's confidence rests on the unique event of Christ's resurrection and the experience of the Spirit in the Christian community. Soleri's confidence rests on the Urban Effect as it has worked thus far in evolution and can be projected into the future.

But when we view Paul and Soleri in the wider context of either Paul's time or ours, we see that what they share is far more important than what divides them. In Paul's time there was a tradition of hope for a new age, but even among most of the heirs of that tradition it had receded into the background. The practical requirements of keeping Jewish liberties, practices, and morality alive under Roman rule absorbed the attention of most of the Jewish leaders. Those who dreamed of a better day occasionally took up arms to overthrow the Roman yoke, only to be destroyed and worsen the condition of those left alive. Paul, however, speaks passionately and confidently of the coming of a world inconceivably new and glorious and finds the meaning of his life in that expectation. The newness is far too radical to be ushered in by arms, but Paul is not led by his hope to sit passively by. Instead he builds up communities which develop that style of life appropriate to the hope.

In our time also there is a tradition of hope for a new age, but even among most of the heirs of that tradition, the hope has receded into the background. Efforts to ameliorate social, political, and economic injustices as well as to maintain some measure of world order without resort to war absorb the best energies of most Jewish and Christian leaders. Those who dream of a better day occasionally resort to violent revolution, but for the most part, even when there is military success, the results are disappointing. They do not match the deeper longing of the human heart. Soleri, however, speaks passionately and confidently of the coming of a world inconceivably new and glorious and finds the meaning of his life in that expectation. The newness is far too radical to be ushered in by force of arms, but Soleri is not led by his hope to sit passively by. Instead, he works to create cities which will move humanity one stop further toward its end.

The situation has not always been like this. The Christian hope transformed the Greco-Roman civilization into an eschatologically oriented one, and down through the eighteenth century most of the leading thinkers of the West lived by hope. The eschatological vision went through many transformations, sometimes individualistic, sometimes corporate, sometimes other-worldly, sometimes this-worldly. Even in the nineteenth century it found powerful new forms in Hegel and especially in Marx. In the form given it by Marx it has profoundly affected the modern history not only of Europe, but also of Asia, Africa, and Latin America.

But while, globally, future-orientation has never been more important than it is today, within the West itself, and specifically among

Christian thinkers, it has faded. Early in the nineteenth century Friedrich Schleiermacher reformulated Christian doctrine in such a way as to detach it from future expectation. Although this did not put an end to Christian hope, it has reoriented large segments of the more enlightened Christian communities toward present conditions and possibilities. In some instances this reorientation is accompanied by explicit polemic against the future-orientation of the past.

Around the beginning of this century, reflection about evolution renewed hopeful thinking on the part of some, especially in the English-speaking world, but the experience of World Wars, of depression, and of the replacement of free institutions by totalitarian ones undercut this optimism. Further, many of the ablest thinkers were persuaded that nature and history must be viewed in quite different ways, with evolutionary categories restricted entirely to the former. Those who follow this tradition, separating the human sphere from the natural sciences, can gain no hope for the human future from the study of biology.

However, despite both disillusionment with historical progress and the increasing separation of the human sciences from the natural ones, a subordinate stream of thought has persisted, which views the human species as part of the whole of nature while stressing human distinctiveness. Its most influential spokesmen have been two Frenchmen, Henri Bergson and Teilhard de Chardin. For them, the human species stands in the flow of evolutionary process and gains its meaning from its place and role in that process. This process is not a gentle or automatic escalator to ever happier ends. On the contrary, it can be brutal and ruthless in its operation. But it does work, over eons of time, toward new forms of order which sustain new intensities of inwardness.

Soleri has entered deeply into this vision and is engaged in its theological reformulation. He shares with Teilhard the conviction that not only are we to anticipate radical novelties but also the whole process will eventually be consummated in a fulfillment of the destiny of all things. He goes far beyond Teilhard in the analysis of what this eschatological vision means for us now as we live from it.

A Christian theologian must look at Soleri's work with keenest interest. The effort of much of modern Christianity to reorient itself from a focus on the future to a focus on the present is one of appalling magnitude. Indeed, it is not clear that Christianity can survive such a shift. In the perspective of the history of religions we can distinguish the quest for salvation through recovery of a primordial wholeness, in pure immediacy, and in the newness of the future. In all traditions all three motifs may be found, but Christianity arose and swept the Mediterranean world as a future-oriented faith. If its confidence in the future declines further, it is not clear what future it itself can have. Other traditions have explored more deeply the potentialities of return and of immediacy. Quite recently there has been vigorous fresh exploration of the dimension of hope, but no image has emerged capable of renewing the future-orientation of the life of the Church as a whole. The Church remains torn between its historic future-orientation and its awareness that it offers no convincing vision of a hopeful future. Soleri's confident expectation is itself a beacon of hope to a Church that must hope but does not know how.

Further, an ultimate hope lacks power if it does not communicate a sense of urgency about present decisions. Teilhard's vision of Omega was inadequate by this standard. Although he called for zeal and work, his vision did not make clear the direction for present action in the world. It appealed too much to forces beyond individual involvement. Soleri, in contrast, offers us concrete implications of his vision. He proposes arcologies as the next step, now possible and requisite, in the progressive transformation of human existence. He even undertakes to build his "city of God."

Despite the rootedness of his vision in the Christian tradition, Soleri's rhetoric accentuates his heterodoxy. He rightly sees that not only in Christian modernism but also in Christian orthodoxy the eschatological orientation has been checked, blocked, and corrupted. It has at times been little more than a system of rewards and punishments for moral virtue and vice. The understanding of the Father-God as eternal and omnipotent has led to the view of an originally perfect creation with the human role only to disobey and destroy the perfection. Such a vision leads to ideas of restoration and of return to the primordial. In it human beings are denied any role in bringing into being something that is truly new and great.

Clearly this is a one-sided and distorted appropriation of the Christian myth for which the Kingdom of God is certainly not the same as the Garden of Eden, but Soleri is not wrong in detecting that distortion in much Christian teaching and popular piety. For him it is the distortion which gives the actual meaning of the symbol, the

Father-God, and therefore he polemicizes mercilessly against this symbol. If the "Father-God" is the primordial reality from which we have broken away, then, he shows, it is the least valuable, most chaotic state of matter, devoid of all that makes our world interesting and significant. It has its importance not in itself but in what has been generated out of it—the infant Son, still being formed. To break all tendencies to religious nostalgia and all longing to return to primordial innocence, Soleri would have us withdraw all religious devotion from the Father-God and direct ourselves instead toward his offspring, the Son-God, who will in the end be all-in-all.

Soleri's imagery accomplishes what images should accomplish: it shocks and reveals. He helps us to see meanings in traditional language that have had great efficacy even when the intention of the more careful users of the language was quite different. Of course Christian theologians have not intended by "the Father-God" what Soleri understands by it. But what he hears in these words has been heard by others too. Thomas Altizer, for example, is not unlike Soleri in calling for the death of this Father-God for the sake of the Son, and he notes a tradition of Western visionaries and thinkers who have shared this sensibility. Soleri's language will not, should not, become a new orthodoxy, but for the present it is consciousness-raising and liberating.

That the Father-God is not the last word about the universe is due to the Urban Effect. This is the principle whereby the interaction of individuals gives rise to new forms and to new levels of individuality and community. It has worked throughout the evolutionary process and it now works through us. The function of arcology is to facilitate the breakthrough to new levels of individuality and community. The Urban Effect will then go on far beyond that to transform the whole universe into the Son-God.

Soleri occasionally recognizes that the Urban Effect is God, but as I read his theology I marvel that its deity is not more fully realized. The Urban Effect is the creative and redemptive principle. It is the basis for our confidence in the future. It is that which we must serve if we are to share in the creation of the Son-God. It is "that thrust which demands from each present a next step which will disclose a more complex and integrated relationship."

I myself stand in a theological tradition in which the deity of the Urban Effect has been recognized and affirmed. I believe that Soleri's theology could be enriched and balanced by stressing this element. That this has not yet occurred probably reflects his sense of deity as realized perfection rather than as creative and redemptive activity. That is, what he hears in the word God is conditioned more by the Greek than in the Hebrew sensibility, although his processive vision in general is more compatible with Hebrew ways of thinking. My major recommendation to Soleri in this paper is that he acknowledge that tradition which defines one's "God" as that in which one places one's ultimate trust and then recognizes that for him it is the Urban Effect that is God.

Others have named the Urban Effect in different ways. Henry Nelson Wieman named it the creative event, creative interchange, and, as I prefer, creative transformation. He pointed out that any vision, such as Soleri's, of where this process will lead is itself a product of the process at that point. We cannot be sure that the vision is accurate. In fact we can assume that as the process continues, our finest visions will be superseded by others. Hence to have our devotion shaped by particular visions of the future is idolatrous in the sense that it places ultimate weight on what can only have provisional truth and worth. What can be fully trusted, and therefore what is properly God, is the process that again and again produces new visions, visions that, precisely because the process is genuinely creative, cannot be foreseen before they arise.

To say this is not to disparage Soleri's vision of the spiritualization of all matter through which even time and space will be overcome and all will be copresent. On the contrary, it is to affirm this vision as an authentic product of creative transformation or the Urban Effect. But it is to say, as Soleri will surely agree, that the future is anticipated today only dimly, and that as time goes by new visions will replace the best that we can manage now.

To avoid the impression that this is merely a verbal suggestion, an illustration of the possible danger of Soleri's rhetoric is in order. In his language about the ultimate fulfillment Soleri suggests that finally matter, the physical world, space and time, will be wholly transcended into pure spirit. In this final resurrection all that ever has been will be everlastingly copresent. Soleri has thus renewed in the context of modern cosmology a vision not uncommon in the history of religions. The connection of finitude and physicality, time, and space has often been recognized, and fulfillment is envisioned as the infinity of pure Spirit. Often this leads to a depreciation of the physical sphere, which is expressed either in asceticism or in license.

Soleri guards against this depreciation by avoiding a dualism of matter and spirit. What he sees is matter becoming spirit. Matter is, therefore, not to be cast aside, but spiritualized. And even this is seen not as our present existential experience but as an ultimate and distant goal. Nevertheless, the ideal of pure spirit can inspire, and has often inspired, a repressive attitude toward the autonomous demands of the body and an indifference toward the physical environment.

A different vision of consummation would be one in which finitude and bodiliness were not transcended. The ideal would be of a psychophysical wholeness centering in Spirit in which every aspect was fulfilled in a way that supported all the others. Such individual fulfillment would be in a community not only of other human beings but also of the multitude of living forms in which the fulfillment of each supported the fulfillment of all the others.

Such a vision would have different consequences for us here and now. First, we would attend to our own bodies and to all aspects of the psychic life, seeking to develop patterns of mutual fulfillment among their too often conflicting demands. Second, we would seek to maintain the complex variety of living forms as inherently valuable.

Of these the second deserves elaboration as a challenge to some aspects of Soleri's thought. By juxtaposing the End of pure Spirit to the beginning of mere matter, Soleri places our present world in between, in the early process of the spiritualization of matter. The various life forms, including our own, have meaning and worth as stages in the process, but they are not to be preserved; they are to be transformed and transcended. Conservationism is, for Soleri, a sentimental obstacle to the ruthless demands of transformation. The planet earth that has borne us forward thus far is not finally to be conserved but to be used as a launching pad for the spiritualization of the universe. In this scenario the consistent meaning of Soleri's vision of consummation in pure spirit becomes clear.

I confess that this feature of Soleri's thought frightens me. What if, after all, the complete spiritualization of matter is not the End of the Urban Effect. What if, instead, alongside this upward and miniaturizing movement there is the entropic decay of order in an ever-expanding physical universe. What if the true End is a harmonious interconnection of all levels of order on this planet guided by a strengthened and developed Spirit that is tender and reverent toward the physical world. In that case the steps that we might take toward the End of spiritualization of the entire universe might irreparably and fruitlessly damage the Earth-home where we have our one chance of accomplishing our true End. I do not know, and I do not believe that anyone knows.

My point in these comments is not to assert that Soleri's vision is false and the one I have juxtaposed to it, true. Indeed, I believe that the inadequacy of both is already visible in their juxtaposition and that they can and should be transcended. This is the work of the Urban Effect. My point is, instead, that Soleri does derive from the specific form of his eschatological vision implications for present policy that, if his vision is faulty, may be misguided. He is encouraged to do this by his deification of the End and his failure to attend equally to the deity of the Urban Effect. If he fully recognized the Urban Effect as the present and living God, the God he actually serves, he could adopt a more tentative attitude toward his own eschatological vision and recognize more clearly the dangers of drawing practical conclusions from it.

If that meant that Soleri's theology would not guide action today, it would be a poor recommendation. But it does not mean that. To attend to the Urban Effect and to serve it gives guidance enough. For example, the theological rationale for arcology flows from the understanding of the Urban Effect and from trust in its further working beyond our present capacity to foresee. Arcology fits both into Soleri's vision of the spiritualization of all matter and into the alternative vision of a strengthened and developed Spirit guiding a harmonious interaction of all levels of being.

Soleri recognizes the dangers of sacrificing the present for the sake of the future, but his theology nevertheless calls for this. This sacrificing the present is a healthy and needed antidote to preoccupation with instant gratification. Further, it is clear that in fact there is much immediacy of enjoyment among those who accept the harsh disciplines of living and working at Arcosanti. A holy spirit pervades the community.

This suggests that although one does not give oneself in trust to the Urban Effect in order to gain enjoyment, the resultant transformation of the self in a new community is immediately rewarding. The old adage still applies—that only those who are ready to lose their lives find them. To cling to the security of what one is and has and to seek to satisfy the desires that express that stage and mode of being leads to stagnation and decay. Life and vigor come from the unforeseen novelty achieved by the Urban Effect. Thus the present and active deity gives present and immediate joy to those who trust it.

There is another reason, I think, for stressing the Urban Effect rather than the Son-God as the primary mode of deity. Soleri's vision like that of Teilhard assumes that the human species will be the bearer of the next evolutionary advance and that it will be through this advance that the universe will move forward toward its consummation. That may be. But we are keenly aware that even now, at this comparatively low stage of development, the human species has achieved the means of its own destruction. It seems that evolutionary progress increases the risk of self-destruction. There have been dead ends and blind alleys in evolutionary development in the past; so there seems to be no assurance that the human species will not be another. Furthermore, the self-destruction of the human species could carry with it the destruction of much of the biosphere.

Teilhard and Soleri have not, of course, been ignorant of these dangers. But they have been persuaded that a convincing vision of future fulfillment can inspire the kind of activity today that will avoid the ultimate catastrophe and carry the human species through this crisis. Certainly there is little doubt that the loss of future which marks so much of our Western culture today unnerves many for the disciplines apart from which the crisis cannot be survived. A positive and hopeful vision of the End may indeed save us from self-destruction.

Nevertheless, we are not justified by such a vision in failing to consider the risk thematically. The possible End may never be reached. We can count on the Urban Effect to move us toward that End, but we cannot assume that the increasing freedom and complexity to which the Urban Effect gives rise will not be used destructively. An adequate theology must nerve us to support and serve the Urban Effect even without the assurance that the process of complexifica tion and miniaturization taking place through human activity will lead to the consummation. We are engaged in a great adventure whose outcome is uncertain. Its failure would not mean the final failure of the Urban Effect; for as a principle it does not depend on this one planet. But it would mean that the human venture had failed.

The possibility of failure in no way minimizes the importance of the envisioning of a hopeful outcome. On the contrary, the dangerous loss of future that afflicts us in the West today is not primarily a loss of certainty that the future will be a consummation. More fundamentally it is a loss of the sense that any happy outcome is possible, that the future *could* be such as to be a source of worthwhileness in the present. If fundamental fulfillment is possible, yet threatened, we are called to act with even greater urgency than if only the timing of the End is affected by our efforts.

The possibility of failure does mean that our ultimate faith cannot be in the successful outcome. Our ultimate faith must be in the process that alone can lead to the successful outcome. We must live today not only from the future vision but from the present rewards of participating in the ongoing transformation that is the Urban Effect. We need the vision of the outcome to nerve us to the subordination of our present desires to transformation by the Urban Effect. But we cannot live from the future alone except as we find in doing so a present meaning and rewarding newness. The eschatological orientation is the basis for present meaning, and the experience of that meaning is required to sustain the eschatological orientation. This polarity is clearly present in Soleri and his association, though it is inadequately developed in his theology.

The achievement of a better balance between future and present raises another question: the relation of Soleri's theology to Buddhism. At one level he is quite correct to polemicize against nirvana. There is a profound antithesis between Soleri's orientation to a final consummation and the Buddhist quest for emptiness. A Buddhist teacher will often begin by ridiculing the remnants of eschatological thinking, arguing that any future will be only another Now and therefore unable to give meaning to the present. The present Now is as good a candidate as any for the fulfilled Now. Hence, the Buddhist concludes, only when we realize this and disengage ourselves wholly from the future orientation can we begin to progress toward the emptiness that is the only true fullness.

Nevertheless, the initial antithesis between Soleri's eschatological vision and the Buddhist stress upon pure presence may not be the last word. There are remarkable affinities in Soleri's vision of the resurrectional state and the Mahayanist doctrine of true emptiness or Buddhahood. If so, then one might see the Buddhist movement toward Buddhahood as another avenue toward the final resurrection that Soleri foresees as the consummation of all things.

Furthermore, although the movement toward enlightenment seems to lead first away from involvement in history and hope for future fulfillment, the Buddha or Enlightened One seems to be an instance of the work of the Urban Effect and to be peculiarly contributive to its further working. Perhaps we need a more pluralistic vision in which we can trace the working of the Urban Effect through the complexity of the many great Ways of humanity even when these ways do not acknowledge it as we do.

Although Soleri polemicizes against the concern to return to or preserve the past, he is not unaware of the claim of all things past as well as present somehow to participate in salvation. He writes: "And none of it, not even the most limited and irrelevant instance, will have been for naught." Yet this concern for inclusiveness does not characterize his sense of the process that leads to the outcome. In that process his awareness of the need for tough-mindedness in sacrificing the lesser for the sake of the greater prevails.

I suggest that reflection on the way the Urban Effect works could infuse our participation in the process with more of the tenderness that is manifested in the final End. For example, in the encounter of two minds which have generated opposing ideas, the Urban Effect does not manifest itself in the sheer victory of one over the other. On the contrary, it appears in the emergence of ideas that are different from those which either party brought to the encounter. But the new ideas are not simply different from those brought by the two participants, so as to displace them. No, the function of the Urban Effect is to generate novel ideas of such a sort that the preexisting ideas are retained but relativized and included in a larger, more adequate whole. The rise of the new is not the abolition of the old, but its transformation and inclusion.

Of course, this is a one-sided view. There are times when the old is simply destroyed, and perhaps this must be, yet it is not mere sentimentality to weep for the permanent loss of some mode of thought or form of life. It would have been better if that too could have been preserved in the larger whole so as to contribute its uniqueness to the complexity and richness of the whole.

Soleri presents the Urban Effect as a fact descriptive of what happens. This is surely not wrong. But it is an astounding fact, so astounding that a great deal of thought has been engaged in the effort to deny or minimize it. And it appears in Soleri's own vision almost magically. There are primordially the myriad of particles, mindless and inert. What we expect from their interaction would be "statistical and fatal." There is more. They interact in "ways which are organic or living." This fact is named the Urban Effect. How can it be? How can there be a "thrust which demands from each present a next step," if there are only material particles?

To this question Alfred North Whitehead has given more thought than has Soleri. He calls this thrust the Platonic Eros. It is a lure by which what is not yet is made relevant to what is. Equally primordial with the myriad of particles is the cosmic longing to realize possibilities that are not absent from these particles as such. This requires the ordering of these possibilities so as to serve as lures for all the conditions of actuality. These lures may be resisted by the particles, but gradually they draw the particles into new forms of order through which they are actualized. Thus even matter is not mere matter; for it, too, in some rudimentary way can respond to relevant aspects of what is not yet. As matter responds to the rudimentary possibilities relevant for it, life appears, with its vastly greater capacity for response to a wider range of possibilities. In short, the Urban Effect as sheer phenomenon is the expression of the power of the not-yet to energize what-is. That power is God.

There may be some irony in the fact that as a Christian theologian I urge Soleri to accentuate the deity of the Urban Effect over against the radically eschatological deity of which he more often speaks. I do not do so in order to bring his thought more in line with historical Christianity. A strong case can be made that Christianity is most true to itself when it is most fully eschatological. Wolfhart Pannenberg, probably the leading systematic theologian in the Protestant world, makes that case today. But he does so on the basis of the resurrection of Jesus as the proleptic occurrence of the End through which the truth of the End is established. Soleri does not want to argue from such a specific historical event. Instead he argues from the Urban Effect. But in that case it is the Urban Effect and not the resurrection in the last day in which we can put our confidence. For the resurrection we can hope and work.

Although this refocusing of theological attention may deepen the gulf between Soleri and traditional Christian faith in one way, it can bridge it in other ways. Soleri does not seem to appreciate the extent to which our human relation to the Urban Effect resembles historic Christian thinking about our relation to God. Soleri sometimes talks about our role as creators of the Son-God. That is not false. But he also recognizes that as we work to create the Son-God we are free instruments of the Urban Effect. Our freedom and our capacity to work are all received from the Urban Effect. Our work is effective when it makes possible the creative novelty of the Urban Effect which we cannot control or direct. When we serve the Urban Effect it works through us to create the Son-God. Only in such service is perfect freedom.

Christianity has long been torn between the vision of a new heaven and earth, on the one side, and, on the other, salvation for some in the midst of an unredeemed world. Clearly Jesus' proclamation of the coming Kingdom belongs to the former, but as time passed, and the world went on, unredeemed, the emphasis shifted to individuals and to communities. A derivative tension was felt keenly in the sixties, when Church leadership, committed to structural change, found itself out of touch with the pietistic majority among the laity. Other groups in our society exaggerated this split, some seeking an instant reform of social structures, and others dropping out of society altogether.

Throughout his writings, but especially in his critique of the Findhorn community, Soleri makes clear that his eye is set on inclusive transformation rather than on personal salvation now. But he conceives this in a way that radically transcends the recent debate and renews the forms of the early Church. He offers little more comfort to social idealists and activists than to pietists; for the End on which his eyes are fastened is so remote, so transcendent of any now possible social arrangements, that focusing upon it withdraws energies as much from the public issues of our time as from the quest of personal salvation. It leads to the call for a new community of dedicated believers not unlike the Findhorn community itself. Thus Soleri calls in the end for a new Church and a new religious order.

In the perspective of the past two centuries it is surprising that one at the cutting edge of our civilization should call for a new religious order. Yet in the larger scope of history it appears fitting and proper.

Special vocations of this sort seem largely pointless when there is no convincing vision of excellence that judges and relativizes the patterns of worldly effectiveness and success. But when, as with Soleri, such a vision is powerfully present and requires actions not rewarded by society in general, then the call must go out for those who share the vision to separate themselves from the world's standards and live by different norms. When these norms require common discipline and shared action, they require new communities in which believers can support one another. Perhaps as the bankruptcy of the conventional affluent style of life grows yearly more apparent, the call will be heard and will touch the depths of spirit which give rise to dedication. If so, the order will grow. In a world hungry for convincing faith, such an order may indeed light the way forward.

1

Religion
as
Simulation

Synopsis: Man's inquietude and sense of loss resulting from his fragmented self prompts the invention of divinity, whole, integral, and loving. This invented vessel is a self-fulfilling prophecy, the miracle of evolution emerging from its preembryonic stages into a willful thrust. The divine is, therefore, practically all in the future and we, life, are responsible for its creation. The divine simulation is, or ought to be, our blueprint for creation.

I accept the idea of God and propose it as the only acceptable model for a significant reality. Because of its inclusiveness, it is a highly improbable model, an improbability which life inevitably pursues in the sense that God is a hypothesis life cannot do without. It is a hypothesis not because man does not know better, but because as yet it is only a hypothesis, a hypothesis that is in the process of implementing fragments of itself.

FOR GOD'S SAKE

Once upon a time, the parthenogenetic mother cell told the parthenogenetic daughter cell of frightful "sex demons" in *times past* who would battle two by two and from the violent mating produce myriads of demon offspring.

Once upon a time, the cold-blooded lizard told the egg-hatched baby about magic-endowed creatures of *times past* whose blood ran warm and kept them alive and active even in the ice-cold hell of glaciations.

Once upon a time, the egg-laying creature of water, land, and air told its progeny of industrious divine creatures during *times past* within whom offspring would develop and grow sheltered in a warm sea of care and attention until the trauma of birth.

Once upon a time, the mammal told the simian baby of naked, erect semigods who in *times past* fabricated fantastic toys and magic machines.

Once upon a time, Homo Faber told his children of an incredible God who in *times past* (Genesis Time) created the cell, the lizard, the bird, the simian, and man. The mineral cosmos, the vegetal cosmos, the animal cosmos, and the mind of man, all God-worshippers working and slaving away at survival, now and then hosting imperfect genes which generated peculiar offspring who would inch closer to the image of their future God, fulfilling reality, by that new inch. All of them—cell, lizard, bird, ape, man, transman—needed to see in the past *that which would come from themselves at some time in the future* and to whom or into whom they could return one day by good deeds and good thoughts.

Early man saw at the origin what in fact could be an achievement at the end: God. An impressive *tour de force* of the mind yielded a total simulation of the mass-energy universe transforming itself into God. This simulation was constructed in reverse putting first what is last perhaps because God-at-the-end is too great a presumption to be harbored in the groping mind of man: but it is also a powerful, if purely potential, catalyst for man to sustain himself with. The theologian mistakenly plans his future through the discovery of his ancestry. He saw and sees as past what he wants for the future; he has explained and partially documented evolution by inventing the kingdom of God and its deployment.

God was not created by humanity joining in mass protest against the lack of divinity. Holy men and prophets, the shaman and the lunatic invented or prophesied the appearance of a transbeing in possession of demonic powers. A structure-form of divinity was designed by those men: the shell of a simulation of what amounted to a hypothesis. The performing that such a shell distilled from man fills history. *We are and forever will be under the spell and the constraints of an idea-form that we try desperately to fill with an adequate, functioning performance.* Not only is the function following the form, but the function constantly falls short of the form which originated it. To maintain that a truly transhuman power guides man, who was the cause for the invention of the form (God), is only to confirm that the shape of the universe of man at that given moment demanded the invention of a form to be the receptacle of events to come. The invention was the brainchild of a few men.

THE OMEGA GOD (GOD AS HYPOTHESIS)

If *religion is the simulation of evolution,* then, as all simulation is structural, it is faulty, skeletal, naïve, extravagant, short-sighted, vain, etc. It is nevertheless one of the boldest and most anticipatory projects ever to come out of the mind of man. It is instrumental, not in discovering our origins, but in creating the future. It is a future-oriented searching and planning that will be joined by science once science has uncovered the past. One could say that religion works in the future and science in the past or, better, the subject matter of religion is the future and the subject matter of science is the past.

From its inception, the evolutionary Tatonnement established the methodology of survival and development: complexity-duration-centration-interiorization; and man is the most willful product of the methodology. Since man was compelled by the onrush of his mind to fabricate a coherent structure out of the phenomenology within and beyond his grasp, he invented a center of the phenomenon, a *center* of responsibility and power: God. Man placed God at the outset and worshipped Him. The critical point is not so much the placing of God at the origin or at the end, but rather the need for such a mooring. If the mooring begins to fade, the mind begins to agonize on the concreteness of its own existence and of its aim.

The God-point of Western theology—I will call it the Alpha God[1] —is a portentous simulation of future reality which, if ever implemented, would become what I call the Omega God. For this Omega God, life is a pain-filled gathering of events with God as the extreme hypothesis of such gathering, fully conscious, fully achieved. By a backstage switch, Plato's shadows on the cavern walls become the radiant projection of one's being, all life's being, against the warp of the space-time outer membrane. The radiance of the spirit emerges from the transcomplex mass-energy bundles of life's quest. In Plato's provinces of reality, the shadows were constructed by man's consciousness and made to be what the real was; in the simulation model, the shadow becoming radiance measures the amount of godliness achieved by life moving on and growing.

Behind and below life is only the god of the statistical universe,

[1] In the introductory paper, "The Two Suns," written after "The Omega God," "The Technological Frankenstein," "The Theology of the Sun," and "The Sacred Spaces," I have broken down the Alpha God into a series of father-son Gods. In that frame, the Alpha God of this paper has become the Gamma God when considered in His aspect of simulation, and is preceded by the Alpha God of mass-energy and the Beta God of the organic world. Omega God has been further defined as Omega God itself and Omega God the immanent particle of it.

split into every granule of matter, fully segregated and moving in logical but blind fury on the space-time path of physical transformism. This incompleteness has its resolution forward, in things to come. It is not the consequence of a fall from past perfections. It is a partial illumination originating from the past and lighting the path into the future. It does not, as in Plato's cavern, originate from prehistorical time and create the shadow semblances of our being, at fault in their stride.

In the evolutionary theology, where God is a pursued hypothesis, partially, immanently present, two of the momentous elements are the conceptual concreteness and the power of doing. The concept of God is accepted, not in the ambiguity of a given Alpha God, but in the clearly problematic possibility of a pursued God. Things do not get done because the wrath of god is suspended above the doer who then bends to the will of an incorruptible God, but rather because the doer has consciously or unconsciously decided that a certain behavior would make possible the advent of a future god. The idea of the Alpha God suffering with and within man can be maintained only through dialectical debate and always leaves a bitter aftertaste. Only a God suffering his own problems within the problematics of life is capable of full compassion. The becoming Omega God is such a God.

Christ, the Son of God as represented by the scriptures, seems an attempt toward making God suffer His own genesis. In this light, Christ is a synopsis of the total theological simulations, miraculously making himself concrete through sufferance. Sainthood could be, then, a specific, concrete, personified synopsis of evolution, the making of the Omega God, or at least that part of it which is trying to wrench itself away from the dialectics of good and evil. Parallel and complementary to this is the esthetic process giving form to an achieved fragment of godliness (see page 41, "The Esthetic as the Immanence of God").

If the structure, the idea God, is preestablished (simulated), then the performance of reality is polarized in the force field of good and evil. Therefore, either within the triangle-structured environment or within the intangible, the idea of God is the structure (form) which defines the performance (function). Nowhere is it more evident than here that performance (function) follows structure (form), and that life is future-oriented. Even with the burdensome prospect of a future too loaded with responsibility, the mind does not totally forfeit that responsibility. By putting perfection at the origin, the scope of such responsibility is limited and the demands are defined in terms of an option between salvation and damnation; but then such an option is perfunctory anyway since salvation and damnation do not alter the balance of preexistent perfection, the Alpha God.

The Christo-Genesis of Pierre Teilhard de Chardin with its convergence at the Omega point is the closest approximation of the Omega God. It is the reverse of the Alpha God, which I see as a simulation of the Omega God on a reverse time run. By such deception, a guidance system is set for the working of the mind from the beginning of consciousness, probably because consciousness cannot operate randomly as the genetic matrix seems to be able to do with survival as its aim.

Thus, from the beginning of consciousness, the existing god of chance, the statistical god, the entropic god, the proto-Alpha God, could in the manner of simulation or anticipation be challenged by the hypothesis of a willful, compassionate god, and, consequently, cosmogenesis could move in successive steps from the approximation of simulation into concreteness, concrete sufferance, and the synopsis of sainthood on one side and, on the other, into fragments of the hypothetical Omega God.

The servomechanisms for this emergence have been biological or, rarely, parabiological structures operating within associations of individuals, nests, colonies, symbiotic cooperatives, etc. Man introduces extrabiological servomechanisms. He can be defined as a creative exomutant. The exomutant man is any person active in performing a task by the use of an implement or machine. He, in close synchrony with such instruments, is an ephemeralizing force, forcing his own will or the will of the group upon extant nature. Examples of exomutant man are the mechanic, the plumber, the linotypist, the cameraman, the teacher, the doctor. They are human mutant combinations of the inner man and his genetic matrix with the outer instruments he uses for his work. If it were not for the primitivism of such exoinstruments, there would not be a line of demarcation between the inner and "instrumented" man. The hope of the species, godliness, resides in refinement of the extrabiological servosystem. (The computer is theoretically at the demarcation line.) Such integration is the interiorization of the cosmos, an interiorization pushed to the outer membrane of existence, once the Omega God is realized.

Homo Faber is a raw model, then, of the Omega God; not a fallen angel searching for sainthood and divesting himself, conditio sine qua non, of earthly servomechanisms. The "plumbing" of life is the harbinger of Omega God, not the enemy of Alpha God. The god of the scriptures is a simulation of the future, a skeletal form to be filled by performance, marker of the path peculiar to the development of the human species.

In His misplacement at the beginning of time, God offered man access to sin and also to forgiveness; but man failed, in his fatal preoccupation with the past, to put enough urgency into the task of closing the immense gap between the present and the achievable aim. This aim is immensely distant in the folds of time, immensely strange, because despite its being of man's making, it is not ever given him to contemplate, and thus it cannot ever be made in any image he could predefine. Therefore, very early in time, man's imagination, prompted by anguish, filled this unbearable void with the Alpha God, the rewarder and punisher, the Father. It is one thing to live with oneself made in the image of God, and another to live with oneself creating a God in one's image, an image that is strange and foreign, beyond anything the "I" might ever conceive presently on its own.

To give man a foothold into the Kingdom of God is to comfort him and make him content as a future-maker. Such a Kingdom is nonetheless, at present, a most terrifying and dreadful promise of the time-space void.

In a way, our destiny is like the destiny of an assembly-line worker condemned to make a bolt, condemned to know nothing more than that what he makes is no part of any mechanism he knows of. He has only the anguished feeling that a monster is developing from his bolt-making, an immensely strange and frightful robot-god beyond his grasp and, more distressing, beyond his desire. This potential God, inherently informed and monstrous by definition, utterly does away with anything familiar, with anything cherished like the idol, the token, the icon, or the Alpha God might be cherished. The Alpha God of theology might leave us a methodology to be observed so as to move inch by inch along the evolutionary development, a methodological imperative overseeing the dialectics of opposites and the yin-yang of existential processes.

The invention of God and His misplacement at the beginning was the most far-reaching invention of the mind of man. Now that God has been invented, He has to be created. The structure must inspire performance. Holiness must construct itself into life.

The only holiness of protohistory (protolife-evolution) is the holiness intrinsic in Something, the physical universe, as opposed to Nothing, the thought of the Absence of Anything. But Something cannot negate Everything. The most it can negate is Everything but itself, that is to say, the Something which this itself is. The existence of this Something is the denial of nonexistence: if Something is, Nothingness is not. Consequently, if existence is a more conceivable alternative to nonexistence, the existence is God-like, inasmuch as it makes the hypothesis of God possible. This hypothesis per se might well be the original cause of life-consciousness.

Such a possible God is always in the future, never in the past, as the past has produced only that which had the possibility of becoming God up to that moment. If even one particle of the physical whole remains untouched by this process of becoming God, that is to say, is not made compassionate, God remains cheated by the statistical non-God, and the implosion into the Omega God is partial, the transfiguration faulty, and, as further hypothesis, the explosion of the spirit into the "next" universe impossible.

Through this future-oriented theology, the lost past becomes a possible future. The measure of failure, the fall and its consequences, becomes a measure of potential achievement. We, therefore, as Adams and Eves, were, are, and will be falling short, not of measuring up to our maker, but of what we will eventually be, given enough time and wisdom. The simple faith of the believer in reentry into the Kingdom of God ranges from nostalgia for paradise past to trust in eventual fulfillment. Christ, like a rough anticipation of God, is not too different from a child's drawing which represents in obscure fantasy a reality far less defined but far more fearsome.

Inasmuch as the theological structure is a simulation, the subject of which is God, such a structure has to be all-encompassing and all-inclusive. If not, the God-point would not be part of it and the premises of Inclusiveness would not be satisfied. The total simulation of evolution by religion is the conceptual transformation of the physical

world into the transphysical world, into duration conceived as the
entelechy of physical time. The causa prima, then, is like a vector
emerging into the future, becoming the causa ultima by the reordering of the whole of things, making mass-energy into the absolute of
the spirit. This God-point at the end of time is the most primeval and
compelling directional thrust for conscious life.

If all religions are seen as theological simulations, not realities, but
not metaphors either, then by this total theological simulation the
physical world is finally, if still only hypothetically, liberated into the
spiritual world where the physical limits are nullified.

The possibility then is of a physical contraction, a consumption
through infinite complexity: a spirit-mass-point and, therefore, a
condition of instant, total information-knowledge-wisdom-love, the
whole of the mass-energy world consuming itself into the God-point
of omnipotence, omniscience, omni-inclusiveness. There, at mass-
zero and energy-equals-spirit is the contentedly achieved, self-same
God-point. (Or, as a further hypothesis, the preconditioned "Big
Bang" birth of a new universe.) Godliness is achieved in toto if and
when the cosmos in toto has rid itself of the constraints of mass-
energy time and space.[2]

If it is pure dementia to think that the whole cosmos might collapse itself into a God-point-Son, it is of the same degree of dementia
to assume that the whole of creation came about from the will of a
God-point-Father. Greater conference can be found in a process
which leads to synthesis than in a process which establishes synthesis
at the origin and then tries to explain why such union was broken or
why it had to give forth something outside of its own plenitude. This
sheds new light on the mystery of Good and Evil, which in the presence of the total grace of the watching-over Alpha God is necessarily
tagged as a cruelty congenital to life and its sufferance. One can almost say that while the first dementia is an improbable hypothesis,
the other is desperate if not absurd.

The wisdom of the theological hypothesis as compared to the evolutionary one might be in the desire of the living to fall back on a
myth as a guarantor of redemption, a goal more pursuable than pure
creation. It is easier to go back home than to have to be constantly
building a new one. Furthermore, human failings and shortcomings
do not detract from the godliness and incorruptibility of an Alpha

2 The resurrectional milieu.

God, a God-Father. Whereas, for an Omega God, the failures of each of us are the failures of godliness; it is a god-deprived universe for which one and all are responsible, not just for individual salvation. Consequently, the different weight of one's own responsibility: All of us, all of life, are more responsible to a hypothetical god of our own making than to a god which is there already and anyhow. For the Omega God, the cosmogony that counts is that our salvation coincides with the creation of the Omega God (not its invention, since that has been done, that is to say, simulated).

The unresolved dilemma of the existence of evil then has an explanation, if not yet a resolution. The embarrassment of the Alpha God's witness to evil is necessary inasmuch as the Alpha God is only a simulation of the totally compassionate, future, and possible Omega God. Instead, for the Omega God, evil exists in the measure in which God is incomplete. Evil withers away by the ever larger presence of the self-creating God.

Religion can then be seen as the simulation of a possible reality which would occur if the process of sensitization going on now on the earth and elsewhere would not cease but would, on the contrary, develop exponentially, calling into cause the whole of the physical universe, transforming its bleak emptiness and the isolation of its sensitized species, man included, into the radiance of the Omega God. If, in this cosmogony, there is nothing after death to go back to (if Alpha God is the simulation of Omega God), there is instead the lifelong exhilaration of knowing that within the self is nurtured an ever-so-dim particle of a most improbable but most willed conscience of the universe. The kingdom-come expectant is the process of the latent spirit of the cosmos imploding into the Omega God. It is as if by the formidable pressure of complexity-miniaturization developing in the universe, the spirit is exuded by the mass-energy stuff of the pristine cosmos.

The piousness and hypocrisy of the devotee, present more or less in the self-righteous true-believer, is shaken by the nature of the Omega God. There is no longer the reward or the punishment factor to fall back on. Behind is the atomistic beat of fate; beyond is the mystery of the uncreated, the potential sacredness of pure spirit. In between is the unrolling of the drama of life, sanguine and radiant, promising and stern, beautiful and cruel, rigorous and compassionate, living and evolving.

There is the conscious confrontation between the immanent anguish of life within enveloping and overpowering nonlife and the eventual transfiguration or metamorphosis of such nonlife into spirit. Anchorage for such confrontation and instrumental to such metamorphosis are the implosions of mass-energy into servomechanisms which heighten the level of consciousness and consequently, in chain reaction, heighten the intensity of anguish because more knowledge means more consciousness. *Thus, the power and relevance of a parallel and continuous genesis which I define as esthetogenesis, capable of supporting the fractional immanence of God, the otherwise desperate struggle of life seeking godliness.*

ALPHA GOD OR EROS

The witch doctor and the theological mind not only see in the past what could be in the future, but also by an even further and somewhat balancing bouleversement, see in the future what has been in the past: the final catastrophe, the apocalypse, the nemesis, the flat sea of entropy, the post-catastrophic condition of the undifferentiated, the oneness peculiar to atomistic identity, the tranquility and plenitude of durational naught. Nirvana?

What of the priest-confessor or the psychiatrist-healer if past and future are interchanged? How much of the Freudian reality would resist, without transformation, the breaking through of the Adam and Eve threshold and the backward journey to the inception of life where not Eros but naught, the dullest of all gods, would sit? Would Eros remain such a totally overriding force in the fate of man? For the Freudian as much as for the theologian, a future-oriented revelation would be traumatically pregnant. (It could not be a true revelation, since revelation presupposes the existence of the revealed.)

Could there be something true in the demolition of the Freudian or pseudo-Freudian crucifixion of man to his genitals by the pure and simple mention of the infinite wisdom of nature breaking away from parthenogenesis into heterosexuality for the sake of infinitely possible permutation (complexification) and the consequent evolution and differentiation of information-knowledge-transfiguration?

The gate opening on all possible combinations of parental genes is a far more powerful determinant of life's destiny than the desperate nostalgia for the loss of oneness in the womb, the hypothetical nirvana still patiently waiting for man's return.

The limits of the Freudian universe might not be so much in the inclination to subsume all of the subconscious under the longing for the past union in Eros, but rather in the hidden consequence of the substitution of the Alpha God with Eros. In the simulation framework, such switch limits the infiniteness of a future whose mirror image is the Alpha God, with the far reduced infiniteness of a future whose mirror image is Eros. In other words, the predictive power of Alpha God is decreased when it gives way to the predictive power of Eros, a weaker prophecy of oneness.

Perhaps the psychological balancing act, which leads to existential concreteness and keeps despair at bay, finds it necessary to load the arm projecting into the future with the reciprocal load of the arm projecting into the past. Therefore, the greater the weight promised by the first (future), the greater the weight of the gifts that the past must deliver. Unless we realize our mistake and reconstruct such a double vision into one, we risk fatal confusion. Each additional paradise lost, seen through the mirror interposed between our forecasting and our efforts, gives us the illusion that that which we seek in the future has already been attained by a holier predisposition. The more attractive this lost paradise becomes, the more discouraging will be the assessment of our existential fate. It might not be absurd to imagine the paradox of an intelligence pervading the cosmos and falling into greater and greater wells of desperation the closer it gets to the realization of its own zenith because its imagination constructs ever more glorious pasts, unconscious simulations of its own possible future.

What is the efficacy of the religious quest if it is going to remain past-oriented? What is its usefulness if it is going to turn around and point a conscious and systematic effort toward the concretization of the future? In the first case, new myths will be invented and new religions will appear, historical events will be transformed into supernatural mythical structures. In the second case, such historical events will not be reconstructed as supernatural facts of time past, reverberating forever into the present, but they will instead be taken as premonitions and premature attempts at transrational modes which life could and ought to create in time.

In the first instance, the supernatural structures will be kept together by faith, wishfulness, fear, naïveté, and a degree of fraudulence (the priest castes). In the second case, the premonitions of transrational modes (which could be conceived as limited and possibly inappropriate warps for the threading of life into spirit) will prod and sustain men in their creational effort.

The contemplation-adoration of the Alpha God would become the pursuit of the Omega God. The idolization of the Alpha God would become commitment to the threading of the future through conceptual godliness reaching for a possible Omega God. The former demands the rediscovery of the innocence of an illusory, pristine wholeness, the child of Alpha God. The latter demands an effort of unfathomable dimension, the creation of the Omega God.

If the historical theology is transformed into the simulation of possible options, then the dictum "what God giveth God taketh away" translates into "God cometh if Life maketh." No longer can man be, God willing; but God will be, man willing.

With this presumption, the burden of life is immensely enlarged, the oneness at the dawn of the universe remains the only granted oneness, but an awesomely dreary and dull one. On the other hand, the oneness of the Omega God is only a feeble hypothesis, as feeble as the want for it which is in each living thing and the operative transformation-transfiguration such want has made around itself (civilization and culture as the latest results). It is definitely not the oneness of myth, of Eros, of theology. It is transmythical, transerotic, transtheological, because it belongs to and is that which has never been and is not, but is only that which could be, ought to be.

The analytical process, which is so much a part of man's life, goes on inasmuch as a differentiation-specification-genesis-synthesis is the operative norm of durational processes. The perfecting analysis in which life is engaged is focused on a new synthesis and can be seen pessimistically (eros-theologically) as a breaking down of divine oneness, the Alpha God, or, optimistically, as creational and transfigurative.

Karma is seen then not as a stepping-stone away from nirvana, but as a stepping-stone toward the Omega God. Nirvana is the raw material, originally homogeneous and ruled by the physical laws, physical law itself; the Omega God is the world resulting from the genesis of spirit evolving through successive stages from the use, consumption, transformation, and esthetogenesis of nirvana. Nirvana is seen not as paradise lost, a past plenitude, but as a protoparadise, the most archetypical of all, the one from which we must move as far as we can as it is the negation, as much negation as can be, of the Omega God.

THE ALPHA GOD	THE OMEGA GOD
THE PARADOXICAL[3] GOD	THE HYPOTHETICAL[4] GOD
OF THEOLOGY	OF ESTHETOGENESIS
Simulated	Suffered
Just	Tragic
Synthetic	Organic
Paternalistic	Existential
Directive	Transfigurative
Static	Becoming
Given	Potential
Cyclical	Vectorial
Nostalgic	Willful
Conservative	Evolutionary
Dogmatic	Problematic
Fatally defined	Disengaging itself into grace
Everywhere-nowhere (steady state)	Utterly centered (Big Bang)

THE ESTHETIC AS THE IMMANENCE OF GOD

"I am, therefore you might be in me" is the dynamism conceded by the Alpha God. "I become, therefore I might be" is the hypothesis of the Omega God. In the Alpha God cosmology, the success of life in returning to godliness does not infringe on the serene, ultimately serene, concreteness of a true and perfect reality. The anguish crowded in the Omega God cosmogony is the uncertainty of its realization, which coincides with life's realization. For life not to sanctify is for God not to realize Himself, a damnation of reality incapable of redemption, that is to say, the dominion of a lower kind of order, the

---

[3] Placed in time before the achievement of itself.
[4] A fraction conjecturing a whole.

brutishness of a nonsentient cosmos, evil as the obliteration of compassion. Such anguish is made even greater as it is shrouded in the knowledge that a future resolution, the hypothetical and justifying Omega God, will have to be monstrously foreign in order to be real, a paradoxical reality which is presented to man tomorrow and would corner him in deepest dread, the devouring splendor and fiery compassion of the True God whom man could not behold and survive.

The more consciousness affirms itself and interiorizes the cosmos, the fuller becomes the realization of the mysteries ahead of us which separate the present from the Omega God and consequently a greater degree of anguish. This is where the exponential demonism of knowledge is. It triggers greater and greater explosions of itself and, consequently, deeper wells of anguish. The longer the throw, the less known is the ground on which the stone falls and the scope (knowledge) grows exponentially. It is my belief that in this journey into creation, the immanent resolution of this existential anguish is a fragmented genesis of the Omega God. It is the concretization in humanly acceptable terms, terms dependent on the historical moment, of fragments of the fearsome phantom of the Omega God. The resolution of this existential anguish is an esthetic genesis. The transfiguration of anguish into a grace which is not conceptual and immaterial, but which is made, instead, of matter metamorphosed into spirit, is the creation of the spirit on and by the bridge of matter. It is, therefore, beyond the hypothetical or the simulative, beyond prophecy and futurism. It is a fragment of the substance of the Omega God. It is legitimate and anticipatory: legitimate, since in the sum of its components, the so-called works of art, the adequate adjourned concreteness of that much of the Omega God has been realized; anticipatory, because its powerful hold on the essence of life tells of things to come. It is not a prophecy but a radiance. Some will characterize this concept as exponential hubris which presumes a conscious effort of life toward the creation of the spirit, the Omega God, and defines the esthetic process not as interpretive, in the service of God, but as God-making. The only way to avoid hubris is to believe in a Father holding and manipulating fate and destiny, that is to say, manipulating evolution. If one cannot accept this view, then every step along the evolutionary path automatically becomes hubris in the sense of emergence from a more modest parent and a thrust toward an even more ambitious offspring. But, since it acknowledges the limitless agenda of the evolutionary process, it can only be humble about its own achievements.

In the ascendence-emergence of reality into godliness, there are two main roads afforded by the deterministic universe of mass-energy. One is the road of sainthood, where vision, faith, and sufferance have the synoptic power of synthesizing in the brief span of a person's (or group's) life the whole hypothesis of a future god. Sanctity is the living synopsis of the Omega God. Through sanctity the discrete can gauge, if not be, the limitless.

The other is the road of esthetogenesis by which the residual anguish invested in a person unequipped for prophecy and self-immolation does not trigger sainthood but does transfigure in personal-universal terms such anguish into a particle of divinity, non-simulative, noninterpretive, nonsacrificial, nonprophetic, but an actual, concrete fragment of divinity, a minuscule, infinitesimal particulae sacra of the immanent, achieved Omega God.

The esthetic genesis is composed of acts, immanent fragments of the hypothetical Omega God, and moves from fragile object to fragile object while constructing its form. Creativity is what sainthood tends to be deprived of since it deals with simulation or invention. Faith is what the esthetic process tends to be without since it deals with creation as definer of reality.

Simulation on one side, a suffered implosion of it, concreteness on the other; totality of structure on one side, forming of foci of radiance on the other; ethical guidance on one side, injection of its drive in historical, discrete opuses on the other. Parenthetically, then, it appears that in the Alpha God universe, sainthood is the necessary and sufficient condition for the return into the Father. In the Omega God potential universe, the esthetogenesis of the real is the necessary and sufficient condition and can be powerfully supported and guided by the synopsis of sainthood.

Ultimately, the theological structure can be seen as the simulation of esthetogenesis, the form of a universe totally conscious that its last hiatus, full knowledge and creation, is nondimensional because it is infinitely complex, and not temporal because it is utterly durational. The esthetic then becomes the immanence of a future and hypothetical God. Esthetogenesis, the genesis of the spirit, its grace, will fully deploy its power once religion, the forecaster, and science, the explainer, can fully embark upon the task with the media and the mechanism being the technological world, the second generation transformer (after biotechnology) of matter into spirit, of mass-energy into God. This emerging creation filling the cosmos in the long cosmogenetic-esthetogenetic evolution is pushing evil, the misdeeds of insensibility, unconsciousness, and ignorance into ever-reducing corners of reality to the point where evil might become a jester sui generis, humoring reality with its makeshift efforts.

OMEGA GOD AND SCIENCE

The theological cosmology of the Alpha God leaves the scientist with a nagging sense of déjà vu, with the perception of a crack faulting the importance of scientific inquiry since it revolves around the independent doing of an Alpha God who preexisted science and will outlast it, and who looks indulgently on the innocent games of the scientist knotted up in the tangle of interpretation. Science as interpretation is what the Alpha God allows. Since the cognitive factor is there in the Alpha God, the cognitive attempt of man has redundance on one side and lack of originality on the other. Its function would be mainly explicative.

This is not so if the cognitive has to be constructed in the absence of an a priori, cognitive Alpha God. Then science is a discoverer of technologies and a preparatory stage for further technological inventions. If God is a hypothesis for the future, technology (physical and biological) would precede science inasmuch as evolution would not be overseen by the knowledge and wisdom of God, the super scientist, but would be a self-developing, self-understanding phenomenon. Reality then would develop by successive and momentous fiats, deterministic and fatal initially but more and more willful and destined in the process of time, bumping here and there on this earth as elsewhere into ferments not wholly submissive to the statistical logics of mass-energy. We call those ferments life. With them the hypothesis of divinity appears and within it is its instigator, man, with his theological simulations in parallel to the esthetogenetic transfiguration.

In this genesis, science is an information discipline. Whatever science spills into technology, art, philosophy, or religion, it spills out of itself. The semantic metaphor "creative science" stands for "science as cognition," true whenever the information stockpile undergoes synthesis and becomes knowledge.

A knowledge discipline is necessarily a past-oriented discipline, the understanding of what has been. A future-oriented science is a contradiction in terms. One can only invent or create the future; one cannot know it.

Cognitive science that is true, pure science is about the "what" of the acted reality and opens the treasure chest for the "hows" of postbiological technology. The reasons and standards for application of those "hows" define the aims established by consciousness. These are teleological (philosophical) decisions in which religion as an ethically imbued simulation of possible future realities lends a powerful supporting hand or, alternatively, comes as the crushing vise of intolerance and bigotry.

It is science, then, via man's consciousness, which attempts to discover what reality is so as to give technology raw material and information adequate for invention and production. But it is technology, preponderantly biotechnology, that invents life, stocking up the pool of reality, to be later discovered by science. Then, technology comes along again to invent and produce that which can be called a neo-nature, the man-made. Sequentially, then:

1) The Physical Universe (Cosmogenesis)
2) (Bio) Technological Evolution (Biogenesis)
3) Scientific Discovery (Within Homogenesis)
4) Extrabiological Technology (Within Esthetogenesis)

Technology comes before science inasmuch as the evolutionary momentum is set in technology before its understanding by the mind can begin (science). One can say that science is but a technology (discovery) of knowledge preceded by a technology of invention, the biotechnology of life. A clear consequence of such chronology is that science cannot decide what life had to be, is, and must become, but only into what and how it has developed up until now and how it can carry on the process. The problem, then, is not technology. It has served life well up to the inception of consciousness. The problem is the *conscious* use of it. It is really the advent of good and evil on the stage set of life that is the source of trouble, something the Alpha God had no way of anticipating since the Garden of Eden was his programmed schedule.

The protomental technology, from virus to beaver, had to contend

for life in biological terms on the relatively clean-cut platform of sur-
vival-fitness-adaptation-mutation. The postmental technology, from
man to transman, has to deal with on the same platform, but as a
primary foundation for the higher platform of fulfillment and creation, a situation of such complexity as to baffle complex and cunning
life itself. The next forms to be function-filled must become compas-
sion-impregnated so as not to be the encasement, the coffin, for the
termination of life. They must be the polis, or fragments, of God
(Omega God), the Civitates Dei (the Urban Effect).

The esthetic is the future-maker, the God-maker, since the esthetic
procreates fragments of divinity and grace from the optional, the tentative, the known, and the pragmatic, making up the anguish of man.
To understand the smallness of the hedonistic niche or the imperviousness to extravagance within true esthetogenetic radiance, such radiance must be felt as coincidental to the art of living at its highest.
The esthetic (not a category, but an objectification) is developing,
creating the reality of the spirit. In this process, it makes use of the
technologies and the sciences, besides being fully stormed by philosophical and religious wonderment. Creation, the esthetic objectification, does not preexist itself, as science does, in the form of technological performance which science is going to discover and explain.
The esthetic comes about as creation.

If science is trying to grasp what technology has made reality into,
history would be that part of reality which science deals with as post-
natural, assuming that natural genetic changes during historical times
can be considered minuscule within the immense evolutionary transformations of prehistory.

Theology, the simulation of a hypothetical, future godliness, a
postbiotechnological and prescientific discipline, is neither an explanation of reality nor a creator of the future, but is instead a driving
thrust pursuing the realization of its own hypothesis. In this view,
religion is the transrational methodology skeletally constructing the
future that only esthetically, immanently, bit by single bit, will be realized, created, objectified. There is then the possibility that, for instance, the symbiotic phenomenon of the Church and the renaissance
flowering of the arts has to be reevaluated in the sense that the
Church is the instrument for the arts and not the arts a vulgarization
of God's word, since the greatness of the Church is in the history and

the influence of her saints and martyrs, the synopses of God, and in this instrumental position toward the arts.

Philosophy, witness to performance and cognition (technology and science), to simulation and creation (theology and esthetogenesis), is part of all of them and acts as a meddler and a crucible, offering ferments and yeasts to the uptide of the future. The sharpest contrast between Alpha God and Omega God is that for the former the effort of man is discovery, interpretive and adaptive, and therefore dynamic only insofar as it attempts to move consciousness from darkness to light, from ignorance to knowledge of the given, a given per se aloof and necessarily not perfectible, the Alpha God. For the Omega God hypothesis, dynamism is the central tenet, a possible god growing itself into fullness, concretizing its existence stage by stage, and also mapping out its quest for better devices for etherealization. Therefore, the quest through the universe and the past so as to know more, so as to do more, so as to create more.

Each person is a philosopher engaged in technology, science, and teleology. Furthermore, everyone is, at least vicariously, a creator; the artist of his or her own life, in any case. Therefore, the boundaries of the different disciplines are blurred or fused into one another. Technology, being the bulk of reality, tends to take the upper hand, be it at the level of the struggle for survival or at the level of the surplus market economy. Technology asks of science the understanding of itself, past and present, so as to invent and produce new mechanisms. One could make the following hypotheses:

1) Technology successfully makes the universe into a working "machine" nested in the middle of determinism (the physical universe, cosmogenesis, and the biological universe, biogenesis).

2) Science adds and feeds the cognitive element into the "machine" by way of consciousness.

3) Theology keeps life turned toward the future in a comprehensive hypothesis that has taken the form of an unconscious simulation resulting from a past-oriented thrust, the Alpha God. Sainthood is a powerful synopsis of such simulations.

4) The esthetic transforms such simulations by fragments into concreteness, the making of the hypothetical Omega God.

5) Philosophy rides the team and is driven by it and by its own private demon.

The theologian is a technologian, a technician whose efforts are toward the understanding of godliness. He is the most hard-pressed and frustrated of technicians, forever engaged with the phantom of his subject matter, never with it, as it does not exist as yet, and yet the divine notion is the most encompassing of all concepts and the most forceful of all hypotheses. *The theologian is a technician fabricating God via simulation, not a scientist discovering God via knowledge or an artist creating fragments of God.* The point is to see if he can transfer his love from a certitude he conceives as concrete and extant, even if difficult to grasp, to a certitude of hypothesis, the love for a hypothesis, a compendium of all that might someday be, given enough love investing it. To love a hypothesis might be the true compassion of the technologian, the technician of God. The technologians of God are not engaged in discovering a nonexisting deity, but rather in the making of sacredness, fragment by fragment, toying in the meantime with the simulation games of an evolutionary theology.

It would be important to read the holy books in the light of religion as simulation instead of as the fragmented documentation of history. They may show themselves to be depositories of radical-evolutionary modes, future-making dynamos, surcharges of the vector matter-spirit. I would suggest an institute for great simulation studies—the rewriting (transposition) of the sacred books, dealing with the Alpha Gods of the past and their creation, into a future predictive instrument, pointing to the evolutionary path constructing the Omega God. The institute would set out to test the idea that the whole body of myth and theology is not, as it is assumed by the transmitted fables and sacred texts, a description and interpretation of past occurrences but is instead a predictive and simulative body of knowledge that can be made into a most powerful beacon pointing at the future. The human mind has constructed such a predictive body through a mixture of awe, fear, imagination, projection, extrapolation, compassion, and basically by the living that man does in a present which is consistently a prefuture. It would be a character of the institute that its own living, living in the prefuture, would be a substantial part of the inquiry.

OMEGA GOD AND SUFFERANCE

The personal trajectory from birth to death recapitulates the evolutionary trajectory. In individual terms the second half of the trajectory is contained within the paradox of inevitable physical deterioration coupled, in the best of cases, with a sharpening of consciousness. *This might more than symbolize the potential disengagement of the spirit from the material frame which is, now and possibly forever, sustaining it.* The comparison of personal destiny to evolutionary destiny aligns personal distress with the total ambiguity of evolution. If evolution suffered from the same final weakness as personal destiny, individual death would mandatorily preclude the emergence of evolution into translife.

To die into the hands of God is the formula of the Alpha God. On the threshold of life eternal, the person is free of responsibility, unmortgaged, and content.[5] If this alternative is as comforting as the churches promise, then both the anguished unwillingness to face personal death and the preoccupation with stunted evolution become frivolous. This promise of eternal bliss, which no one has ever had the privilege to verify, is not only cruelly ambiguous, it is a teasing screen faulting man's most noble moments. It is not a yeasty uncertainty but rather an influence which colors actions with sinfulness, with doubts and rebelliousness, with resentments and fears.

The Alpha God in all his possible compassion still seems to break man the more he attempts to understand. He breaks man's fiber by making demands that only conceptual acrobatics can answer, acrobatics that often the "man in the street" can dismiss with small wit.

The Omega God is not ambiguous in His demands and promises. He demands all, promising only "more of the same" endlessly. He is manifested by fragments in which He has been realized, immanently, for good and for evil, without an ounce of mockery or cruelty, in all candor and vulnerability. The anguish of man is immanent in him and can only find resolution, momentary and short of target, in the creative act, a particle of the esthetogenetic process. God-like particles, not at the wake of a dead God, but attending at the birth of the

---

[5] After a possible quarantine in purgatory.

simulated God, can, in the martyrdom of physical or mental sufference, or in sainthood, render the hypothesis of God suddenly believable, giving sufferance a divine sanction.

Physical suffering and illness, inasmuch as they are of fate and beyond human control, are cause for specific sensitization to life's predicament, like a border town for which periodic invasion by alien forces works as reminder and punisher: reminder of the precariousness of being, punisher by the dread of an ever-present enemy. It is martyrdom even though it might not reach the peaks of anguish caused by the viciousness of man and institutions. It is viciousness of the deities forming the clan of fate. All of them, an immense mob housed in the immense vats of the physical cosmos, the Alpha God's fractions of its fractured self.

Wouldn't it be an atrocity if the expediency of an elite, the priest-kings making up the forbidden apple of knowledge, could or would once and for all preclude the Omega God? Isn't it more fruitful, more promising, at least more self-explanatory, to share in the anguish, the true distress of him who cannot dismiss his own fatal destiny as irrelevant because he feels that a similar end might expect evolution? In the struggle to find a satisfying or commensurate answer to the massiveness of the problem, though sainthood and creativity might be elusive, there is still total immersion in the tidal wave of matter bridging into spirit, and, vicariously or by mimesis, man is sufferer and creator, creation indeed.

What is inferred from the Alpha God is a palpable reality which is an immense reform school. What is implied in the Omega God is a reality which is an unlimited crucible for creation. What of a reformatory with a lot of crucibles lying around? Those crucibles at best would be receptacles for mimetic fragments of the Omega God; at worst, fakes put there to soothe the pride of man believing himself good enough to compete with God. No matter how good the deed of man, God would have done it already, and done it better. Good-bye creation, radiance. Come in contrition, envy. The crucible excludes the reformatory inasmuch as the reformatory goes for false crucibles. We must choose one or the other: a poor mimesis of the Alpha God in contrition and envy, or the creation of the Omega God in fiery radiance.

OMEGA GOD AND MEANS

The radiance of the achieved Omega God (a pure speculation about the future) cannot be of a political nature, nor of a social nature, nor of an economic nature. It can only be of an esthetic nature, of grace and harmony pervading all and setting up the conditions for further synthesis. This makes clear that politics, economics, and social structures are means to ends. They are technologies in quest of content (the ultimate harmony). They cannot dictate to life, they must attend to its demands. They can be made into fetishes, idols, false gods. They cannot be God-like. They can partake of a methodological imperative, but left to themselves, they are expedient and subservient, servants of all. This is an old story but worth repeating because it falls most often on deaf ears, and the price of such deafness can be staggering: the enslavement of man to political, economic, and social machineries.

Political, social, and economic options are many, and for hundreds of generations man has sought to find the least crude or cruel among them. The centration methodology is not an option, it is a necessary and operative condition with which can be associated any degree of grace or disgrace, inasmuch as in both cases life is still the subject matter. As instruments for fitness, the political, economic, and social options must be parts of the coordinative effort of life. Fitness is a premise to performance, it is not performance per se. Unless we pursue health with grace in mind, even health will fail us. Therefore, to engage in political, economic, and social action without having our eyes on grace is to unleash blind forces with little purpose in mind, displaying a desperate or cynical trust in the future.

The most verisimilar analogy to God is not the economist, the politician, the lawyer, the legislator, the technician, or the priest. It is the artist, and it could not be otherwise, as it is the artist who is end-oriented while the others are means-oriented.

The artist is end-oriented because his subject matter is residual anguish itself which he does not try to circumvent or abate but which he transforms into fragments of the Omega God. He is the dancer among the acrobats, the one among the multitude, the one making emergence out of emergency, and, out of necessity, making spirit out of matter. The noncontradictory corollary is that we are all participants in the act of creation since none of us could make it alone.

If oneness in the Alpha God is achieved by a return to innocence, then everything is expedient for reentry into that which preexists from the beginning of time. Consequently, it becomes hard to sustain man in his odyssey because along the journey he has no absolute to anchor himself to but only ritualistic procedures whose goodness or badness is relative to the perspective one surrounds them with. One does not become better inch by inch if reality is itself the only true god, existent and perfect. One fails inch by inch through exclusion from grace. Eternal damnation of a phenomenon whose fall from grace is existentially perpetual is a failing actually attributable to abortive duration, to seeing growth as past-oriented, growing into the past.

OMEGA GOD AND GREED

Greed seems to be a pragmatic wall against which any rationalization of our mind comes to break. The quiet greed of the affluent, the vociferous greed of the new rich, the potential greed of the poor. The best projections, the most optimistic ones, are made meaningless by economic pragmatism stating that wealth will move more and more where wealth already exists. It might well be, then, that a vow of relative poverty is the most direct, realistic, and influential road available to us if we are seriously engaged in human affairs. Thousands of people are living such a vow within the affluent society. They do it by choice. If this were not true, then they are poor only because they have not found the way to get rich. Their poverty is then part of their limitations, not part of their design. They are the unsuccessful members of a "success society." To be relatively poor does not mean not to produce wealth. It means to produce wealth but to have a life which is congruent with the condition of man, the true condition of man: his fitness in the earthly reality and his moving into the realm of the spirit.

Why is a vow of relative poverty a theological decision? Because it entails an acceptance of the demand for a responsibility toward life that can only be firm and lasting if life itself is viewed as directed, purposeful, and sacred. It is future-oriented theology in which the responsibility for the existence of godliness (purposefulness) is purely human.

Relative poverty is a condition which encourages the transformation of more matter into more spirit since it is not prey to the gluttony of greed nor to the brutalization of indigence. It must not be the dull condition of contented survival but the burning action of persons pursuing godliness.

OMEGA GOD AND ECOLOGY

If present reality is a fragment of the possible Omega God, then the ecological context has an inherent sacredness of which we can make use only if by such use this sacredness is enhanced. At the same time, it is imperative that such use be made inasmuch as a fragment of godliness is a suffering reality, a fragment of being in the pursuit of wholeness, of grace, of fullness. But, if the present is a runaway infant whose father has both the right to life and to death and toward whom the infant feels the weariness caused by protracted and unwanted submission (that is to say, the ambiguous desire of the man-invented god to be not only the only and final authority but also to be divested of power since God's power signifies the foreclosure of life's freedom), then the infant can claim innocence even for the most savage act. After all, he had no voice in his conception and his development is overseen by the contradictory paradox of a maker and breaker who is neither a maker nor a breaker. The piety of the conservationist is reflected in the father-knows-best assumption, an injunction to one and all that what we see in nature is the will of God, that the infant is and cannot be but pure and wholesome, and, furthermore, cannot ever be improved. What this kind of conservationist fails to see is the fearsome unfolding of the enfant terrible, the theological process, which will not stay put in spite of man or god. There is the dangerous possibility that the Apha God and pollution coincide.

For the evolutionist, the present God is a pale anticipation of the future God. Therefore, godliness is pursued according to the methodology of complexity-duration-spiritualization and the consequent dynamism of the ever-changing ecological balance. The limits to growth have to be found in theological simulation since it is that in-

vestigation which at the outset includes in its parameters the final
parameter, the paragon, in the emergence of matter and spirit.

OMEGA GOD AND PANTHEISM

The immanent God is not a pantheistic being since it has not
preexisted what it is in each moment of the present. It is only and
purely the total, vital charge present in each moment following the
past moments.

The pantheistic God is all-achieved and ubiquitously acts upon
life. The immanent God, of which the Alpha God is an attempted
simulation, is in a continuous process of augmentation toward the
fullness hypothesized in the Omega God. While the pantheistic divinity is just, the evolutionary divinity is wanting.

OMEGA GOD AND MUSIC

The identification of music with organized noise, the sounds of
matter, fits more the Alpha God theology as it refers to times past. If
one does not stop in time, genesis time of the Bible, one finds music
and "the harmony of the spheres" to be one and the same thing. This
position claims a loss of grace resulting from the acquisition of consciousness and subsequent creative interference with the state of
grace pristine before man's intrusion. A point for John Cage epi-
gones, perhaps, but a mystification of sentient life and the engrossing
process of creation.

OMEGA GOD AND LEISURE

For an Omega God model, leisure can only mean a higher kind of
activity, as the work of creating God must go on unremittingly. It is
again the Garden of Eden which must be seen as the origin of the
pollution of the spirit because it was in the Garden of Eden that the
mind was told to remain idle since in such idleness the vision of the
Alpha God would appear. A fraud, such vision, if God is not attend-

ing to our well-being (Alpha God) but is begging for His making (Omega God) from us, life.

OMEGA GOD AND ATHEISM

The Omega God hypothesis can reconcile the theologian and the atheist. To the theologian it gives yeast to the most ambitious hypothesis ever to touch the mind of man. To the atheist it does not demand any irrational trust in powers he cannot believe in. It just tells man that inasmuch as he fulfills himself, he adds an ounce of spirit to the quivering of life enveloping the earth. It demands that he not refuse the tenuous hypothesis that, in time, enough of those ounces of surmatter coming together might tip the balance from the prevalence of nonlife, nonconsciousness, to the prevalence of life, consciousness. That day, or much sooner, perhaps now, theologian and atheist might want to shake hands and get down to work, one in making the love of his life a little more concrete and the other in making the hypothesis of his mind a bit more compassionate and immanently divine.

The Theology of the Sun

SYNOPSIS: The mass-energy universe is a knot which unravels in space and time at the direction of life. In no way can life do without the energizing of the physical universe. The consumption of matter into spirit is just that, a consumption, and, by it, a transfiguration.

If one considers that the primeval earth was not much more than molten rock, one can vaguely gauge the miracle of the life-spirit and the massiveness of its ecological transmutability. Life itself is the transformer, made of mass-energy particles, extruding spirit from stone. From molten rock to the present is indeed and all the way a theological journey, in its minuteness and strangeness not less than in its spatial-temporal enormity. If reality is focused on this transformation of mass-energy into spirit, then the dynamics of ecology are theological. Ecology is theology: theoecology. In other words, if there is any substance to the assertion that life is the slow evolution of matter into spirit, the making of an immanent God worthy of as much reverence, if not more, as the historical God, then it is difficult to separate ecology from theology.

It is common wisdom to say that we are all children of God. What if it were truer to say that an infant God is moving toward adulthood through the actions of all of us, provided that life continues to evolve? Then the long journey of divinity into adulthood is neither a return to something old and lost nor a commute between two specific stations; rather, it is a journey into the unknown. It is primarily the uninterpreted technological feat of the impregnation of matter with the radiance of spirit achieved and augmented by the economics of life (in the ultimate sense of the term "economy") in all of its manifestations. The possible journey into the adulthood of divinity, the lengthy evolutionary venture, feeds upon the physical universe—the quasi-inexhaustible repository of raw materials and energy needed for the task of creating the most glorious of all conceivable gods. If this seems to echo the gross national product ethos, one might consider that:

1) The Western Ethos cannot accept the theology of a God who expects man's repentance in exchange for the promise of return to His arms or womb. This is, as we will see, the

advocacy of a steady-state ecology and we must be aware
that the idea of steady-state contradicts the most telling
characteristics of Western civilization: self-reliance, drive,
pioneering, perseverance, and the underlying Faustian inquietude.

2)   There is also the ever-present risk of being caught in idolatry. Our dominant idols may well become greed, intolerance, mediocrity, etc. Since the thesis is that we become coresponsible for making the new divinity, the Omega God,
failure to create the "right" God builds failure into our entire future.

The birth and becoming of a true God is the measure of reality.[1]
This is as yet a hypothesis because only the conceiving stage of the
process can be postulate. If the making of the Omega God (as distinct from the assumed Gamma God of traditional theology) is the
thesis of the living in the process of becoming, then we must recognize within this long development an iron logic, regulating the process of experimentation which is inherent in the journey called evolution. Each experiment which does not conclusively support such a
logic bears the seal of failure. Before considering such a logic, let us
look at one attempt in this direction which has gone astray.

One can say, generally, that the door slamming behind each experiment not conclusively supporting such logic is the determinism into
which the experiment falls. This seal can be the death sentence for a
species or the caging of it in a self-made prison of determinism: the
insect world, for instance. The fate of the insect tells us that the technological instrumentation which carries out the extrusion of the spirit
from matter, the invention of life in its numberless forms, is a dou-
ble-edged sword. One edge opens windows on landscapes of interiority; the other cuts the jugular through which flows the sap of
metamorphosis, physical as well as metaphysical. The armored insect
is physiologically deprived of access to consciousness, one of the
possible conquests of such metamorphosis.

Technology developed by man—an offspring of biotechnology—can
imprison human development in a cage as deterministic as the one
that imprisoned the anthropoids. The tragic, joyful music of life be-

[1] The reality of the banker and the pauper as well as the reality of the priest
and the atheist.

comes then a naked confrontation with fate; the magnificence of the biotechnical machine containing the whole hordes of crabs and beetles yields a muted cry for an unachievable God. The ultimate consequence of disconnecting ecology from theology is to risk the fate of the crab, a grand fate as far as crabs go, but pure despair for humankind. For the human mind, to separate ecology from theology is to move blindfolded on a landscape covered with booby traps. The health of ecological habitats and any meaningful future for mankind and evolution at large can only be realized if ecology and theology are seen as aspects of each other.

Because evolution from brimstone to consciousness-spirit has been a lengthy process, eventful and immensely costly in sufferance, the continuation of this process has to be assured for the sake of the legacy of a meaningful future. This is the same future the evolutionary phenomenon has begun to outline forcefully and convincingly as the attempt toward the making of godliness. The *guiding* logic is therefore the paradoxical-hypothetical lighthouse set at the end of time, not because as yet undiscovered by man, but because as yet uncreated by life. The simulation of such a possible reality, a skeletal structure at first, is a challenge and a responsibility which we must face, for if we do not, we retreat into naught. Going by the theology of the day, things look dim, if not grim. We are not at all ready to carry on responsibly but are more like a protean beast, self-punishing and revolting against the self-inflicted pain.

The evolutionary process seems to say that part of its strategy is to come up with new forms (mutations) which, now and then, generate new and useful activities (functions). Forms predispose elements for new contents (form before function).

Now, since the totality of the living process is not a linear event but rather a frontal tide of feedback loops, the only access to the future which is not purely an illusory reprint of the past is in the constant appearance of new forms, the loops being capable of eliciting new contents.

EVOLUTIONARY
THRUST TOWARD
THE SPIRIT

PRIMARY LOOP

SECONDARY LOOP

The primary, or creation, loops are forms which define function and are woven perpendicularly to the direction of themselves and all along the thrust of such direction by the secondary loops of the manutentive aspects of reality whose genesis and development is an inversion of the primary loops' genesis and development. The secondary loops, the sum of which can be identified as the routine of life, form a support to all those actions and activities which sustain the development of the present.

These minor loops, the maintenance and continuity crowds with their fantastic machines (us, most of the time), are forced to transcend themselves by transforming routine into ritual through grace and reverence. These rituals are offerings, if one chooses, to the existential, immanent, fragmentary, helpless Omega God; ritual offerings otherwise expressed as the reverence for life.

Illustrating the significance of the metaphor of the loops are two main cases:

Case A) The creation loops prevail; one of two things happens:

1) If the cosmos is saturated with spirit, that is to say, the Omega God is incipient, then the routine supported by the maintenance loops accordingly dwindles away because it is becoming less and less necessary.

2) If the cosmos is far from being close to the radiance of the Omega God, the disappearance of maintenance loops spells the breakdown of the evolutionary machinery.

Case B) The maintenance loops prevail; one of two things happens:

3) For the cosmos well on its way toward the Omega God, there is the catastrophe of loss of creative power, the derailment into stagnation.

4) For the cosmos in proximity to the Alpha God, there is quiescence with success of a sort which is the trap precluding further development.

Of these:

1) is a possibility only in the most distant of futures when the metamorphosis of matter into spirit is quasi-total;

2) might well have some equivalence to the Eastern commitment which prematurely discredits the importance of instrumentalizing the spirit with adequate physical machinery, psychosomatic man included;

3) is the case of the Western mind confounded by the exhilaration of physical-technological prowess, marring the most intimate and intangible domains of the spirit;

4) is the case of fossil species, arthropod insects, etc., whose survival success story is the triumph of automatism over routine-grace and creative power.

One can imagine a human condition where the withering of the creative loops to the advantage of the maintenance loops might produce a kind of reality in apparent agreement with a static, nontheological structure. This is comparable to the self-balancing countenance of an ecological fragment composed of the mineral support, climate, bacterial, vegetal, insect and animal life for which the future is in too many ways the reenactment of the past. Steady-state ecology is the advocacy of such equilibrium. A relative staticity, since the larger reality of which it is a part is involved in the constant and irreversible reordering of things from which emerges new challenges whose pressures will transform, more or less beyond recognition, all the component parts. This is the totality of the evolutionary phantasmagoria.

The creation and maintenance loops woven together make for the prefuture, the transparent, the emergence of the spirit. The well-balanced strength of the primary creation loops and the secondary maintenance loops weaving the continuity and resilience of the primary loops is the optimum condition for the emergence of reality, of new futures, and of the power of the immanent god, the simulation, extrapolation of which, by religious doctrines, fathoms a final Omega God. Imagining for a moment the evolutionary swell to be completed, and calling such an image a simulation of its eventual concreteness, this simulation is what we call religion. The prophets, saints, and martyrs of a religion are its living and suffering manifestation, the instantaneous revelation of its sacredness.

The cool head that science has had to keep is quite necessary since the secondary maintenance loops are the bulk of life-reality. But the substance of such reality is progressive complexity originating from the primary loops which science, as the discovering discipline, is entitled to acknowledge, a posteriori, as a posteriori, as past events whose logic and rationale are in continuous metamorphosis, and the development of which is not the province of science but the province of technology of the spirit. This technology of the spirit emerges into reality once the level of consciousness has been reached by the technology of the flesh, the vegetal, and the animal kingdoms.

The central importance of theology is revealed by the presence or absence of the transrational in the man-made world since it is in the transrational that the spirit dwells. A strictly rational environment, the technocratic city, for instance, is a reality in which the primary loops have shriveled to nothing and the secondary loops of maintenance-continuity have become a linear but blind diagram which fails to support the creative primary loops and also fails on what is its own prerogative, the continuum of routine-grace. Strict rationalization is mandatory squalor, the 1984 dead-end situation. But then, where is the rationale for a transrational phenomenon? It can only be found, as is to be expected, in the one transrational reality we know: life, a speck as yet within the cosmic reality. Here is where the iron logic of evolutionary success comes into the picture. Certainly the success is not to be explained by reductionist theories in which life is a purely mechanistic, deterministic, rational phenomenology.

Out of the monumental transformism of evolution and its confounding complexity only one thing seems to emerge clearly and constantly: that such complexity is the deus ex machina of the degree of its transformism and the pressure of its intensity. It is not difficult to see why. Life is a measured, informed response to the challenges of the inner and outer realities, whatever those might be. Since, at least theoretically, the degree of understanding of the challenge defines the fitness and impact of the response, fitness and growth are directly dependent on the quantity and quality of information appropriated and digested by the organism. From this comes the privileged position of the complex, as the most knowing and responsive, the most spirited, and, ultimately, the sacramental. Complexity and intensity are the spatial and durational parameters of consciousness, the stuff painstakingly generated from the primeval Alpha God (the sun). But the spatial, the durational, the complex, the living have for entelechy the utterly centered character of the Omega God—the God-point of total spiritualization, maximum complexity, maximum consciousness-knowledge-creation, and, therefore, not surprisingly, the mandatory physical parameter of miniaturization. This element of miniaturization that could have been detected all along the evolutionary phenomenon seems to fit to perfection even the greatest of all extrapolations, the Omega God. This is "more done with less," not in the simplistic ethos of simplication-disintegration but in the demonism of spiritualization-etherealization.

To put it another way, since the genesis of the spirit is the sensitization of matter, the methodology of the process of matter becoming spirit must be in agreement with the modes which life has been defining and testing in successfully fostering such genesis. They are interiorization, complexification, and centration-convergence. For all of them, the physical miniaturization of the spatial structure is characteristic and mandatory: Do the same thing with less because by doing so such same thing becomes better than itself and is more able to plug itself into other similar-dissimilar things. From this arises the access to a new round of information-knowledge-sensitization, more matter becoming radiant with more spirit, and the consolidation of the bridge between matter and spirit. The bridge between the Alpha God of the sun and the Omega God of the spirit is the lengthy purgatory of matter transfiguring itself into fragments of god under the pressures of complexification, intensification, understanding, sensitization, and miniaturization. Thus, the inescapable nature of the theological path on the methodological guidelines of the transrational destiny of life.

What is fueling the crucible that can concert matter into surmatter, that can initiate and foster the chain of evolution? There is a single power source (in terrestrial universe), tentatively elected by various theologies as a divine body whose acting presence is indispensable to the development of what I have called the theological ecology, theo-ecology. It is the sun. To view this immense furnace purely as a center of brute energy is correct enough. To dismiss it as a divine body, primeval as one pleases, might reveal a misplacement of values. As far as we can conjecture and rationalize, the "god of the origin" is pure, brute mass-energy, an unlimited savagery, predetermined and deterministic, the single reality most authentically antithetic to what we now apprehend as spirit. For us earthlings, such a powerhouse is the sun and none other than the sun. From such negation of the spirit, the fate of which per se is to step down the length of the entropic ladder, comes the origin and development of life whose destiny is the stepping up the length of evolution toward the Omega God.

In the cosmic context, the fury of the suns, isolated from each other by the naught of intergalactic space, is the rule, while the yeast of life, ever more tenuously scattered and utterly isolated within the same cosmos, is the rarest of exceptions. It is only in view of the wisest use of times, spaces, occasions, opportunities, energies, and agencies that life has access to a future. Only within the guidelines of such wisdom can life, such an exception within the rule of an inanimate universe, hope for a future whose maximum radiance might still be the radiance of a minor sun of all possible suns of the spirit.

Therefore, the physical sun, the true Alpha God of dawn and symbol of the hypothesized spirit-sun of a distant future, the Omega God, is the reservoir of those energies that the life-transformer is manipulating into the asentropic journey toward this other sun, the god of the spirit.

On the other hand, the physical sun when invested with divine power becomes only the raw, brutish simulation of its own possible entelechy, the other radiant sun which is painstakingly originating itself from the father-furnace. Since this is not a metaphor but a hypothesis on its way to realization and since it has been tested by more than 3,000 millions of years of history, to cling to a nontheological ecology would be a dispirited game.

Setting the contemporary scene somewhat between the Alpha God, the sun and crucible of life, and the Omega God, sun of the spirit, we are immensely closer to the crucible than to the Omega God and must remind ourselves that, of the whole diagram, only the minute fraction which has transpired up to the present is more than a hypothesis. We are presented with the paradoxical proposition of a theological simulation framed by the relatively fragile precedents of past history which say that God is this and that because secretive life might be that and the other. At the same time, it speaks of the urgency of knowing as comprehensively as we can what the hypothetical god needs to become if we concede that his making is conditioned to, and in fact is, our own making.

In the framework of matter becoming spirit, the pursuit of happiness is no more than a fringe benefit, an accident illuminating some substance of the process. Individual self-gratification is drowned in the onrush of the divine whose radiance can only pause and illuminate that of the person who is intensely reverent and given, donated, as a component of the vector, matter-spirit. If this seems to be an indefinite postponement of fulfillment and an acceptance of existential hardship, it is not. On the contrary, it charges life with the responsibility of creating itself into the divine, and can, as it should, fill the most humble effort with a singularity in which attainment above many more self-righteous things is the one made to glow by spiritual radiance. It points to the grace of theology which is not the theology of sin, redemption, and longing for identification with the Alpha God; it is the theology of creation whereby the hellish oneness of the original crucible is tamed and transfigured in the demonic-divine intensity of the other sun, the son of the sun, the Omega sun of the spirit.

That contemporary man might lack the strength to see beyond himself and thus for the sake of sanity might reject his metaphysical nature is possibly our single most tragic fault. If this is so, what remains to be contended with can only be handled in a pious or sanctimonious manner in which action is at best a retardant of catastrophe, the ultimate catastrophe of a killed future. The rhetoric of practical man and his spite for the intangible spirit is the incapacitating factor that makes reality rush by him unnoticed and unenjoyed. This makes him fail ultimately, as said before, even in his task as energizer of the secondary loops of practical maintenance-continuity. If proof is needed, note the catastrophe of the automobile as an etherealization machine. The fact seems to be that the nuts and bolts of practical man are to be stringently controlled, submitted to the priority of the spirit, the theoecology, otherwise they are nothing more than the sand of entropy in the cogs of the surmachine constructing itself into the Omega God.

What, of all this, trickles down to the average man, to underprivileged man, to elite man, to suffering humankind? The crushing responsibility of the God-makers. If the acceptance in principle of the theological simulation that sees fulfillment in God-speed is human, there arises the necessity of seeing as human not the short-cut, the way out, the self-righteous, the secure and comfortable, the ingrown, the expedient, the obsolescent, etc., but rather the conscious option toward reverence for life and the efforts it entails and with it all the despairing ambiguities enveloping these efforts.

It is because of the double difficulty of the demanding nature of humanness and its inherent ambiguities that when we are clear on something we should desperately but hopefully hold on to it. Rare are the moorings available to us in our construction of the future. The mooring of complexity-duration and miniaturization is clear and unequivocal and as such is the most direct, promising, nonex-pedient launching platform toward an equity of social condition and a congruence with the ecological substructure. The two combine their creative best in the theoecology of the Civitas Dei where the ecologi-cal gates will be kept open. Open also will remain the access to a more compassionate family of man and, finally, open will be the gate to the progressive creation of the Omega God. The nonultimate char-acter of the Civitas Dei is in its being still only a simulation of its own entelechy, the esthetogenesis of mass-energy.

To conclude: at the possible zenith of the materialistic age and in the wake of many pronouncements on the death of God, the theolog-ical question knocks ever more persistently at the door of man's con-sciousness and presses hard on his conscience. The pantheism of the aging flower children is far too innocent. Their recommendation of indiscriminate respect for all things touches on escapism; love that is value-free (valueless?) rather than invaluable provides far too easy a bridge between narrow experience and hypocritical irresponsibility.

The scientific insight, or the vacuum it created, has displaced the hypothesis of an eternal God with the genesis of spirit which points toward the possibility, dimly perceived, of a future godliness. Premo-nitions of this direction are the sacramental strands which run per-petually along the fibers of life.

The Two Suns
(Alpha and Omega God)

Synopsis: The pristine universe is made up of 10^{80} particle-godlets. It is utterly polytheistic and, therefore, immensely weak, tenuously spirited.

The final universe is God of total integrity and total consciousness; logos will be. Logos will be all and everything, everywhere, for any and all times because in that ultimate resurrectional condition there will be no raw matter (media), but only pure spirit (message). Neither space, time, mass, nor energy will impede its being since they will have been consumed in the process of creating it.

RELIGION AS SIMULATION
THE THEOLOGY OF THE SUN
THE TECHNOLOGICAL FRANKENSTEIN

These papers are presented in the order in which they were written. More than chapters of a thinking process, they are the reiteration, elaboration, and modification of a central idea: God as a postulate of a possible (or unavoidable) future and, consequently, the presence, in every moment, of immanent particles of such God as they are produced by the spirit. This paper is a synopsis of the theory which is expanded in the other three papers.

The paradoxical thesis presented here is that the physical universe is media patiently working at its own metamorphosis into message. McLuhan's language is used to propose the non-McLuhan view that the message is never the media. This is explained through the presentation of two extremes ad absurdum and one very important exception. The two extremes are:

ALPHA. An original condition in which the absence of any message leaves the whole of reality as pure media. If one category, the message, is equal to zero, the total is equal to the other, the media. Within those confines one could therefore say that the media is the message, a worthless immensity from the standpoint of teleology.

OMEGA. A final condition of reality in which the message, by its own advent, has burned up the media in toto. Since this is the stage at which the media has finally been dissipated into the message, one can say that the media is the message, a teleological centration.

Between these two extremes, one assumed to be the beginning and the other hypothesized to be the end, are instances unlimited in number and infinite in variety where media are the means by which the messages gather themselves. Since both media and message are constituents of the event, one is influential in the definition of the other, which is the element of truth in the McLuhan dictum.

The exception is esthetic reality, where media and message are bound together to a degree which yields one indivisible event. To isolate one is to destroy the whole and, consequently, the other. The morality play is media with a message, one distinguishable from the other; the tragedy is an indivisible, irreducible esthetic event. To put it another way, the function of the bicycle is transportation, the function of a specific sonata is that sonata, not the sonata form which is the framework. Whatever other function we attach to it is a fringe benefit. The bicycle is an invention. The sonata is a creation. The bicycle is a means. The sonata is an end whose character partakes of the finality of the Omega condition where the media is consumed into the message.

Then, in the thesis of the universe as the medium metamorphosing into the message, the lengthy process has an immanent percentage of realization. Consequently, every "present," every moment of history, carries within itself fragments of the message, the immanent, realized part of it. This metamorphosis implies the activation of every speck of mass-energy into a conscience, the conscience of itself as part of a whole (Eastern being) and the dynamic imperatives such conscience produces (Western becoming). Within the activation inherent in each mass-energy component of the force field is infused the new activity: the sensitization of consciousness.

But consciousness is not yet the message. It is a preliminary quivering of matter, so to speak. The message is the further transformation of such conscience into a new synthesis with the surroundings—a creation. One could call it the interiorization of the cosmos which starts with the partial interiorizations of organic nature, the organisms, and surges in time into the associative-cooperative-cultural forms of society and beyond, involving larger and larger parts of the cosmos.

Consciousness, the attribute of conscience, is then in a very primitive, primeval way, or in a very sophisticated way, a cognitive category which acknowledges contiguous reality and acts accordingly but whose ultimate concern is to transcend self and otherness by an act of creation.

As there is not such a thing as pure science, but instead a cognitive process called science which seeks to understand a phenomenon and apply it to the formation of manipulative devices (Western), so there is not such a thing as pure consciousness (Eastern), but a perceptual-cognitive process which, by way of the brain's powers of generalization, tries to acquire, and does acquire, the ability to transubstantiate matter into surmatter.

I will now restate the thesis:

The physical world is the media, *which I call the Alpha God, patiently working at His own metamorphosis into the message, which I call the Omega God.* The term "God" is used for the concept because intrinsic to the word is the attribute of all-inclusiveness, the inclusiveness attempted by the proposition.

One can expediently fill the gap between these two extreme Gods by following this chart:

OMEGA GOD	THE POTENTIAL GOD
OMEGA^1 GOD	THE IMMANENT GOD
GAMMA GOD	THE SIMULATION OF GOD IN MAN'S IMAGE[1]
BETA GOD	THE ORGANIC UNIVERSE
ALPHA GOD	THE PHYSICAL UNIVERSE

The Alpha God and the Beta God are, respectively, the physical universe and the organic universe; pantheistic dynamism exclusive of man. The Gamma God is a symbol or simulation of what the human universe, inclusive of the preceding universes, ought to become. The Omega God exists inasmuch as it is realized in the immanent Omega^1 God which is the human universe at present. Therefore, the Omega God is not a symbol as is the Gamma God, but a possibility attached to and conditioned by the actions of sentient life.

1) In ascending from Alpha to Omega: each God is suppositive of the next; each God fathers the next.[2]

2) In descending from Omega to Alpha: each God is inclusive of the one preceding and carries its matrix.

3) In the absence of the next God, the Son of God, the Father-God becomes the immanent God. For example, if the Beta

---

[1] See "Religion as Simulation."

[2] God the Father or the Mother are posthumous titles since fathering and mothering waited ten to twelve thousand millions of years to make their appearance in the heterosexual mode of reproduction. The terms "originating condition" and an "originated condition" do more justice to the notion.

God of the organic universe is, but the Son-God, the Gamma God of simulation, is not yet asserted by human consciousness, then the Beta God is the immanent God.

4) Before the appearance of the Gamma God, the immanent God coincides with the total God. The reason that the Gamma God does not coincide with the immanent God is because of the escape of self-consciousness from reality into a constructed simulation of it. That is to say, the Gamma God works as an anticipatory power, with all the advantages and defects inherent in the intellectual-abstractional processes.

This simulation phase, the Gamma God, is unavoidable in the process of matter becoming spirit since:

A.   The stresses of life demand that it transact itself;
B.   An instantaneous and total transaction into spirit is impossible;
C.   The acquired technology of generalized structures in the thought process of the human mind favors simulation as an instrument for such processes; and
D.   Anguish reveals itself at the core of self-consciousness. The anguish of being a fraction (the immanent Omega[1] God) of the Omega God, which might never come to be, begs for a structural guideline hypothesizing the possibility of such finality or entelechy, "the form that actuates this realization" (Webster).

Therefore, it is necessary to have a substitute, the Gamma God of simulation, who will support consciousness in the struggle and will comfort it in its most discouraged moments. Only after and beyond the Alpha God is the immanent God, a fraction of the Omega God.

The theology proposed here is a theology of evolution, in contrast with the original Christian theology which is a theology of salvation; the Catholic and Protestant which is a theology of transformation (capitalism); and the Eastern theology, a theology of return or rediffusion. Granted that all this is oversimplified, all these theologies are unwillingly deterministic since they substantially preclude the advent of the truly new, the uncreated, the Omega[1], and the Omega God. The most deterministic theology, at least in words, the Marxist-

Communistic theology, wants the new man but through the reduction determinism of economics-politics-science.

To conceive of more than one God is to open the door to all sorts of deities. But since the categorical imperative of the Omega God is utter centration wherein all other gods are engulfed, it is only with its full advent that theology can rid itself of polytheism. For instance, the Beta God of the organic universe fathered by the Alpha God of the physical universe coexists with the Father-God, but assuming the incipient advent of the Omega God both father-Alpha and son-Beta are consumed in its radiance.

The reason for this is in the nature of the Omega God for whom all of reality has been made into conscious creation, the full sensitization of mass-energy and the recreation of it into the Omega God. The further down and away we move from the Omega God, the more fractional divinity is. Indeed, in the physical world, the Alpha God is fractionalized among every particle of the cosmos, myriads of encapsulated gods, all prisoners of their own deterministic fate. (But since they are so similar to each other, "seen one, seen them all.") The cosmos, as we perceive it now, is one step away from pure homogeneity of an even older Father-God, the pure entropy God, the utter negation of any possible differentiation. The immense pull of such past, like an afterimage that does not fade, could be the explanation of the persistent and formidable trend of Alpha God toward the pure chaos of entropy. The sins of the fathers . . .

Every time the door to the prison where the fractional Alpha Gods are kept is unlocked, each imprisoned Alpha God particle takes cognition of its neighbors and may decide to enter into an association with one or more of them. This is the organic advent.[3] One could hypothesize that the interaction which existed before such a decision was an interaction forced upon each particle by an exterior power (gravitational, atomic, magnetic, etc.), or, which amounts to the same, by a power which was and is most fatally determined, durationally nil, entropically single-minded: the real anti-Christ, fate.

The organic event is the first synthesis of the Beta God from two or more elementary particles of the Alpha God. In what might appear as a paradox, taking into consideration the full evolutionary process, we move from no diversity and total segregation, the one-

[3] The Urban Effect.

per-particle Alpha God, ignorant of everything and each identical to the unknown neighbor, to maximum diversification and total desegregation and, finally, the ultimate synthesis, the Omega God. From ignorance to comprehension, from complexity to simplicity, from analysis to synthesis, from indifference to radiance . . . from randomness to oneness.

At the Alpha God level, the effect is readable into the caused; transcendence is only a distant and remote hypothesis, proposed by no one because no one is there to do so. Self itself is not conceived nor conceivable yet. As soon as the deterministic prison doors are ajar, transcendence moves on to the stage of reality and creation becomes operative.

As of now, in the cosmos we know, transcendence is still primitive, and it has been organically operative for 3,500 millions of years, give or take a few eons. If man is taken as the paragon, this itself gives scale and dynamism to the phenomenon. Thus, if on one side we can feel the immense smallness of the Omega God as measured by the amount of it (Him?) immanent in life the Omega[1] God; on the other side we cannot ignore, even if we want to, the formidable thrust of this hypothesis literally sweeping us from our feet while unlocking matter to wrestle from it the Omega component of the Gamma hypothesis. Stone, the petrified hypothesis of the spirit, ultimately needs the hammering of a compassionate component, a conscience, to deliver itself to the building crew, the organic-mental, to press its own limited self and the parts not yet appropriated, i.e., interiorized, into the total self of the Omega God.

We are not building in the image of God since that is idolatry—the adoration of Alpha God (mass-energy); we create God or we fail to do so. There is no third alternative, since a third alternative is a diminution, to say the least, a negation really, of the Omega God.

Translated into contemporary terms and viewed from the perspective of the eye of the spirit, the most comprehensive definition of pollution is the segregational mode of mass-energy, that is to say, the Alpha God or, better yet, its father, if seen as a situation of origin. This original pool is segregative, polluted, and entropic, the antithesis of the God-Father of traditional theology. If this condition were to be the result of a breakdown of the highest synthesis, then, it would become an evil working against the zenith of diversification in the oneness of the Omega God.

The Church, in its contention that a fully achieved God exists, has to accept the dialectic of an all-powerful, all-knowing God confronted by an exterior "thing" upon which His love has no power of redemption and a weak power of persuasion. No power of redemption since the fall from grace by the "thing" implies faulty omniscience or omnipresence to start with. Only by clearly admitting this original faulty condition in the nature of the Alpha God can one really make head or tail of the fall from grace. That is to say, the understanding is reached that what is in the Alpha God and Beta God is only the first step of numberless steps to come, moving toward the true omniscience-omnipresence of the barely conceivable Omega God. The power of persuasion is weak since the stated contention is that of an existing perfection axiomatically nonperfectable, and therefore the direct consequence is that the less-than-perfect "thing," life, must be outside such perfection and is only incidental, ephemeral, and fraudulent. Then the motives for persuasion become reasons for frustration, if not downright damnation, since they are working on the fragile scaffoldings of joy or sufferance which are illusory.

The consequence is life as a doomed and inescapable spinoff of divinity (the Greek fate), or, quite the opposite, life seen as the eye of the storm making matter into spirit. For the first condition, life seems like one of the last steps down toward the pollution of pervasive entropy, supervised by an impotent God. For the second condition, life is one of the first steps up toward the asentropy of divinity.

To reaffirm the wholeness of the temporal-spatial, energetic-conscious universe and the perceptible and strong thrust that seems to indicate an irresistible, if not automatic, irreversibility of the vector, matter-spirit, in the direction of the last, one can consider the solar system as typical of situations where such irreversibility affirms itself, and where the sun, case by case, is the original, if local, Alpha God, and the spirit developing from it as the sun's offspring is an Omega God that with all the other Omega Gods developing around the other suns throughout the universe sums up into the immanence of the Omega God.

This theology does not intend to be a metaphor but rather a "true or false" situation,[4] a barely structured representation of what we

[4] There is no such thing as a true or false future since the future *is not,* but there is a desirability or undesirability of a future to which true or false might refer.

call reality. To verify it means to realize it since the proof of its veracity cannot be found in simulation. It is, in fact, this impossibility which makes the God of the Church into the Gamma God, the simulation God. This is the equivalent of saying that ultimately the mystery of reality is one with reality itself and the resolution of it, mystery and reality, will have to wait for the most remote of all futures to explain itself to itself.

This is the tautological condition in which creation finds itself. Creation is self-explanatory. Its advent is the reason for its advent. In any other light, creation is not creation, but development. Therefore, the mystery is the creation. The chain of events of every successive link is supported and instrumentalized by, but not traceable to, the preceding. Creation is a folly with secretive intent, part of which is to further another folly with a secretive intent. The folly with a secretive intent of the solar system has been to pollute the terseness of space with bundles of mass-energy in a gravitational, electromagnetic net, the planets. By successive chains of follies with secretive intents, one of these bundles, the earth, through the alchemy of the whole system, has come up with more and more pollutants of terseness: stone from naught, life from stone . . . Alpha God from the unnameable, Beta God from Alpha God . . . and so on.

The position of the Gamma God is critical because it partakes both of falseness and trueness. Only by renouncing the illusion of gazing at the real can the believer find the true sense of its simulated God and trust in the possibility of its advent through faith and deeds. That is to say, as soon as I know that the Gamma God is the false God, I come to know that it stands for a remotely possible true God, the ultimate folly with a secretive intent.

Therefore, the God of traditional religion is a false God, and, at the same time, a necessary guide toward an utterly remote and improbable true God. The sun, the earth, the leaf, the virus, man . . . this chain of ancestry cornering a speck in ongoing, surging space-time and imbuing such speck with the feeble sound of life is the barely conceivable hypothesis of an immense metamorphosis of matter into spirit. Put into the context of man, the hypersensitized part of the immanent Omega God of today, it appears that the city is at the center of the storm, where, to be repetitive, the hypothetical eye is the Omega God. This is so for the elemental-fundamental reason that the city stands as one of the links, and today as *the* link, in the chain of intensification, synthesis, or metamorphosis that sees the Alpha God giving way to the approximation of its own entelechy, the Omega God.

The good city is the center of intense processes where awareness is fed by the abundance of environmental information characteristic of the performing city, supplemented by the more specialized but remote audiovisual, printed, and electronic information, and where, optimally, such information-awareness is transformed into knowledge-wisdom, the attributes of godliness. The good city becomes the city of God when such knowledge is put to use and the ensuing condition is the transcendence into creation, the central attribute of God, the Omega God.

The two suns, the Alpha God of pure matter and the Omega God of pure spirit, one concrete, the other hypothetical, separated by the immense time gap of all futures and linked by infinitesimal moments of consciousness past and present, are not in contraposition to one another. Indeed, since one is the necessary premise for the other, they form an indivisible becoming of media into *the* message.

Revelation, Invention, Creation

SYNOPSIS: Life and consciousness will not touch upon the total radiance of the divine through revelation but through creational genesis. Revelation does not give us a god, only a blueprint for his creation. Religion is not a revelation but a powerfully inspired invention, inspired by the blossoming sacramentality of man's conscience.

As a dilettante theologian I have been tinkering with the ambitious notion of a Universal Church. In looking around for an instrument or instruments capable of this religious unification, I stumbled on the apostasy, or perhaps heresy, of seeing the many existing theologies as instruments themselves. Not that the churches are instruments of God, but that those gods themselves are instruments constructed by the mind and soul of man.

This conclusion didn't come about neatly and suddenly but was the product of a persistent state of dissatisfaction and a certain amount of probing. The churches seem to be the means through which the instrument-God affects man. As a parallel and balancing factor came the realization of the necessity of churches and often the intensity of their sacramentality. But the God of these churches could not divest itself of its true garments, its instrumental nature; the churches will not surrender their status as the closest upholders of the revelation of an extant reality, the true God. Yet this revelation cannot be the word of God for the simple reason that God *is not,* and God is not because God is in the making. God is not as a house is not, even when only a sketchy outline of it is conjectured. God is not as a house is not, even when the process is much further along and walls and roof are constructed. God is, however, in the same sense that premonition, will, design, and partial existence document the advent of a completed, functioning house.

The key concept can be stated as follows: *Religion, a theological structure, is a human design, not conceived around a revelation* but conceived around a longing which prompted man to construct the simulation of a possible future reality. If by revelation is meant the *discovery* of an existing supernatural reality, and if by simulation is meant an *inventive* process by which the future can be prognosticated, then religion is based on simulation, not revelation. Religion is something which stands for something else which does not as yet exist.

Conceding the above, one is struck by the following implications:

1) There is no longer a just and loving power to turn to when things are out of hand.

2) There are no longer two responsibilities (and consequent moral knots):
   A) God's responsibility and   B)   man's (life's) responsibility.

3) There is no longer access, vicarious or direct, to past perfection free of pain and sorrow.

4) There is no longer access to salvation at the end of the personal experience of life, nor is there the threat of personal damnation at such end.

5) There is no one true God who is the God of one's own Church and a false God who is the God of other churches.

6) There are no longer the words spoken by God or by His spokesmen. There are words of men, good men and bad men, and their deeds.

This is, in a way, a belief in God, but a God who does not exist as yet. The position is, thus, as far apart from the orthodoxy of religion as it is from the dogmatism of the nonbeliever, the atheist.

If it is true that in most religions there is a current of futurism, a tension which is achievement-oriented, it is also true that central to all religions is the assumption that one or more gods are overseeing the whole of reality, God or gods who are more than what they watch over. On the other hand, the concept of religion as simulation (see "Religion as Simulation") stands on the premise that such God or gods are not really there, which is why man had to invent them and then had to write the parts such gods have played and are going to play.

In the simulation theology there are incremental conditions of sacredness that can be labeled as gods of certain limited powers. Since such gods are subject to the evolutionary flow, aspects of their power become obsolete and they are superseded by more evolved gods, more inclusive gods. Never at any instant are there one or more gods who are beyond extant reality for the simple reason that the two are but one and the same thing, differently interpreted.

This religion does not fit many of the pantheistic molds since the pressure which characterizes it is the need to transcend whatever it is up to that point. Transcendental action is ill-fitting to the harmony of those pantheistic scenarios.

How does a theological simulation come about? Since man is an inventive species it would be strange if he did not, sooner or later, turn to the greatest challenge of all: *how to extend one's own life beyond one's own life* and to invent in the process the greatest of all structures, God. Since we are not dealing with reality but with an engrossing hypothesis about the future, what is the efficacy of a theological simulation? It is more than that of being a rail on which evolutionary momentum can develop. There is an immanent element in the invention-simulation theology which stands for nothing less than the essence of the living phenomenon. If in this theology the outlook on the future is but hypothetical or anticipatory, the past, in contrast, is eventful and concrete.[1] But, by an inversion of the perspective of orthodoxy, what we see is that if there is in the past something we like to call a God to return to, this Father-God is none other than the limitless polytheism of the mass-energy universe. Then, contrary to the orthodox view, there is a Son-God to be created incrementally through the evolutionary process, and to be fully expressed at the end of time. Indispensable to this process is sustenance of the thrust which transforms matter into conscious matter (spirit) and continual increase in its momentum and magnitude.

Few men in different times and different places built theologies whose nature was to be in place of something desirable which wasn't there. They built theologies as a function of the condition of man there and then: his longings, his terrors, his hopes, his fears, his power, his grace, and his temptations. With those elements as a basis, they constructed models for the future as a technician builds models of mechanisms possibly capable of performing given tasks. A way, perhaps the only way, to sanction such theologies, such models, to put them beyond doubt, ridicule, and chastisement, was to make them oracular, that is to say, revealed. But revelation is only that which is revealed by the author of the revelation to the receiver of

---

[1] Sacred, indeed, because it stands as *it is,* the causation of the present and the premise of the future.

the revelation. There is no malice inherent in the ambiguity of the invention and simulation which is called revelation. When one believes strongly enough in what one is doing, one becomes possessed by it. In that state of being, a mental construction can well strike the soul as revelation. In countless instances, man hears voices from within that he sincerely believes must come from without, or from a "within" which is much more profound than one's own.

If, to keep the theology legitimate, there had been the need of a revelation and thus, necessarily, an author for it, God, then there was no room for doubt that such an author had to exist. Once the theology is accepted as revelation, God exists because only he who exists can reveal. Inescapably then, religion had to be turned upon the past: God is because God has always been. The best thing man can do for himself is to hope to join the eternally blissful being, someday, somehow. The return into the Father is the main objective of man, *the reaching toward a condition of perfection and fulfillment as a reentry.* This is why and how man made a gigantic step backward as he was making a gigantic leap forward: a retreat behind the shield of revelation so as to avoid ridicule or stoning, while declaring for himself the power (invention-simulation) of prediction (and of self-fulfilling prophecy?).

The consequence of such expediency is part of the burden everyone has to carry. Could this burden be the closest approximation of the concept of original sin? An original sin in reverse; to be guilty, not of having bitten the fruit of knowledge, but of lacking the courage, after the tasting, to accept the knowledge and what it would give to man, demonism and anguish together with brief explosions of joy. The sin is in glossing over man's debts toward life, the immense responsibility of inventing sacredness and becoming, in so doing, the prime mover of consciousness, understanding, knowledge, love, and creation.

To invent sacredness was to become aware that with life a new dimension was being added to reality, the dimension of consciousness-passion (compassion). Among the components of consciousness are joy and sorrow, elation and pain. With them was to come forth reverence and with reverence the necessity to proselytize the sacred through the universe, a mandate as inescapable as the thrust that keeps life begetting more life. To proselytize the sacred means to cause sensitivity where sensitivity is not, to sensitize the universe, to inspire the metamorphosis of mass-energy into spirit. It may have been hubris for the founders of religions to demand that the whole world be converted then, when the center of the whole world was the earth; now that this whole world is the cosmos which astronomers, physicists, and mathematicians conjecture about, to proselytize sensitivity throughout it is exponential hubris, a quasi-grotesque gesture out of proportion with the miserable minuteness of the earth and its spirit. But the real question is, does life have any alternative to this responsibility? I think not.

With the onset of consciousness, a progressive and potentially immense dislocation of power has begun to work its effect in the granularity of the physical universe. It is the power of a God in the making, a power which is moved, while transubstantiated, from a reality dominated by statistical laws to a reality constructing ever more compassionate events. It is fate, so to speak, transfigured into destiny; the destiny of convergence into the Omega God, the God hypothesized by the simulative efforts of theology.

There is much talk today of a religion of action, of commitment, as if there were another kind of religion. And indeed, for a theology which depends on an a priori God, action and commitment may only increase the distance from the eternal, self-same God.[2] For this theology, there is a grain of truth in the Lutheran contention that faith alone will suffice for the return of the sinner to the father, inasmuch as this view tends to limit the durational thickening of action. On the contrary, in the fulfillment of the simulation-prophecy, in the process of God creation, of creating a God, it is action, the true action of transformation, transfiguration of the existing, that is the only path taking man and life into the divine.

The most an a priori God can demand of man is inspired stewardship, the good keeper doing the will of the master, which includes the laundering of God's dirty linen, sufferance, toil, the amendment of His mistakes and shortcomings . . . It will not do. It will not do, notwithstanding the clamorings of the pious and the priests, the conservationists and the nostalgic. The spirit is a demonic thrust which cannot stand appeased or quiescent. The demonic com-

[2] If it is true that action makes for durational increments, living time, then the sum of those durational increments may well measure the swelling separation interposed between the lost past of bliss and the believer's present immersed in the immanent dynamics of history.

ponent is inherent in a process which knows that more sensitization implies, with more joy, more sufferance. The soil which becomes a leaf, which becomes flesh, which becomes passion, which becomes spirit, necessarily produces sufferance, the sufferance of living and living in ways increasingly dense in events, in contrast to the nonsufferance of a soil deaf to the call of sensitization. The sufferance of a cracked stone and the sufferance of a cracked skull do not compare. Sensitization, the miracle brought forth by the complexity of the living organism, is the chasm separating the two.

Nothing might be more necessary to break the existential indifference of today's man than to make him sense his responsibility as God-maker. As soon as he forfeits such responsibility, he becomes God-breaker. It is my contention that the new religion humankind needs is the religion of God-making, a continuous realization of the responsibility bearing on any and all thinking beings for taking charge of the evolutionary thrust by putting into it their own personal component in a manner each can handle and a bit more. The God of infinite love and infinite beauty will be, if and when we will it with all of our strength. The more our ways are devious and our souls dried up, the further away in the future moves the advent of such a divine hypothesis.

The God of infinite love and infinite beauty is seminal within ourselves. It is our responsibility as God-makers. This action will in time pervade the universe. We cannot dismiss the immensity of the task and, therefore, the necessity of a humble, a correspondingly, immensely humble, attitude toward that which makes the world a condition of unreserved reverence.

To release ourselves from the bonds of past-oriented theology, it would help if we could make and maintain a clear distinction between nostalgia and religion. Since many emotive notions are nostalgic (fatherland, "those were the good old days," etc.) and since religious notions are highly emotional, we can be, and often are, easy prey to states of being where nostalgia and religion intermix and taint each other. The mixture is explosive, not necessarily in constructive ways, since it is a past-oriented mixture. As a "has-been" Catholic, I cannot separate the Catholic Church from nostalgia for the events of childhood and youth. One's emotional bias for the rites of one's own Church, at the expense of an equitable assessment of other religions' rites, is too evident to need long consideration. There is, then, an emotional block to rationalization, the imprint left by events that touched the psyche before the mind could make any assessment of a logical-rational nature. One is then rationalizing a posteriori under the a priori constraint of psychoemotional nature. In this ever-existing condition, leaders, good and bad, find the handles with which to hold the masses—us: whiteness, blackness, Christ, Mohammed, fatherland, etc. Religion as part of the experience of any individual has such a hold and each of us must try to deal with its power, since it is really a holding power on our being and thus is a molding power on our becoming. It is, therefore, quite understandable that my proposition of a potential Omega God, some fragments of which are immanent in the present, strikes as heresy of the grossest kind or as a useless exercise in hubris.

To those who say that life's struggle is but a struggle of reentry into the Father by a prodigal progeny, I say no. There is only one outcome of reentry. It is the loss of consciousness, the loss of spirit, the loss of life, since the Father is nothing else than the immensely dumb if immensely grandiose universe of mass-energy, the Alpha God.

To those who say that turmoil is illusory because sameness is the true nature of the universe, a universe imbued with beatitude, I say no. There is a seminal and fundamental anguish that is manifested throughout nature as soon as such nature becomes organic. Such anguish is the pain of incompleteness suffered by a living creature for which self-sameness is nothing but annihilation. Nirvana is not a paradise lost. It is an abandoned equipment yard, since life, God, has moved to higher ground.

To those who say that pure senselessness characterizes both the mineral and the organic world, that where indifference is substituted by sufferance and joy is where irrationality supplants senselessness, I say no. Senselessness and indifference belong to the polytheistic kingdom of the Alpha God; sufferance and joy belong to the tide of consciousness sweeping away the senselessness of the mineral world into the cognition-creation of a future God.

To those who say that today, the present, is all there is, that a day stolen away from sufferance and death is all that counts because it is all that can be hoped for, I say no. The present, immanence, is the synopsis of the past, a synopsis measuring how much of the Omega God is achieved or fulfilled; it is the springboard for those next achievements and fulfillments which will inch closer to the full divinity hypothesized by man in his religions.

To those who say that the universe is a perfect engine with which the intellect, given free rein, can overconstruct a super-engine, a shining, polished, rational, logical, mathematical, quintessential structure running itself for itself, I say no. The splendor of the spirit is not made of reductionist mechanisms. If it does make use of them, as it does with technology, it is also beyond them. It is an effect whose cause could not be found in a self-fulfilled mechanistic universe but rather in a universe whose deprivation was the spark for a chain of events in which every effect was transcendental of its own cause, the successive splendors of a becoming, escaping ever more powerfully from the claws of entropic and statistically driven reality.

To those who say that the divine spark which develops as life develops is but a mirror of the divine splendor of a preexisting God, I say no. There is a divine spark developing and such a divine spark is the life spark and there is none other.

To everyone I would say that what we are is no more than a premonition of what we will be, ought to be, if we absorb the fire of prophets and holy men. The journey has hardly begun, life is an infant God plagued by strong drives and inexperience, by physical hunger obfuscating the budding hunger of the spirit, the impatient infant God, a seeker more than an achiever, a fumbling God, often and easily mystified by an immensely powerful and awesomely beautiful cosmos.

The cruelties of the infant God are of the same nature as the cruelties of any infant. The infant is a totally self-centered organism blessed by double luck: a mother is there willing to put up with the "little beast"; and the infant has evolutionarily achieved a physiological automatism which prevents it from self-destruction. It is indeed this perfect robot which unflinchingly demands nurturing and attention for survival. In the infant there is no limit to the indifference toward the sufferance of others. The ego is the center of the universe. All else is for it or against it. Much the same is the behavior of infant life, humankind included. Racial drives, for instance, have the same self-centered fury. Under various pretenses we group ourselves in infant societies and we strike out obsessed by fear, driven by the need to insure survival and dominance in the face of an enemy which is seldom where we think we see it.

In the process of growing up in quest of the self, life will shed the ego. The enfant terrible will begin to have a more reverent perception of itself while acquiring a firmer and more compassionate grasp of the blind and dumb reality of the physical universe. The infant God will increasingly radiate the grace of its sufferance, since sufferance will have been the bread and wine nurturing its emergence.

2

An Eschatological
Hypothesis

INTRODUCTION

THE ESCHATOLOGICAL HYPOTHESIS

THE THEOLOGICAL MODEL

THE URBAN EFFECT

THE NORMATIVE GRID

THE PERSONAL RESPONSIBILITY

INTRODUCTION

Years ago, if asked about the intent of arcology, my standard answer was: the definition of a plumbing for society. Such statement was meant to point out the overdue restructuring of the human-societal environment in its tangible, indeed, physical context. The logistics of the urban system were collapsing and in their physical breakdown flesh and psyche were mesmerized. They still are, in fact, more than ever.

In pursuing effective responses to this nemesis in residence throughout the urban landscape, it becomes ever more clear that there is nothing which expresses itself in a human associative, cooperative, compassionate way that has not been originated and nurtured in and by the physical world. That is to say, a plumbing for society is a sine qua non element on the road to the spirit. What was left out in my statement was a specificity about that which would or could or ought to be found beyond the instrumental threshold of the plumbing for society.

There are two main reasons for this void, one subjective, the other objective. The subjective reason is my limited perception and knowledge of the human condition and consequently limited ability to set or suggest normative guidelines to extend the plumbing to the performance. The objective reason is the real and insurmountable barrier between the creational process of becoming. And any kind of regulatory governing, supervising, and engineering of such creational process. It is a barrier because the province of engineering and the province of becoming, though both strung on the warp of the real, do not match. They do not match for the same reasons that science and esthetics do not match.

The art of living, that sought-after chimera, and the engineering pursued by the social sciences have as many things in common as an engine has with a minuet. And those things in common are more numerous than a cursory glance might indicate. Significantly, they are both consequences of mental processes. But in the final analysis, the nature of the engine and the nature of the minuet differ, one could venture to say, diverge. Left at that, it would appear paradoxical that a good plumbing for society might have anything to contribute to the dance of life. To dispel the paradox is to assert that without the mechanism, any mechanisms specific to the phenomenon, there is no dance. This does not rid life of the mortifying fact that, more than often, the most opulent display of machinery fails to generate even the most timid effusion of joy.

It is the case of a necessary but not sufficient condition: the piano is not the music but without the piano there is no piano music. That is to say, music which is uttered through the necessary instrument called "piano." The arcology is the piano but the design of the arcology is also a musical composition. Therefore, the arcology is machine and minuet in one. And naturally, it can be a good or bad or indifferent machine-minuet.

Where then is the niche of the social engineer? The piano tuner? It has yet to be found because it is difficult to separate the dance of life from the mechanisms of living. Most of that which we have dependent on good engineering, for instance, contentment, really belongs to a far more ambiguous discipline. Transcendence. And that is why from plumbing I had to jump into theology (eschatology) in the strong belief that engineering (or science) must come after the fact, balancing, compensating, throttling, analyzing, systematizing, informing, tuning . . . but never incarnating.

The eschatological hypothesis presented next, as native as it might be, has become mandatory for the definition and conduct of arcology. Without the eschatological hypothesis, or without trust in an eschatological process, the guideline turns out to be fragmentary at best, or pure license by "higher authority" at worst, since it would move into a tunnel with no light at the end. This eschatology is not an attempt after truth since truth is not. Only true processes are (a tautology). But is it that kind of hypothesis which can effectively restore faith in the human condition because it is a hypothesis that can have great normative force and, therefore, is a valid model to be kept in one's mind's eye? As far as I can see, the only way to dismiss it is to offer a more normative conjecture.

For adherence to this hypothesis one can ask science to work out the methodological grid for its denouement. To appease the religious mind, one can suggest that, at worst, the goal would be the cloning of logos, since the hypothesis does not accept the existence of logos (in toto), but it takes as the normative guideline the attainment, that is the creation, of it.

Religiousness[1] is therefore taken as the most serious of all notions and is seen as inseparable from the ecological, evolutionary discipline which automatically anchors it to the question of survival. There is no religiousness without survival, but religiousness transcends survival as any end transcends the means applied to it.

Then what is really to be dealt with at the moment within the eschatological hypothesis is a certain amount of plumbing and then a lust for life which asks to be illuminated and guided by an eschatological beacon. Between the two are the observational processes of science which alter and set up, a posteriori, grids of anticipation. Those grids of anticipation eventually become part of the plumbing in the feedback synergy of the whole. But all along what empowers and signifies is the more or less befitting art of living which by definition is a boundary-speaker and a prophecy-maker (simulation). Calling prophecy anticipation has the advantage of injecting in the question the full charge of ambiguity and indeterminateness necessary to keep planning from becoming deadly déjà vu. Man anticipates. He is an anticipatory animal and his anticipation is colored by its own eschatological hypothesis or the absence of it (a model also).

This synopsis of four religious paradigms (eschatologies) is necessarily limited but hopefully some of the substance is preserved.

1) For the (non)eschatological model of the existentialist, anticipation is at best a heroic but ill-fated, irrational guide; at worst, it is laissez-faire capriciousness masquerading as responsibility.

2) For the pantheistic eschatology, the divine is automatically incarnated in the living stuff and, therefore, the incarnation machine is always right.

3) For the eschatological model of nirvana, sufferance or joy are illusory but overcoming them is optional. It is sufficient to separate oneself from the appearances constructed by senses and ego.

4) For the eschatological model of Christianity there is a fall

[1] Because it endorses the concept of transcendence in the sense of process theology leaving science and philosophy at least uneasy.

from grace which demands man's redemption through faith and/or deeds to sustain the struggle which will eventually return man into the arms of the Father. It is the God incarnated, Christ, who is the anticipatory radiance of all existing divinity, of that which will be if man wants it.

For the eschatological hypothesis put forth in these papers, none of the preceding grid is fitting. Not the first, where the present is all that there is and in it are only unconnected moments of elation and sufferance ultimately meaningless and reaching into nowhere. Not the second, for which all is well since relative incompleteness is the only sin of a world otherwise fundamentally good-natured and predetermined. Not the third, where there is only one unalterable and absolute reality from which life is obscurely separated but into which it will have to fall in due time by way of a dole measured by the sufferance of illusion. Not the fourth, where nirvana is personalized and willed into the Father, for which birth from the Father is both necessity and malediction, and in which denouement is the reconciliation with the Father by the redemptive process of becoming.

However, the eschatological hypothesis proposed here sees in existentialism the importance of immanence, the present, and defines it as the achieved and imperfect if not brutal fraction of a divinity ultimately belonging to a remote future which is possible but not inevitable. In pantheism it sees the justness of a perspective which makes reverential the sight and the response of the beholder, the sufferance of being transcending into becoming. In considering nirvana, the forcefulness of the condition of being is distinct from the condition of becoming in the otherwise fallacious contention that becoming is illusory where being is all that there is. In Christianity there is the powerful anticipatory mechanism of the redemption of the flesh and its resurrectional paradigm.

But this eschatological hypothesis is quite distinct from all four above (even though it could be read into the Christian eschatology if the latter could be turned head to toe). The fundamental difference from them is that this hypothesis is critically wedded to the creational evolutionary process for which truth is not discovered but created and in which revelation is not revelation but discovery, invention, or anticipation (the Christian-Marxist synthesis).

This has a critical bearing on the dignity or indignity of the evolutionary process and its integrity, that is to say, its validity. For those religions postulating a supreme being, to be chased, thrown, or to sneak out of paradise, nirvana, or oneness seems to be the critical act of the consequence of a critical default of life vis-à-vis the supreme being. What is incomprehensible, in fact savagely unloving as well as logically untenable, is the reason behind the generation of imperfection by perfection, of finitude from infinity, etc. Can we seriously endorse the idea that to be innocent animals is satisfying to the Father but to become inquisitive and tormented individuals is an (original) sin unbearable to the Father? What makes innocence become malice if not the existence of the seeds of malice in the Father, the Causa Prima, from which innocence cometh? Theologies have traveled a dead-end road but stubbornness does not break the unbreakable. Fossilization is the nemesis, the "ragione ultima." The only plausible explanation is that the supreme being is imperfect even though nothing else originally constituted a paragon.

But if the supreme being is wanting, then there is no fundamental discrepancy between the hypothesis offered here and those others. My Alpha being is absolute but lacking. Creation is the sufferance of the Alpha being on its way to a transcended nature of itself. Then the return into the Father is indeed a flight into Sonhood, the creation of Omega being by way of becoming.

None of the four eschatologies are satisfactory because for them nothing that life does or does not do really alters the essence of being, be it brains, Jesus, God, Allah, or existence as a beautiful construct (pantheism) or as a deceit (existentialism). Perhaps they are not eschatologies since they do not propose an ultimate end as much as an originating magnet (existentialism excluded).

This introduction is to affirm that the necessary if not indispensable prelude to a fully developed arcological concept is the definition of an eschatological hypothesis.

The Genesis

It starts with the preoccupation about the problems of moving things (and ourselves) from here to there: part of city planning. It ends by seeing the matter of moving things from here to there as the mechanics of God-making . . . by way of perceiving knowledge, etc. . . . as the direct consequence of sufficient concentration of things (complexity), etc. . . . bits of information in specific spots and the power to get to them, concentration made possible by a sufficient reduction of the space-time parameter entering the system (miniaturization). At the ultimate end is an ultradurational system in which complexity is at its paroxysm and is centered within a nonspace, notime system: LOGOS.

THE ESCHATOLOGICAL HYPOTHESIS

1) Is there a need for a causa prima or is it sufficient to observe that to be or not to be are the only two possible stations from which anything can originate?

2) Of the two possibilities, being and not being, it is a matter of fact that being, whatever that might be (a figment of being), is. Nonbeing is forever a discarded possibility.

3) This choice is, by necessity, antecedent to or inclusive of any interceding divine power, since such divine power would itself be.

4) Therefore, being itself, divine or whatever, is not conditioned on antecedent origination. Being is itself original, the original choice between two alternatives: being and nonbeing. A third alternative is impossible.

5) Since being is self-same, nonextensive and undifferentiated, it has to be spaceless and timeless. Not to be self-same would mean to contain becoming. To be dimensional would mean to be surveyable, that is to say, to present more than one self to itself. To be part and to be itself.

6) To be of time would mean to be constantly reforming itself, instant after instant, becoming. Since neither space nor time are parameters of being, questions of where being is and how lengthy it has been are meaningless. Being is being, period.

7) For being, there are two possibilities: to be itself or to be other than itself, to become. Being has chosen to become. What has caused being to alter itself and by so doing to abandon being in favor of becoming is a nonanswerable question. To say that the transition is the will of being is no answer since the question then becomes: What is that which we call the will of being? A better explanation might be that as between being and not being the choice has been being, so as between being and becoming the choice has been becoming. Is being then a superfluous notion? Perhaps not, since becoming demands a staging point which nonbeing could not provide.

8) Being has chosen becoming. The choice is tantamount to the beginning of space, where being can deploy its becoming, and the beginning of time, where being can perform its deployment of becoming.

9) Deployment and performance according to a self-constructing discipline, be it logical, statistical, random, erratic, or other, enact the physical universe (mass-energy manipulated in space-time).

10) For reasons of the law of large numbers and length of the process ("unlimited" availability of mass-energy, space-times), within the logical, statistical, random, erratic, or other discipline, a nonlogical, nonstatistical, nonrandom, nonerratic process has taken hold: the living phenomenology. The living first originates consciousness within itself, then self-consciousness.

11) Therefore, a statistically inevitable point of departure is the origin of a process which eventually makes becoming perceive itself and consequently act willfully upon itself (self-consciousness).

12) One begins to see in sequence that at each bifurcation (fork) the option chosen somehow negates the other. Being negates nonbeing. Becoming negates being, will negates fate . . . negation is part of transcendence.[2]

13) Since becoming occurs in space and time, self-consciousness is a transformed, transfigured manifestation of a being (in the process of becoming) through peculiarly organized arrangements (the psychomatic, social, cultural systems).

14) Given the three media of A) mass-energy (being which space-time has put into motion), B) space, and C) time, as pervasive, it is plausible or perhaps inevitable that that which is going on sporadically throughout the universe (consciousness) will eventually extend itself and totally *pervade* (the) becoming.

15) Therefore, consciencization, which is now an exception within becoming (the fated cosmos), might be "destined" to become the rule, the totality.

16) Then being which opted for becoming is now opting for consciencization and through the "more of the same" rule might progressively dispose of itself totally into consciousness.

17) Totality of consciousness is totality of intellection, integrity of intent and achievement, integrity. At such point, time and space,

[2] Therefore, for instance, God cannot coexist with man since being (God) cannot coexist with becoming (man).

the instruments unraveling the knots of being (into the evolution of becoming), cease, since copresence and timelessness are the necessary conditions for totalizing intellection: logos.

18) Being and logos, the being of the origin and the being of the end, Alpha being and Omega being, have two things in common: they are both outside of time and outside of space. For them, past and present, here and there, then and now, do not have meaning. Alpha being, the father, precedes time and space. Omega being, the son, succeeds time and space. The first is the original media, the second is the final message.

19) If the process (evolution) of becoming into consciousness is not synchronized with the physical pulsation of the universe (Big Bang cycle), then the final being is nothing more than the original being which has traversed space and time essentially unaltered in its becoming and has finally reentered into itself, self-same, unredeemed, unconscious. In this model, instead of creation of Omega being out of Alpha being, there will be the reentry of fragments of consciousness and their dissolution into the Alpha being through the unjustifiable, that is to say, unatonable, becoming. The evolutionary sufferance will have been for naught.

Taking granite as the symbol of the matter-energy universe, it might not be a poor allegory to call this eschatology a granite eschatology since it needs only granite as a starter. It is a granite eschatology reaching for the spirit. It is down-to-earth, stern, demanding, unforgiving, unphilanthropic, and merciless but its denouement is pure radiance-love. It is unequivocal and unambiguous in its broad outline but paradoxical because it is radical. It is truth-maker and not truth-seeker. It is not a spinoff of something nor does anything spin off it. It encompasses and includes. It is totalizing. It is not fatal (fatally coming about). It is willed. It humbles life to glorify its deeds (the Father glorifies the Son, fathering the Son). It cannot be charitable since it has to be compassionate. It cannot set boundaries to the possible since it anticipates boundless radiance.

This eschatology is constructed with the bricks of matter. It is ecological, an ecology which poorly suffers the constriction of the conservations. Landscape, even though (at present) it has to go along with the slow time beat of organic evolution. The end result of this ecological dynamism (demonism if you will) is self-extinction into the Omega being, a fiery being that flowers or forest, fish or fowl, ape or man could not behold, and will not since it is beyond them. The offspring of their sufferance is the Son-God, the Omega seed.

This hypothesis offers the possibility of depriving us of a theological model which is closer to our notion of a religious creed.

THE THEOLOGICAL MODEL

1) The being of the origin is undifferentiated substance. Alpha being is the Father. Alpha being is the base for which there is no baser base.

2) The becoming is instinction within Alpha being, the Father. Distinct entities constitute the pristine becoming.

3) If 10^{80} is the number of distinct particles constituting the being at its first step into becoming, then the Father is parceled into an Olympian gathering of the same number.

4) Therefore (in hindsight), those 10^{80} singularities are the infinitesimal godlets that becoming triggered out of being when time-space began.

5) Characteristic of those 10^{80} godlets is sameness, segregation, determinism, predictability, dumbness, and the outer directness that the totality 10^{80} has on the part $\frac{1}{10^{80}}$. A divine mob, the primeval ultimate in polytheism, the least divine of all conditions . . . nirvana?

6) Only in hindsight is becoming directional toward logos. The original godlets are forced here and there only by statistical mandate to crack their own isolating armor and to look out of themselves. Life originates, therefore, as soon as the 10^{80} godlets turn out to be $10^{80}x$ where x indicates the number of activated godlets, the associated divinities. Once the process of integration is triggered, directionality is originated (survival of the fittest, at first).

7) Polytheism has thus originated its own nemesis. The tragic sense of life is sufferance of the conflict within the universe which involves the consumption of Alpha being by becoming at the beginning, and then the consumption of becoming by Omega being at the end. The consumption by Alpha of itself incarnates becoming, and the consumption of becoming incarnates Omega. The loss of the Father and the unknowability of the Son are the components of anguish.

8)   Since what has happened to some of the godlets—the association into more complex divinities—is a fact demonstrated by the evolution of life, is there a teleological reason why the same might not happen for all of them and to all of them? If not, then somewhere in the future there will be the Omega being, the monotheistic God.

9)   The theological model says, then, that what is at work is the creation of the spirit on the bridge of matter (mass-energy-space-time) between being without cognition (Alpha) and being as cognition itself, logos (Omega).

10)   Therefore, the temporal and spatial process of and/or upon mass-energy is the transfiguration of brute matter, the original being, the Father-God, into divine substance, the final radiance of the Omega being, the Son-God.

11)   The God-Father of orthodoxy stands for the necessary media which transubstantiation will see ultimately as the total incarnation[3] or logos. Or, more hopefully, it stands as an anticipatory blueprint of logos.

12)   In this process, which is consumed within the spatial-temporal domain, there is an incremental degree of grace being incarnated: the immanent, practical Son-God.

13)   Since the transubstantiation of Alpha being into Omega being is mediated by consciousness (intellection), and consciousness is the sufferance of matter becoming spirit, then sufferance is contextual to divinity (Christ).

14)   This theological model is proposed by other religions, for instance the Christian theology, but on a reverse sequence. In such reverse sequence Omega being is seated in the place of Alpha being and the becoming which bridges the two becomes a convolution attempting to reintegrate that which corrupted away from the original plentitude. This is a reentry in the father-mother womb, whole perhaps in some obscure way, but more plausibly tainted and flawed.

15)   This reentry can be seen as the objectification into an eschatological stress of the individual (subjective) dialectic of reach and withdrawal experienced in the birth-development-death process of each individual (ontogenesis). The call of Alpha being is powerful, if not overwhelming, therefore, the individual wants to deify Alpha to

---

[3] Since the transformation is in the nature of etherealization, we really deal with a process of disincarnation (matter becoming spirit).

insure salvation and resurrection. Alpha is thus made into the loving Father or into nirvana.

16) But resurrection (salvation will turn out to be unworthy) is not in Alpha being but in Omega being since in Alpha being nothing is there to resurrect if not an opaque perception of infinite dullness as yet unredeemed by any grace. Omega being is resurrection itself since all and everything are copresent, coactive, with knowledge of all that ever was (time and space are zero).

17) To keep a semantic connection with theological orthodoxy, the Omega being is the Omega God-Son of Alpha being the God-Father, which in the initial step of becoming breaks down into 10^{80} godlets of the polytheistic mineral universe.

18) The Christian theology points to the fatherless condition of life and man in the myth of the Virgin birth. Jesus had a mother in the flesh in Mary and a standby father in the person of Joseph, but truly the Son of God is an apt and in fact powerful symbol of a father-deprived offspring, which is what the eschatological hypothesis proposes. A triangle, then, is made of the mother, the son, and an unlimited but indiscriminate stock of material represented by the physical universe, thus, two persons and a media.

Feminine and Masculine in the Theological Model

1) A father earth and a mother in the flesh nurturing the Son-God gives a clear notion of what the outer environment and its elements contribute to the living inner environment of the womb generating within itself the son (daughter). But the mother acknowledges in the son the real father of her offspring (since there is no other father but man), therefore the mother is the lover of her son. And the son acknowledges in the lover-mother the receptacle for his semen, the tabernacle for his birth, the crucible for his extinction. The three components form the act of love that makes the son into the lover. The mother becomes a lover through the conceiving and generative act in which the son is both engulfed and given birth.

2) There will be no fairness or splendor in the human family where this fundamental distinction and specificity of roles is not intrinsically recognized. The taboo of incest is only the teaser or alert system about the dangers and ecstasies of the heterosexual universe.

3) For the male to lose himself in the generating womb and by

the womb to be (re)generated is the double event relived at each encounter. The son as the son-lover is extinguishing himself and is reborn in that which is not just metaphorically the tabernacle of life. To the support of the mother-lover comes, in the form of nourishment, etc., the somehow wanton father nature, the miscast God-Father of religion. It is, therefore, inescapable that the fundamental relationship that bonds the female and the male is that of the mother-lover and son-lover with secondary attributes of daughter and father, brother and sister.[4]

4) It is not simply because it is possible that incestuous relations might go on between father and daughter, and mother and son that the incest taboo has to be so powerful, but because to sustain the incestuous act is the nature itself of the heterosexual condition in which one kind, the male, while in his role of son-lover, is quasi-perfunctorily fathering, and the other kind, the female, in the role of mother-lover becomes the nurturer at whose breast the new life is fed and cared for.[5] But if the fathering is ultimately secondary to the generative process,[6] the loving is primary in its eschatological cogency and the loving is the loving of the mother-lover for the son-lover because it is in her where the rite of extinction and birth of the male son is celebrated.

5) But while death, dust to dust, is a return (temporal) into the Alpha media, which comes from the father, the extinction in the womb is an anticipatory enactment of the rebirth into the Omega being (resurrection) which is, therefore, bathed in the feminine radiance. To reinforce this rebirth is the fathering of an offspring which is a link and a component of that ultimate being, the Omega being (the entelechy of life's self-incest), which is the final act of the mother-lover and the son-lover joined at last outside of space and beyond time.

---

[4] Theologically, the Women's Lib movement is at best a shot in the dark with a precarious chance of success since a more balanced staging of the parts is yet to be composed.

[5] To incest one might add rape as the second knot of the male-female bond.

[6] It is secondary inasmuch as, for two "perfect" beings, male and female, the conjunction itself *is* the event since in it is the conclusive, total, integral grace. See last two lines of 5).

THE URBAN EFFECT

What is it that spills over from the formulation of a theological model, directly and immanently, into the condition of man. In pursuing such connection it becomes useful to present and explain the Urban Effect.

1) When being becomes, time and space operate. As becoming fills space and grows in time (ages), there is the explosion of the cosmos, the knot of the being, which unravels in space-time.

2) Within the general unraveling and on specifically apt sub-knots of becoming—the earth for instance—life appears as a new type of nodule of perception–conscience–self-perpetuation.

3) Since those nodules, those organisms, are eminently characterized by the same characteristics which are the main attributes of the city (they are cities), it has been found of important normative value to term the specific and distinct effect they portray the Urban Effect.

4) The Urban Effect is fundamentally that original phenomenon in which two or more particles of physical matter begin to interact in ways other than statistical and fatal (the laws of physics), that is to say, in ways which are organic or living and eventually instinctive, conscious, self-conscious, mental, cultural, and spiritual. The Urban Effect is the progressive interiorization and urbanization of the mass-energy universe initially deploying itself in space-time, and eventually recollecting itself, through the transfigurative process of evolution, into spirit.

The initial act of Urban Effect is the breaking of being into becoming, the first acknowledgment of otherness. It originates the space-time coordinates necessary to unravel the mass-energy latent in the Alpha being.

The final act of the Urban Effect, at last exhausting space-time in the transfiguration of the last mass-energy particle, is the denouement of becoming into the Omega being

5) The Urban Effect is the operative presence of that thrust which demands from each moment a next step which will disclose a more complex and integrated relationship within the relative param-

eters of space and time, a greater amount of vivifying stress, a greater degree of miniaturization.

6) This is a condition sine qua non since eventually the resources represented by the mass-energy universe will exhaust themselves and only a quasi-infinite complexity, a maximal miniaturization will be sustained by the present energy field (then near zero).

7) Therefore, the Omega being is a "puntiform" being, outside of space and time as the Alpha being is, Omega having consumed space and time, and Alpha not yet having been touched and eventually unraveled by them.

8) To be true to itself, the Urban Effect has to embody immanently (moment to moment) the norm of its own nature. Therefore, complexity and miniaturization are conditions sine qua non for the nature of the Urban Effect.

9) In the unlimited escalation of the Urban Effect one can trace a reversal of the physical explosion of the universe into an implosive process, the outer limits of which will be the "puntiform" being Omega.

10) This would be the yin-yang pulsation if it were not for the fact that the Urban Effect is nothing other than the total transubstantiation of mass-energy into logos. This incarnation of logos is really the transcendence of mass-energy not into the Civitas Dei but the Deus Civitas, the God-City. It is not the case of logos preexisting, descending into the flesh of the cosmos, but of the ascent, the etherealization of the flesh into the integrity of the Urban Effect by the creational escalatory evolution of intellection.[7]

What then is the imperative defined by the Urban Effect?

THE NORMATIVE GRID

The normative grid is not a rule of conduct but a framework which, if accepted, can guide in establishing one's conduct because it implies definite social, political, economic, and cultural orientations.

1) Since the eschatological model indicates that the responsibility of life is the transformation of the universe into logos, and since the Urban Effect is the mechanism by which the incarnation process has had its origin and its early development, the norm to

[7] See "Logos as the Omega Seed," p. 109.

abide by is that one which sees the process sustained, extended, and intensified.

2) Therefore, the incarnation paradigm defines the urbanization of the universe as a mandatory process. At the end is the Omega being and the resurrectional condition: logos.

3) The urbanizing of the human race is, therefore, not an expedient but the expression of the essential stress of life and intellection toward less and less remote distance from the Omega being.

4) Since the Omega being is an anticipation and not a reality, its creation is contingent on the will and action of our intellection and that of others who might be elsewhere in the cosmos.

5) The urban nodes are approximations, remote approximations of Deus Civitas, the God-City. They must exemplify more and more stringently the normative guidelines.

6) Those guidelines are delineated by the paradigm of complexity-miniaturization, which is not purely methodological but defines, even if indirectly, meanings and priorities.

7) Effectiveness is the basic ingredient of urbanization. Therefore, the development of frugality is not expedient but is contextual to the Urban Effect. The frugal maximizes the effect proceeding from its own cause and in its paroxysm does not simply maximize but makes the effect transcend the cause (the tangibility of this phenomenon is given in the esthetic synthesis).

8) Since the eschatological model postulates creation as the development of evolution and not as an uncovering of a preexisting creation, it well befits the Urban Effect to be an escalatory transcendental (creational) process in which the effect is not implicit or explained by the cause.

9) The norm is then not to set up causal stresses that will have the effect of giving us a closer look or contact with an existing if elusive truth but instead to recognize causal stresses ordained by the past which have to be put to use by self-conscious life in ways which will render, even so slightly, less improbable the outcome of Omega being, that is to say, not the pursuit of truth but the creation-causation of logos as the guiding norm.

10) If the effect were in the cause this creation would be a travesty. It is, therefore, indispensable for each condition to transcend itself so as to incarnate that which as yet is not (but is an anticipation).

11)   To make creation the normative stress is then the imperative, even if not totally recognized, moving force.

12)   Creation is operative if there is a supportive structure that
allows for its blossoming. The supportive structure is to be within the
guidelines of the normative grid which, as the term implies, has to
have a normalcy of spatial deployment and temporal development.

13)   What is normative then is not simply a code of behavior
since it directly involves the space-time parameters. This is easy to
understand because our perceiving, understanding, and responding
are constricted and are constantly constructing around themselves
the physical landscapes of civility (or uncivility).

14)   This behavior and the Urban Effect are distinct but inseparable. It is somewhat a sign of coarseness or arrogance on the part of
the behaviorist and the social scientist to believe that the environment does not speak of social, political, economic, religious, and esthetic commitments and directions.

15)   Articulation of the message implicit in the urban landscape
is the task that must be performed. With articulation, care must be
taken not to dogmatize that which needs to remain ambiguous since
it is the principle of uncertainty which has to govern the quivering of
matter in the process of transcending itself.

16)   This ambiguity is to be upheld now more than ever because
it is now that the engineering of behavior tends to follow the steps of
the engineering of instrumentality (electrochemical technology).

For the participant in the arcological prototype project the normative grid is to be taken as a serious definer of one's own action.

Nature of the Process

To condense the preceding, one can say that the nature of the
process is the transformation of an original Alpha state characterized
by utter elementariness and utter isolation. The unlively and the un-
knowing, into a final Omega state of utter complexity and utter integrity, the lively and the knowing. The process is endless since it ultimately entails the participation-transcendence of the whole cosmos.
The process is creational in the sense of flowing into ever new and
improbable processes, moving further and further away from the
original state (Alpha being) to approximate more and more the final
state (Omega being).

In order to define the process, intellection advances an eschatological hypothesis which outlines the characteristics peculiar to the process (I call this the Urban Effect as it focuses directly upon the human condition) and with which to develop a theological model.

Participation in the Process

Every living thing is participating in the process, consciously or not, willingly or unwillingly, but to be willfully and concretely part of the process and to do so within the parameters of a human family beset by definite and specific wants is to abide by the theological model and to define by it the normative grid. The normative grid outlines personal responsibilities which are maximally proposed by the Christian ethic but to which new ones are to be added.

THE PERSONAL RESPONSIBILITY

1) Each person is a focal point, an Urban Effect, surrounded by a sea of looser traceries. This sea is in turn host to myriads of other focal points, one of which is the I.

2) As a focus, things converge upon the I and things diverge off it. The I is responsible, within limits, for both convergence (interception) and divergence (radiance).

3) The I is a coresponsible parameter of what the I becomes and of what it broadcasts to the neighboring focal points (I's).

4) The right of the I to be invested with a certain amount of benevolence is to be reflected in at least an equal amount of benevolence radiating from it. Otherwise, the total economy of the composite I is stifled, flawed by parasitism which is the destruction of that amount of benevolence absorbed but not in turn radiated by the flawed I.

5) On the other hand, if output only equals input then the process becomes a steady state and the loss of time that results is more substantive than the waste of personal life, since it is a condition which echoes the nature of the Father, the original lifeless storehouse of mass-energy, the Alpha being. It is an entropic fall within the asentropic flight.

6) The dimming of personal radiance, which is the true damnation in store for it, is a constriction operating on the composite I, a

constriction declared by the rule that the sins of the Father will descend upon the children.

7) An opaque performance disavows the performers' position. It is up to the mercy of the composite to keep a parasite within its folds. Considering the wanting nature of each focus it is obvious that charity turns out to be self-charity and as such has to be evaluated and constrained (which are the intrinsic, inner, limitations of charity).

8) Forgiveness is eschatologically possible and desirable; forgetting is not, since resurrection is unconditional and includes as much the resurrection of the unforgettable action as the resurrection of the act of forgiveness.

9) Resurrection is not the replay of a tape which has been manipulated and thus rendered palatable, but the reenactment in utterly new light of the whole evolutionary span between Alpha being and Omega being wherein every fragment becomes a portion of a clear thread woven into the warp of the space-time grid in total relatedness and now rendered infinitely small and infinitely short by the complexity-miniaturization of Omega being.

The dignity of life, in contentment or in sufferance, can only be affirmed if individual action makes a difference, and for a difference to be true, it has to cause a polarization (as small as necessary) of the future. What is in store at the end depends on this differentiating action.

Otherwise, the dignity of the person is reduced to a bargaining capacity with this or that superpower which ultimately will have the last word . . . in Thy name I deliver myself . . . It is a limited dignity, a slave syndrome dignity, at best it is the dignity of the object of revelation setting itself at the task of obeying the command of the revealer.

The dignity of the creational is something else altogether. Nothing will become which is not the specific personal responsibility of someone. All will add up to a possible if improbable ultimate denouement. The Omega being is none but the offspring of an immense mothering and fathering, or nurturing and loving, stretching the full breadth of the time and space, consuming the full content of the universe in the compassionate light of an ultimate total integrity and sensitization.

The personal task is then an imperative, a responsibility for which accountability is direct and focuses on the sufferance imbedded in life, human and prehuman. We can certainly escape from this responsibility by becoming irresponsible.

The Unborn Constituency

Since the eschatological hypothesis is predicated on the future as the uncreated bulk of reality, the whole process has to act today for the sake of tomorrow. Tomorrow has its own constituency. Who speaks for the unborn and with what authority?

Since much ado is made of the right of the individual to have his/her voice heard and listened to, and since more and more of society's actions reach into the future, how is the universal suffrage meant in nonabusive terms? The right to life of the antiabortionist crusade is an example, and perhaps not the most convincing, of a struggle put up by the future at the hands of present forces (people).

Is a society that is oriented toward instant fulfillment and gratification capable of reaching decisions intended for and directed at the well-being of generations to come? Only by chance, when self-interest, measured in political shifts (elections) or in very short processes, happens to coincide with long-term improvements. Parts of the environmental battle which might improve fishing conditions or camping conditions, for instance . . . But in general there cannot be true regard for the children of one's children when the most important index of well-being of a nation is measured by the gross national product.

In times of tragic imbalance, when famine and bleak poverty are finally perceived as unnecessary, societies have found leaders (Marxist and others) who were able to originate a commitment that made them transcend their own need, then so essential, and design and work for a more distant good. There has been much justifiable criticism of those movements that promised little to the present for the sake of futures more human. But a good dose of philistine self-pity is also traceable in the resistance to actions which are not immediately rewarding.

The notion of personal responsibility is locked to the necessity of planning and implementing so as to transmit to the unborn effective premises for their actions. The feeble voices speaking for them need reinforcement and reinforcement must come from deeds. The altruism implicit in such deeds need not be sacrificial since there are substantive rewards intrinsic to the deeds themselves, but the rewards do not fit the mold of the behaviorist ethic (reward, punishment, reinforcement . . .). This also applies to the realization that since the present shows no interest in the substance of the existential dilemma, one has to turn to future generations in the only way possible: staging of favorable conditions, those which might leave the best options open. This implies the acceptance of all the friction caused by the demand that people work perhaps against their strongest inclinations.

The resurrectional conclusion of the eschatological hypothesis closes the cycle and sees responsibility flow into fulfillment because it maintains that we will be resurrected only if our deeds and those of our progeny are up to the creative task of God-making. Therefore, by working for our progeny, we do work toward our own resurrection.

Logos as the Omega Seed

SYNOPSIS: Life, conscience, and spirit are not generated by other than themselves. They are a fatherless phenomenon powerfully and irreversibly urging the winding up of the cosmos into the synthesis of divinity. What the process seems to suggest is that ultimately a universal genetic matrix, the Omega seed of resurrection, will contain the totality of all that has been.

THE SELF-SEEDING OF EVOLUTION

The proposition is that reality is not so much an evolutionary unfolding as it is a seedless phenomenon, a fatherless offspring. In pursuing the creation of its own seed, reality will eventually reenact itself in the full self-knowledge intrinsic to the resurrectional radiance of the ultimate "tree," the offspring of the Omega seed.

The premise is that a seed, any seed, vegetal, animal, or human, which develops in the organism, vegetal, animal, or human, is a living instance of the complexity-miniaturization paradigm in process. As *ultimate being,* the seed is, at present, a blueprint, a hypothesis, and therefore only a potential fulfillment. The conclusive ultra-being is not the development, in the force field of mass-energy, of the potential process packed in the seed's genetic matrix; it is instead the self-creating process whose aim is the causation of the final entity, the seed itself, in constant metamorphosis because it is pursuing its own image, its own entelechy.

In the field of human concerns, the hypothesis which anticipates the seed is the theological concern (the what). The development, in accordance or discordance with it, is the technological concern (the how). The accounting, a posteriori, of the process and the feasibility models for its substenance (the rationalization of the how) are the scientific concern. The assessment of the truth and impact of the theological concern and the process of its actualization (science and technology) is the philosophical concern (the why). The bits of transcendence scattered along the path blazed by the process are the esthetic acts (fragments of the what).

But this whole process is the same kind of process underpinning ontogenesis. That is why the human hypothesis is present in the first quivering of the earliest living substance. By the same token, the seed of the oak did not initially appear in final form, ready to go, but came about by mutational, adaptive stages. In the perspective of the Omega seed, the difference between the theological anticipation of ultra-being and the oak organism is that then there were no prophets anticipating the oak species since consciousness was still an unthinkable possibility. Therefore, though the ontogenesis of an oak tree is predefined by the acorn, the genesis of the oak species was not predefined. It could only be anticipated, as Omega is anticipated. Neither genesis fills a predefined niche in time-space, neither is genetically determined. They go about creating their niches, creating themselves, that is.

The eschatological hypothesis is an anticipation of that ultimate seed which nature, in its evolutionary development, has the power to produce as the whole total cosmic tree (being), the resurrected evolution of the universe. But, if for the oak tree the process was to construct itself by selecting a few elements from the cosmos at large, then for the Omega seed, the selection has to become a total, participatory involvement in space-time of all of the cosmos. Then, things appear to be as if the universe were like a tree which is working at the production of that tiny kernel of substance which will contain in essence the tree in toto. Since the tree is self-creating, the true nature of the seed is as yet not only imperceptible, but also inconceivable. Therefore, the seed is not at the origin but at the end. This explains why everything is beyond comprehension, since the matrix, the seed, is nowhere to be found if not in and by the conclusive act which will see it appear in the summer of time, at the end of time.

Reality is a seedless phenomenon engaged in the task of creating the seed, logos. Once the seed is created, reality (the tree) will be able to "repeat" itself in all the singular variations peculiar to the individuals involved in the repetition. Each will be instantaneous, since all have lived precedently, but in the obscurity of fragmentation and not in the radiance of the total comprehensiveness and inclusiveness of divine ecstasy.

Therefore, the difference between cosmogenesis and the growth of the oak tree is that while the tree can find itself by seeking itself according to its own genetic matrix, the cosmos has nothing like that to turn to. The cosmos is seedless, fatherless. It has to invent, indeed create, its own matrix.

The anticipatory work of saints and prophets is like a kaleidoscopic blueprint which seeks to be such a matrix. This pursuit of the final total seed, logos, is consigned to different provinces of the real so as to cause the advent of local seeds, those that could eventually come together for the conclusive implosion into logos.

In speaking of the necessity of introducing more zones of automatism into the evolutionary process is meant the intent of originating those new matrices, those new seeds, which will perform automatically from within, the living processes of ever greater complexity: the self-seeding of evolution. But, then, is this not the same process that constrained the determinism of matter to give way to the demonism of life and cause the creation, step by step, of the seed of a tree? The seed of a tree is the "final" monad which has resulted from a tâtonnement, eons long, of elements belonging to the living kingdom assembling one link at a time the genetic helix of that specific tree. It is, therefore, in the offspring (the chain of offspring) that the essence gathers, and at the origin what is to be found is not essence but longing, at most, chance, at least. That is the nature of the original divinity: the consequence of being, surprised in the act of becoming, and being anguished ever since by the awesomeness of the task of creating its own seed.

The resolution has become total participatory involvement (in time-space), the injection of meaning in every remote and dull corner, the loving metamorphosis into limitless understanding of a progressive, total densification of complexity obtained by a progressive and total miniaturization. At the point of convergence of those two totalizations is the Omega seed, explosively resurrectional and manifesting itself in the cosmic tree.

OMEGA SEED AND RESURRECTION

Most often, the poetry of religious fervor reveals more the nature of the author than the nature of the subject, God. Of Him, one has the characterization as the creator, the loving maker, the careful administration, the invincible bastion against evil, and so on.

My God has to be far more specific and awesome, totalizing, comprehensive, encompassing, being, acting, engulfing, performing the what, the where, the when, and the how so as to be the why of its own whatness. Cosmically, it has to have the same kind of specificity one can find in the discrete genetic matrix of an organism. Isolating an organism from the rest of the world, one could imagine that the seed it carries is the repository of its history, that is to say, the evolutionary progression of acts whose end product is the organism itself. But since such organism has not exhausted all there is as media for its own evolution, its own matrix not only is not cosmically whole but is not in the position of reflecting its own history upon itself. It exists but is not knowledgeable of its being. It is an end product but not an instance of total recall, of being in itself and experiencing it, as the complete process that has eventually reached its own present identity. Its history is still made of past dead histories. Resurrection has not irradiated the matrix and the matrix is a silent repository of a past which has existence only in the genetic archives. It is a contrived, synoptic, skeletal, disposable landscape stretching across immense spaces, immense times, immense events.

But the Omega seed, if it is the genesis, comprehensive, conclusive, and all-consuming of the cosmos in toto, is then the genetic matrix of the real, a real made all-present in the consumed parameters of time, space, mass-energy. The seed has imploded within itself the whole creational process which has brought the cosmos to Omega. This resurrectional stage is then the specificity of the Omega seed, inasmuch as it says unequivocally that the final conclusive act of the evolving cosmos is reactivation in the light of total understanding, e.g., enjoyment and sufferance of absolutely all the past, the history of every speck of has-been matter in its participatory process of making the Omega seed.

From the most impersonal act, a stone being consumed into dust, to the most personal, private, and mental act, a person living his own life, all actions are reenacted as hierarchical parts of the evolutionary process, reenacted as conscious knowledgeable coauthors of the whole, the whole being for all of them transparently perceivable to the hierarchical degree justly pertaining to each of them. The fact that the perception of the stone will still be a stony perception will be seen in that context which will also see those same particles in the stone being involved, incarnation after incarnation (disincarnation), in the making of lichens, birds, lions, humans, transhumans, and so on up to Omega.

Individuality will then be not just preserved, it will be bathed in the light of understanding as in a sphere of transparent identification with all that has been an agent in the making of Omega. Then one will experience *the being* of an atom, of a virus, of a flower, of a dinosaur, a forest, a galaxy, a Giotto, a Lincoln, a Christ . . . Omega.

If this infinite experience and the plentitude which comes with it are desirable, then it has *to be made true*. If this infinite experience is not given now but assumed somehow in fragmented ways for our divinities, then *it has to be made possible*. If this infinite experience does not yet exist, since history is in the making, then it is not revelation which impinges on man as an imperative, but rather *its creation which imperatively presses upon man*. If this infinite experience is a future, then science, the discipline of what is, is to be taken as instrumental in the divine beautifying process of the cosmos becoming grace. If this infinite experience is immensely more engrossing than our personal worth, then fulfillment is not in salvation but in the resurrectional Omega seed.

Therefore, the eschatological model of the Omega seed is not:

Intended to deal with the truth but with the desirable.

Intended to deal with the given but with the possible.

Intended to deal with the revealed but with the creational.

Intended to deal with the scientific but with the esthetic.

Intended to deal with personal salvation but with resurrection.

THE RESURRECTIONAL LENS

The equity implied in the Omega seed has to be absolute. Only with it can love be infinite. How can equity be absolute? It can if the nature of resurrection is such as to render to each exactly that intensity of recall which reflects the relative trueness of each.

The desirability of Omega seed has to be maximal since the sufferance involved in its advent is also maximal. Such desirability would be perhaps disputable if the end result were simply understanding (logos?), but if with the understanding comes also the experience of the radiance of Omega in its infinite capacity for recall within the light of an Omega perception, then Omega seed is irresistibly desirable.

Who would not want to be all and everything while knowing all and everything to the degree of one's own trueness?

Since resurrection is not a survey of the past but is the past being lived in the present of Omega as it has never been experienced before, totally knowledgeable, i.e., totally loving (a transego trip), then it is in that condition where the fullness of life, from the most primeval to the most complex, is fully and ab eternum performed. This performance will not entail simply the reliving with astonishing brilliance of each life by each life, but the reliving in utter ecstasy by each life of all other lives (to the degree of one's trueness, again).

Through the resurrection lens, each particle will relive, *be,* all the other particles in all their most particular vicissitudes. Since motivations and drives, intents and action will be integral parts of the equation, the justness of the reliving and redoing will be by definition the supreme justice of Omega seed where nothing gets forgotten but all is forgiven (loving).

Where the notion of logos might be wanting is in the possible lack of the experiential side of Omega seed. Omega seed does not just know; *it is* also all that it knows and, since it knows all, it is also all. It is all of its becoming since it is the genetic matrix of all, not a synopsis of all but the actual, total, self of evolution.

The cactus out there in the ground reenacts itself in Omega seed, then as a polarity of the cosmos in all of its originality, now transmuted in all its universality. Then the cactus and all finds itself to be the means for its own end and for all other ends, and in such a position sharply focuses upon its own specificity as forever impregnated of finality, a true end in se and per se.

This end is not shelved away in some cosmic archive but is instead alive and kicking in the resurrectional radiance of Omega seed. But in a way, unless such grace is reached, the end nature of the cactus and all is so ambiguous as to become irrelevant. The final act is the one which transfigures all the means of the process into an endless and awesome tidal wave of ends.

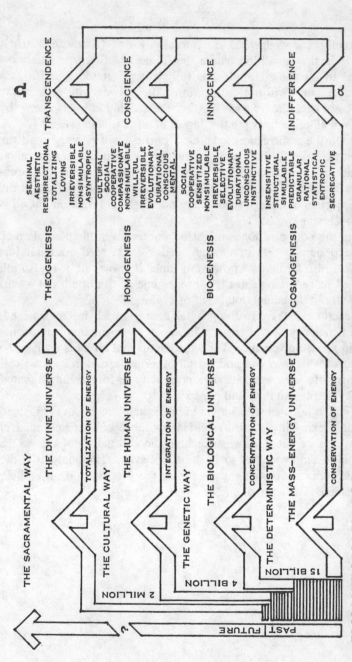

EVOLUTIONARY ESCALATION SUGGESTED BY THE HISTORY OF THE EARTH

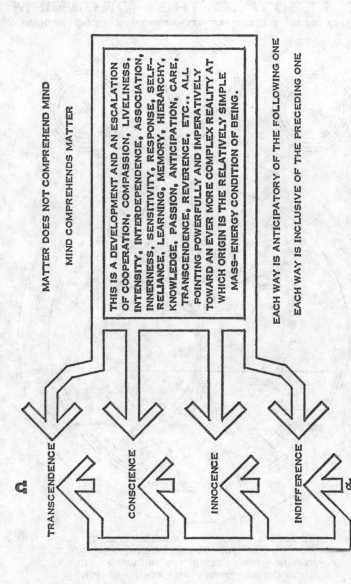

MATTER DOES NOT COMPREHEND MIND

MIND COMPREHENDS MATTER

THIS IS A DEVELOPMENT AND AN ESCALATION OF COOPERATION, COMPASSION, LIVELINESS, INTENSITY, INTERDEPENDENCE, ASSOCIATION, INNERNESS, SENSITIVITY, RESPONSE, SELF-RELIANCE, LEARNING, MEMORY, HIERARCHY, KNOWLEDGE, PASSION, ANTICIPATION, CARE, TRANSCENDENCE, REVERENCE, ETC., ALL POINTING POWERFULLY AND IMPERATIVELY TOWARD AN EVER MORE COMPLEX REALITY AT WHICH ORIGIN IS THE RELATIVELY SIMPLE MASS—ENERGY CONDITION OF BEING.

EACH WAY IS ANTICIPATORY OF THE FOLLOWING ONE

EACH WAY IS INCLUSIVE OF THE PRECEDING ONE

Ω

TRANSCENDENCE

CONSCIENCE

INNOCENCE

INDIFFERENCE

α

THE NATURE OF THE EVOLUTIONARY ESCALATION

THE SEED AND THE ORGANISM

AS INSTANCE OF THE COMPLEXITY—MINIATURIZATION PARADIGM

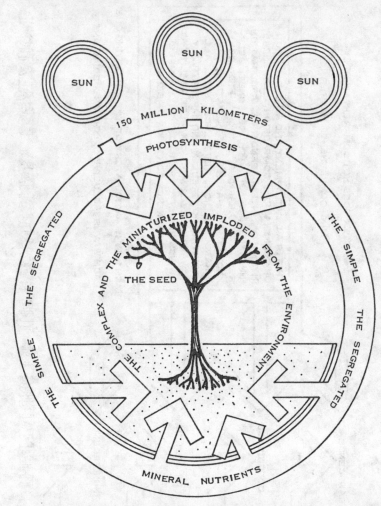

FOR A UNIVERSE TOTALLY INVOLVED ALONG EONS OF TIME, THE "TREE" WOULD BRING TO FRUITION THE ULTIMATE GENETIC MATRIX, THE SEED CONTAINING WITHIN ITSELF THE WHOLE OF CREATION EXTANT AND OPERATIVE: RESURRECTION.

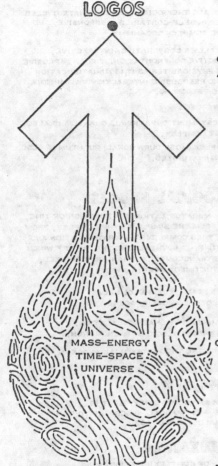

LOGOS

MASS–ENERGY
TIME–SPACE
UNIVERSE

THE NATURE AND EXISTENCE
OF COMPLEXITY ARE
POSTULATED ON MINIATUR-
IZATION. ONE COULD HYPO-
THESIZE A UNIVERSE WHICH
CONTAINED ALL THE
SENSITIVITY AND KNOWLEDGE
OF LOGOS BUT WAS SCRAMBLED
AND SEGREGATED IN ITS PARTS,
MAKING IT INEFFECTUAL AND
USELESS. SUCH A UNIVERSE
WOULD BE TRANSFORMED
INTO LOGOS BY THE REUNION,
RECOMPOSITION, INTEGRATION
AND ACKNOWLEDGMENT OF
EACH PART WITH ALL THE
OTHERS: A MINIATURIZING
TRANSCENDENCE OF THE ONE
INTO THE OTHER.

DO WE HAVE CASES WITHIN
REALITY WHICH MIGHT
ANTICIPATE SUCH A TOTALLY
ACHIEVED CONDITION, AND
IF WE DO, WHERE, HOW MANY?
SUCH CASES EXIST ON THIS
EARTH, MYRIADS, MILLIONS
OF BILLIONS OF THEM, FROM 3500
MILLION YEARS OR SO OF
THE PAST. A TIDAL WAVE
DEMONSTRATING THE
COMPLEXITY-MINIATURIZATION
PHENOMENON; A TIDAL WAVE
THAT HAS TRANSFORMED
THE EARTH GEOLOGICALLY,
CHEMICALLY, ENERGETICALLY,
ECOLOGICALLY, THEOLOGICALLY:

A DIVINE SUBSTANCE
IN THE MAKING

THE COMPLEX
IS POSTULATED IN MINIATURIZATION

THE PARADIGM OF
COMPLEXITY - MINIATURIZATION - DURATION

THE SEED

THE VEGETAL, THE ANIMAL, THE HUMAN AND THE SOCIAL SEED ORIGINATE CYCLES
OF GATHERING AND ORGANIZING MATTER IN SELF—CONTAINED, RESPONSIVE, AND
PROGRESSIVELY MORE COMPLEX ORGANISMS.

LIVING IS THEREFORE AND FUNDAMENTALLY A COOPERATIVE, INTERACTIVE, AND
CONSTRUCTIVE PROCESS, NOT A DESTRUCTIVE CONFRONTATION. IT IS AN IMPLOSIVE
PROCESS, NOT AN EXPLOSIVE ONE. IN PHYSICAL TERMS IT IS MINIATURIZATION
FAVORING THE EVER MORE COMPLEX AND RESPONSIVE INTERACTIONS WITHIN THE
PROCESS OF BECOMING.

THEREFORE

(1) IN ANY GIVEN SYSTEM THE LIVELIEST (MOST DURATIONAL) QUANTUM IS ALSO
THE MOST COMPLEX.

(2) IN ANY GIVEN SYSTEM THE MOST COMPLEX (MOST DURATIONAL) QUANTUM IS ALSO
THE MOST MINIATURIZED.

THE THEOECOLOGICAL PROCESS

SINCE IT APPEARS THAT COMPLEXITY—MINIATURIZATION IS A FUNCTION OF TIME,
THAT IS TO SAY, EVOLUTION MOVES FROM THE SIMPLE TO THE COMPLEX, FROM
THE SCATTERED TO THE GATHERED, THEN COMPLEXITY—MINIATURIZATION AND
DURATION ARE POINTING TO THE FUTURE. IT IS THEREFORE THE FUTURE WHICH
IS THE POTENTIAL WITNESS OF THE TRANSCOMPLEX, TRANSMINIATURIZED,
TRANSDURATIONAL: THE OMEGA SEED: LOGOS.

BUT THIS EVOLUTIONARY ESCALATION IS ECOLOGICAL,
THEREFORE IT IS A THEOECOLOGICAL PROCESS.

MAN, AS ALL OF LIFE, IS THE EVOLUTIONARY ESCALATION.
MAN AND LIFE IN TOTO ARE A THEOECOLOGICAL PHENOMENON.

THE METHODOLOGICAL PRINCIPLES WITHIN THE THEOECOLOGICAL PROCESS ARE:

COMPLEXITY

THE PROCESS IS COMPLEX AND COMPLEXIFYING. IT IS
A COOPERATIVE, SELECTIVE, PEDAGOGICAL, DISCRIMINATIVE,
SPACE—TIME IMPLOSIVE PROCESS.

MINIATURIZATION

THE IMPLOSIVE CHARACTER OF COMPLEXIFICATION, MORE
INFORMATION—INTERACTION LINKAGES IN LESSER TIME—
SPACE QUANTUM, MAKES MINIATURIZATION THE PHYSICAL
PARAMETER OF THEOECOLOGY.

DURATION

THE TEMPORAL DEPLOYMENT OF THE PROCESS ALONG THE
NOT PURELY ATOMIC CLOCK BEATS BUT ALONG THE TRANS—
FORMATIONAL BEATS OF LIFE IS THE DURATIONAL
CHARACTER OF THEOECOLOGY.

EVOLUTION

EVOLUTION AS THE GENESIS (THE CREATION OF GENES) OF A TOTALIZING
ULTIMATE Ω SEED WHICH BY ITS OWN APPEARANCE (THAT IS AT THE
POINT OF BECOMING CONCRETE) TRIGGERS THE INSTANT RECALL OF
RESURRECTION. THE WHOLE COSMOS IS THEN "REPLAYING" ITSELF IN
FULL SELF-KNOWLEDGE. MASS-ENERGY, TIME-SPACE ARE CONSUMED
BY ITS BECOMING.

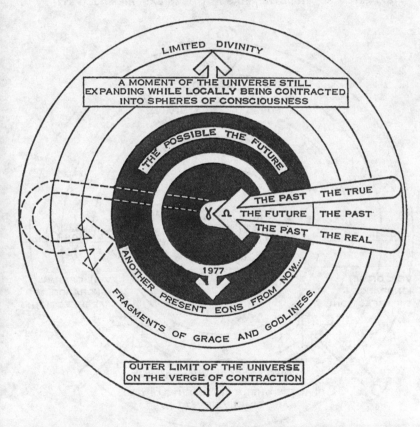

CROSS-SECTION OF THE EVOLUTIONARY SPHERE ORIGINATING AS MASS-
ENERGY AND ENDING INTO Ω SEED AS LOGOS (RESURRECTION) IN THE
TIME-SPACE PULSATION.

REVELATION

AMBIGUITY OF CREATION
AS ACCEPTED BY (DOGMATIZED) RELIGION.

ULTIMATE REVELATION AS THE FALL OF THE LAST VEIL INTERPOSED
BETWEEN THE EXTERNAL "INDIVIDUAL SOUL" AND THE ALL INCLUSIVE,
"PERFECT" DIVINITY.

PAST AND FUTURE ARE EQUALLY "PRESENT": ONE HAS BEEN
EXPERIENCED, THE OTHER HAS NOT BEEN EXPERIENCED (YET).

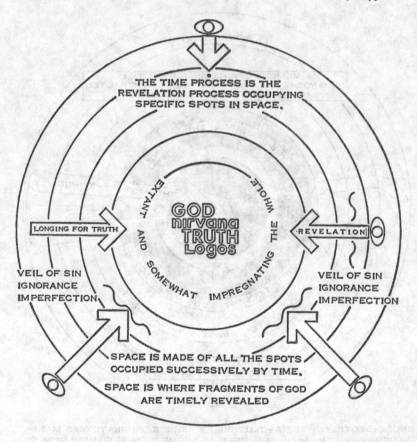

THE TIME PROCESS IS THE
REVELATION PROCESS OCCUPYING
SPECIFIC SPOTS IN SPACE.

EXTANT AND SOMEWHAT IMPREGNATING THE WHOLE

GOD
nirvana
TRUTH
Logos

LONGING FOR TRUTH

REVELATION

VEIL OF SIN
IGNORANCE
IMPERFECTION

VEIL OF SIN
IGNORANCE
IMPERFECTION

SPACE IS MADE OF ALL THE SPOTS
OCCUPIED SUCCESSIVELY BY TIME.

SPACE IS WHERE FRAGMENTS OF GOD
ARE TIMELY REVEALED

GOD, LOGOS, NIRVANA AS ETERNAL AND SELFSAME.

BIG BANG (α) · LOGOS (Ω) MODEL

MATTER–ENERGY, SPACE–TIME ARE NOT "GONE" BUT ARE CONTAINED
IN THE Ω MATRIX (THE INSTANT RECALL OF RESURRECTION)

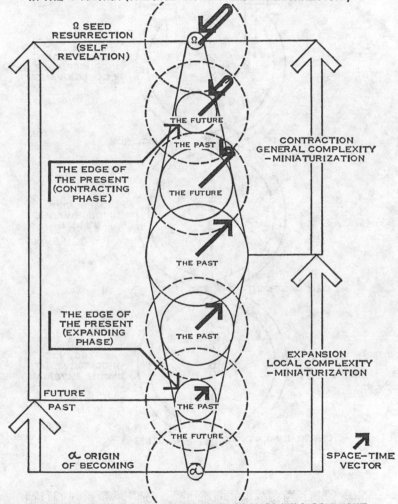

Ω SEED
RESURRECTION
(SELF
REVELATION)

THE FUTURE

THE PAST

CONTRACTION
GENERAL COMPLEXITY
–MINIATURIZATION

THE EDGE OF
THE PRESENT
(CONTRACTING
PHASE)

THE FUTURE

THE PAST

THE EDGE OF
THE PRESENT
(EXPANDING
PHASE)

THE PAST

EXPANSION
LOCAL COMPLEXITY
–MINIATURIZATION

FUTURE
PAST

THE PAST

THE FUTURE

α ORIGIN
OF BECOMING

SPACE–TIME
VECTOR

BY THE ESCALATION OF COMPLEXITY, THE COSMOS WILL CONTRACT
(MINIATURIZE) WITH THE CONSUMPTION OF THE MATTER–ENERGY,
SPACE–TIME PARAMETERS INTO Ω.

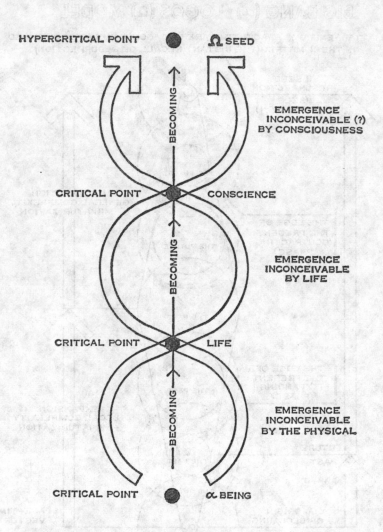

HYPERCRITICAL POINT ● Ω SEED

BECOMING

EMERGENCE
INCONCEIVABLE (?)
BY CONSCIOUSNESS

CRITICAL POINT CONSCIENCE

BECOMING

EMERGENCE
INCONCEIVABLE
BY LIFE

CRITICAL POINT LIFE

BECOMING

EMERGENCE
INCONCEIVABLE
BY THE PHYSICAL

CRITICAL POINT ● α BEING

THE SHORTSIGHTEDNESS OF EVOLUTION

THE COLLECTIVE (SPECIES) PATTERN IN CYCLES OF CIVILIZATION.

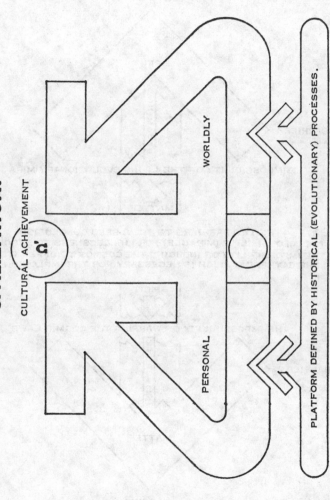

CULTURAL ACHIEVEMENT

c'

WORLDLY

PERSONAL

PLATFORM DEFINED BY HISTORICAL (EVOLUTIONARY) PROCESSES.

DOUBLE JEOPARDY OF Ω SEED

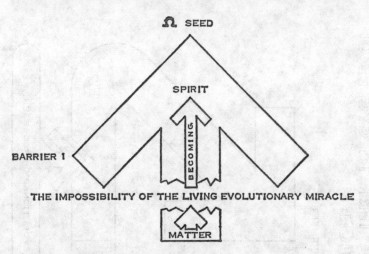

Ω SEED

SPIRIT

BECOMING

BARRIER 1

THE IMPOSSIBILITY OF THE LIVING EVOLUTIONARY MIRACLE

MATTER

THE TWO BARRIERS TO THE Ω SEED CONCLUSION:
① THE IMPOSSIBILITY (MIRACLE) FOR LIFELESSNESS TO BECOME LIFE.
② THE IMPOSSIBILITY OF INDUCING THE COSMOS TO OFFER ITSELF FOR
THE GATHERING WHICH IS NECESSARY FOR THE IMPLOSION IN Ω.

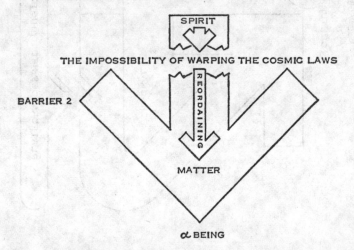

SPIRIT

THE IMPOSSIBILITY OF WARPING THE COSMIC LAWS

REORDAINING

BARRIER 2

MATTER

α BEING

BOTH BARRIERS HAVE BEEN BROKEN THROUGH BY EXTANT LIFE AND BY
NUCLEAR PHYSICS (A CRACK IN THE BARRIER AT LEAST).

THE INDIVIDUAL PATTERN IN THE LIFE CYCLE.

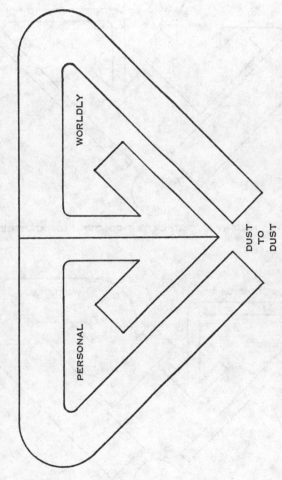

WORLDLY

PERSONAL

DUST
TO
DUST

THE INDIVIDUAL DEVELOPS ALONG A PERSONAL PATH AND ALONG A SOCIOCULTURAL (WORLDLY)[1] PATH TO REENTER AT THE END INTO THE "WORLD OF NATURE".

[1] WORLDLY IN THE SENSE OF OTHERNESS.

INDIVIDUAL IMBALANCE

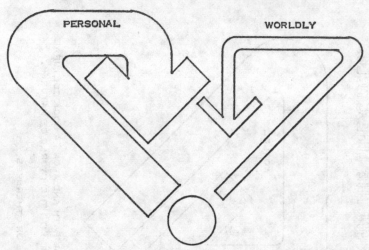

IMBALANCE CAUSED BY EXTREME SELF-CONCERN (EGOCENTRISM).

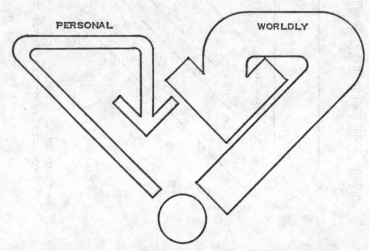

IMBALANCE CAUSED BY EXTREME OTHERNESS (SELFLESSNESS).

FUSION OF THE TWO MODELS

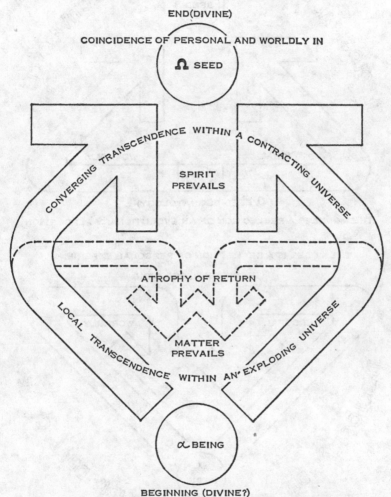

END (DIVINE)

COINCIDENCE OF PERSONAL AND WORLDLY IN

Ω SEED

CONVERGING TRANSCENDENCE WITHIN A CONTRACTING UNIVERSE

SPIRIT PREVAILS

ATROPHY OF RETURN

MATTER PREVAILS

LOCAL TRANSCENDENCE WITHIN AN EXPLODING UNIVERSE

α BEING

BEGINNING (DIVINE?)

LACK OF ANY DISTINCTION BECAUSE OF UTTER FRAGMENTATION

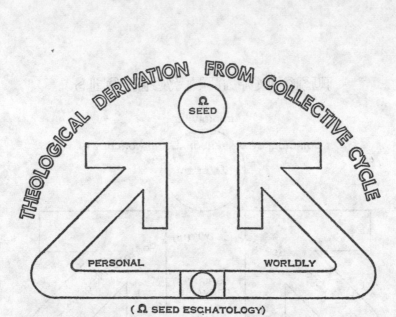

THEOLOGICAL DERIVATION FROM COLLECTIVE CYCLE

Ω
SEED

PERSONAL   WORLDLY

(Ω SEED ESCHATOLOGY)

THE MODEL IS A REFLECTION OF AN EVOLUTIONARY PERCEPTION

THE MODEL IS A REFLECTION OF PERSONAL EXPERIENCE

(TRADITIONAL RELIGION)

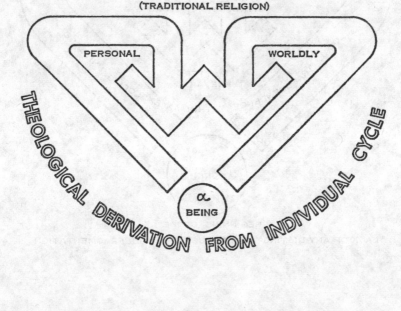

PERSONAL   WORLDLY

α
BEING

THEOLOGICAL DERIVATION FROM INDIVIDUAL CYCLE

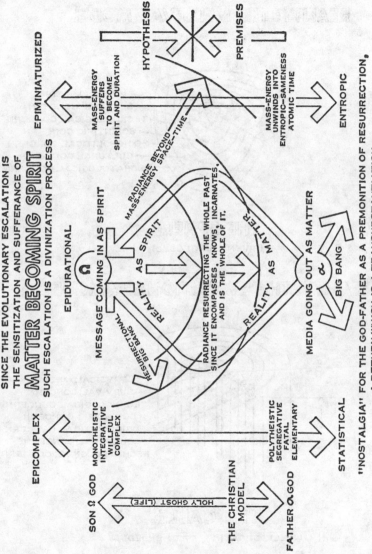

REALITY: THE MEDIEVAL MODEL

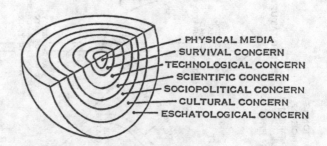

PHYSICAL MEDIA
SURVIVAL CONCERN
TECHNOLOGICAL CONCERN
SCIENTIFIC CONCERN
SOCIOPOLITICAL CONCERN
CULTURAL CONCERN
ESCHATOLOGICAL CONCERN

THE SPHERE
(GIVEN AND CLOSED)

REALITY: THE EVOLUTIONARY MODEL

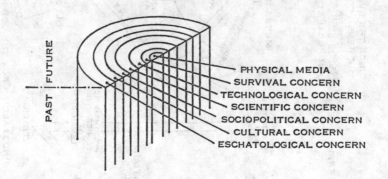

PHYSICAL MEDIA
SURVIVAL CONCERN
TECHNOLOGICAL CONCERN
SCIENTIFIC CONCERN
SOCIOPOLITICAL CONCERN
CULTURAL CONCERN
ESCHATOLOGICAL CONCERN

THE CABLE
(SELF-CREATING, OPEN-ENDED)

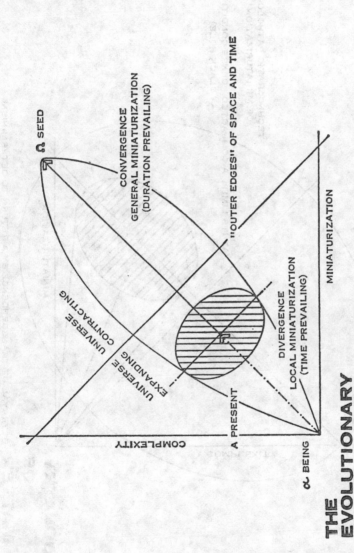

THE EVOLUTIONARY CABLE BETWEEN α BEING (BEGINNING) AND Ω SEED ("END" – RESURRECTIONAL EXPLOSION).

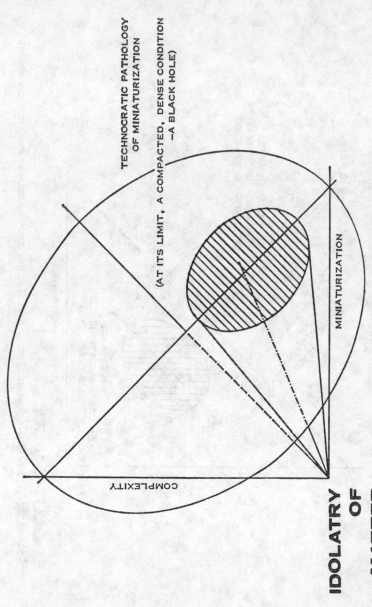

TECHNOCRATIC PATHOLOGY
OF MINIATURIZATION

(AT ITS LIMIT, A COMPACTED, DENSE CONDITION
—A BLACK HOLE)

MINIATURIZATION

COMPLEXITY

IDOLATRY
OF
MATTER BETRAYAL OF TRANSCENDENCE BY A RETURN TO DETERMINISM

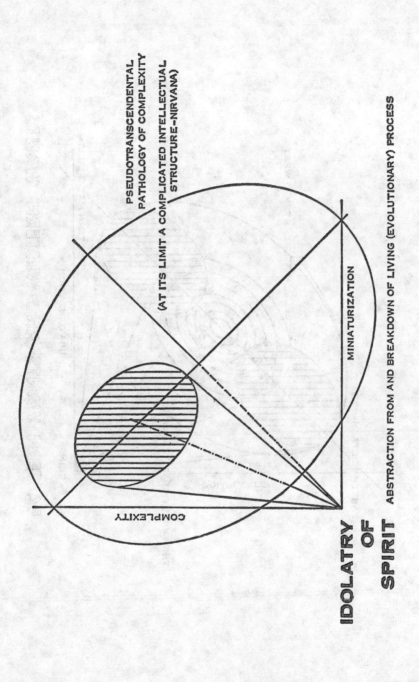

PSEUDOTRANSCENDENTAL
PATHOLOGY OF COMPLEXITY

(AT ITS LIMIT A COMPLICATED INTELLECTUAL
STRUCTURE-NIRVANA)

MINIATURIZATION

COMPLEXITY

IDOLATRY
OF
SPIRIT   ABSTRACTION FROM AND BREAKDOWN OF LIVING (EVOLUTIONARY) PROCESS

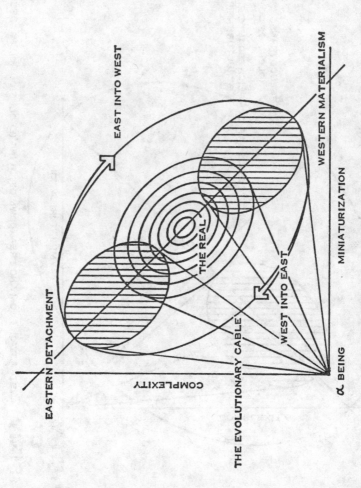

EASTERN WANTS AND WESTERN WANTS

RECAPITULATION

(1) LIFE IS A TRANSHUMAN PHENOMENON.

(2) THE THEOLOGICAL COMPONENT OF LIFE YIELDS THE RELIGIOUS NATURE OF THE ECOLOGICAL EVOLUTION WHICH SUSTAINS AND IS LIFE.

(3) THEOECOLOGY HAS METHODOLOGICAL GUIDANCE IN THE COMPLEXITY–MINIATUR– IZATION–DURATION PARADIGM.

EXTRAPOLATION

AT THE END OF SUCH PROCESS IS THE MONOTHEISTIC GOD. THIS GOD IS THE GOD–SON, NOT THE GOD– FATHER. THEREFORE THE α GOD OF ORTHODOXY IS AN INVENTION–SIMU– LATION OF A POSSIBLE AND REMOTE Ω GOD–SON OF WHICH WE, LIFE, ARE THE MAKERS OR THE UNDOERS.

SUCH GUIDANCE IS THE MOST CRITICAL DEFINER OF THE HUMAN ENVIRONMENT.

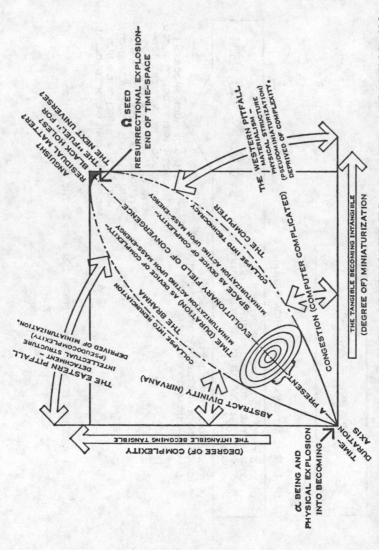

THE EVOLUTIONARY CABLES ORIGINATE IN α AND, FOLDING IN UPON THEMSELVES INTO Ω, COMPOSE THE EVOLUTIONARY SPHERE.

URBANIZATION AS THE ONGOING NATURE OF THEOECOLOGICAL EVOLUTION

LIFE HAS BEEN URBANIZING ITSELF FROM ITS INCEPTION

THE FIRST ORGANIC MOLECULE WAS THE FIRST URBANIZATION, THAT IS TO SAY, THE APPEARANCE OF THE FIRST BOND OF COOPERATION—INFORMATION—KNOWLEDGE—RESPONSE—INTERDEPENDENCE CAPABLE OF TRANSCENDING THE DETERMINISTIC DOGMAS OF MASS—ENERGY; EVENTUALLY SUCH BOND WILL BLOSSOM IN THAT WHICH WE CALL LOVE, THEREFORE TRUE URBAN—IZATION IS A LOVE BONDAGE.

ARCOLOGY, THAT IS, ARCHITECTURE AS HUMAN ECOLOGY, IS ONE OF THE MANY STAGES OF SUCH URBANIZATION.

THE COMPLEXITY, MINIATURIZATION, DURATION METHODOLOGY AS IT APPLIES TO THE CITY.

1. CONSEQUENT TO THE FORTUITOUS OR DIVINE TRIGGERING OF LIFE, THE UNIVERSE OF MASS-ENERGY IS IN THE PROCESS OF ETHEREALIZING ITSELF INTO SPIRIT.

2. INTRINSIC TO THIS METAMORPHOSIS OF MASS-ENERGY INTO SPIRIT IS THE EVER-INCREASING COMPLEXITY OF THE SYSTEMS CARRYING ON THE TRANSFORMATION.

3. THE SPATIAL MECHANISM OF PUTTING MORE INTO LESS TO ALLOW FOR THE INCREMENTATION OF COMPLEXITY IS THE MINIATURIZATION PROCESS.

4. ON THIS EARTH, THE MOST COMPREHENSIVE STRUCTURE EMBODYING THE BECOMING OF ETHEREALIZATION IS THE CITY: A DURATIONAL, LOVING, UNFOLDING PHENOMENON.

A. THUS THE CITY, THIS ETHEREALIZATION MACHINE IS RIGOROUSLY GOVERNED BY THE PHYSICAL ENERGETIC RULES OF COMPLEXITY-MINIATURIZATION.

B. AMONG THE MANY OPTIONS OFFERED TO CONTEMPORARY MAN, THE COMPLEX MINIATURIZED CITY IS THE LEAST OPTIONAL INASMUCH AS IT IS MANDATORY FOR THE SPIRIT.

C. THIS CITY IS A SOCIAL, POLITICAL, ECONOMIC, MORAL, AND CULTURAL IMPERATIVE AND UNDER THE CURRENT DEMOGRAPHIC PRESSURES IT IS ALSO A SURVIVAL NECESSITY.

D. THIS GIVES THE LIE TO MOST OF OUR PRIORITIES AND DEMYTHOLOGIZES PRACTICAL MAN, AS HIS PARADIGMS ARE BANKRUPT. REAL MAN IS MAN OF THE SPIRIT.

THEREFORE, FOR REAL MAN, THE TRUE CITY IS NOT THE CITY OF GOD, THE CIVITAS DEI, BUT THE DEUS CIVITAS, THE CITY-GOD.

THE ARCOLOGICAL COMMITMENT

ENDS

BUT ALL THESE ELEMENTS ARE INSTRUMENTAL FOR THE WELL-
BEING OF HUMAN KIND. THEY ARE MANUTENTIVE AND RESTORATIVE,
THEY ARE NOT SPECIFICALLY CREATIVE. THEY ARE ONLY A THRESHOLD
TO GRACE. THEREFORE, THE ARCOLOGICAL COMMITMENT IS NOT INDIS-
PENSABLE BECAUSE IT IS THE BEST INSTRUMENT FOR SURVIVAL, AL-
THOUGH IT IS JUST THAT.

ULTIMATELY, THE ARCOLOGICAL COMMITMENT IS INDISPENSABLE
BECAUSE IT ADVOCATES A PHYSICAL SYSTEM THAT PERMITS THE
CONVERGENCE OF THINGS, ENERGY, LOGISTICS, INFORMATION,
ACTIONS AND THUS CAN FOSTER THE THINKING, DOING, LIVING, AND
LEARNING OF MAN AT HIS MOST LIVELY AND COMPASSIONATE. THE
CONDITION OF GRACE IS POSSIBLE FOR AN INDIVIDUALLY AND SOCIALLY
HEALTHY HUMANKIND IN AN ECOLOGICALLY HEALTHY EARTH. IT IS
A THEOECOLOGICAL ESCALATION TOWARD THE DIVINE.

THE ARCOLOGICAL COMMITMENT

MEANS

IF LIFE IS A GOD—MAKING PROCESS AND IF THE METHODOLOGY OF COMPLEXITY, MINIATURIZATION, AND DURATION IS REAL, THEN AN ARCOLOGICAL COMMITMENT IS NOT AN OPTION BUT A NECESSITY. IT IS THE URBAN EFFECT IMPERATIVE.

THEREFORE THE ARCOLOGICAL COMMITMENT IS INDISPENSABLE FOR:

1. THE ALLEVIATION OF THE ECOLOGICAL CRISIS.

2. THE REDIMENSIONING OF OUR USE OF LAND, AIR, AND WATER.

3. THE REDUCTION OF THE POLLUTION CAUSED BY TECHNOLOGICAL SOCIETIES.

4. THE PERCEPTION OF THE NATURE OF WASTE, AFFLUENCE, AND OPULENCE.

5. A REASONABLE SHELTERING OF MAN ON HIS WAY TO BECOMING 9 BILLION OR MORE IN NUMBER.

6. RESOLVING THE PROBLEM OF ENERGY DEPLETION, DISTRIBUTION, AND CON—SUMPTION.

7. RESOLVING THE PROBLEM OF SEGREGATION OF PEOPLE, THINGS, AND ACTIVITIES.

8. RESPONDING TO THE INCREASING ENCROACHMENT OF REMOTENESS BY WAY OF GIGANTIC SERVICES AND THEIR BUREAUCRACIES.

9. A RENEWED TRUST IN THE FUTURE OF LIFE IN GENERAL AND MAN IN PARTICULAR.

SYNOPSIS OF OPPOSITION

MEGALOPOLY (ACTUAL)	ARCOLOGY (THEORETICAL)
BIGNESS	SMALLNESS
EXPLOITATION	FITNESS
SEGREGATION	INTEGRATION
MATTER	MIND
POWER	AUTHORITY
DESTRUCTION	CONSERVATION
POLLUTANT	NONPOLLUTANT
ENTROPIC	ASYNTROPIC
DIMNESS	INTENSITY
EDEN–LOST	POST–EDEN
FRAGMENTED	STRUCTURED
EXCLUSIVE	INTERIORIZED
COMPLICATED	COMPLEX
BUREAUCRATIC	PERFORMING
OPULENT	FRUGAL
GREEDY	CULTURAL
INCONGRUOUS	CONGRUOUS

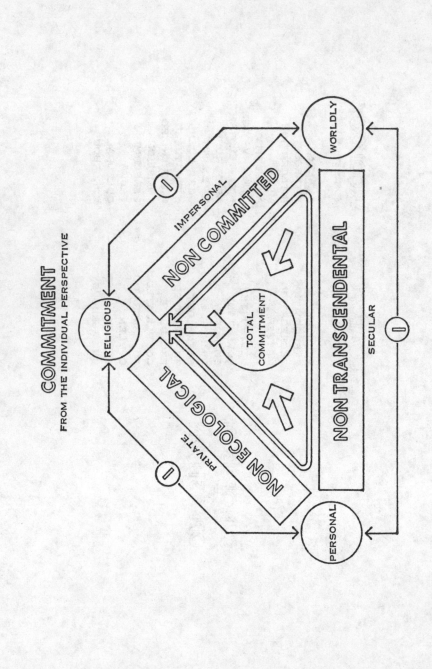

COMMITMENT

FROM THE INDIVIDUAL PERSPECTIVE

WORLDLY

IMPERSONAL

NON COMMITTED

RELIGIOUS

NON TRANSCENDENTAL

SECULAR

TOTAL COMMITMENT

NON ECOLOGICAL

PRIVATE

PERSONAL

3

Space and Man

SYNOPSIS: If science is correct in determining the earth to be composed of the same stuff which makes up the cosmos, and if life is the technology through which such stuff becomes animated, then life, which now appears to be the exception to the rule within the physical cosmos, could eventually become the rule. If, in addition to being feasible, this potential animation of the cosmos is also desirable, then the responsibility of life lies in the transfiguration of an immensely powerful physical phenomenon into an immensely loving spiritual one. An eschatological imperative. The esthetogenesis of the universe.

On what can be defined as the threshold to the infinity of space, the human species is going to make momentous decisions. Some of them will be unconscious and irreversible, some will be conscious and crucial. First, if the space colony venture is to be developed, we must seek consensus. In an undertaking of this magnitude, it has to be a transnational consensus and it must be knowledgeable. This will be impossible if the pioneers and promoters themselves are less than clear about the scope and impact of the enterprise.

What follows is a tossing in the air of a few points of concern about which consensus might be sought, the sooner the better.

A)   The technological concern: I am not well equipped to tackle the technical underpinnings and therefore assume, for the sake of what follows, that we are capable of doing what the scientist and the technologist say can be done. At the same time, since its end product will be habitat, the technological concern is very close to my interest. Ultimately, the technological concern is subservient to the eschatological[1] concern and the habitat will have to be imprinted by it and imbued with it.

B)   The political-economic concern: It is per se a tangled knot to which we respond or react in more and more empirical ways because the inertial stresses pervading it are increasingly beyond our limited wills and wisdom.

C)   The eschatological concern: There will be renewed religious unrest, caused by the space probe, focusing on eschatological issues which will embrace social, environmental, cultural, ethical, and esthetic concerns. All operate directly upon the human condition in conjunction with the questions of health and genetic preservation.

This last concern will be largely unspoken and intentionally

[1] Eschatology: a study or science dealing with the ultimate destiny or purpose of mankind and the world. (Webster's Third New International Dictionary)

brushed under the rug of hard facts and technopolitical imperatives. And yet, the stakes are frightfully high; we must face what we are about to plan and implement. Under the pressure of scientific and technological "progress" stimulated by the space venture, the eschatological concern will give rise to new or pseudonew theological models. Thus, as I perceive it, the probe of life into space is, ultimately, not a technological, political, or economic problem but a theological one.

The eschatological implications of space colonization are fundamental and critical. I will consider the following aspects:

1) *The eschatological concern.* The question of the ultimate aim and purpose of life, the eschatological paradigm as such.

2) *The genetic concern.* The splitting of the human species into subspecies (which has prehistoric precedent) as a direct consequence of space being invaded by humanity.

3) *The urban concern.* The space probe is the urban probe on new grounds. Therefore, the urban question looms ever larger in the destiny of the species.

Depending on how these questions are approached, hope or despair will emerge.

In despair:

1a) We see ourselves as well-worn sorcerer's apprentices, incapable of halting the plunge into technological hubris which more and more forcefully brings upon us the wrath of our indignant Father, the Lord, and our merciless expulsion from nature's bosom.

2a) The human species, abandoned by the Lord, Providence, and instinctual wisdom, will tear itself apart under the stress of new (evil) environs and spawn inimical subspecies which are foreign to each other. These will find their own nemeses in specialization, genetic or otherwise.

3a) The human species will make an ever more compromising step into the urban syndrome, seen as the sum of all evil, since space colonization will be directly informed by those conditions which per se define the current urban context.

In hope:

1b) We are making (reaffirming?) a promethean commitment to the spirit by taking action to release it from the gravitational vise of the earth and by opening the cosmos to urbanization, that is, to logos.

2b)   The human family recognizes its genetic and other limitations and willfully seeks morphologically new cognitive forms for the purpose of outfitting itself for the immense journey into the spirit via the flesh (mass-energy), the process being a lengthy series of transcendences of psychosomatic self.

3b)   In stepping off the earthly landscape, man is turning (by necessity which will become virtue) toward a frugality of environs and hardware specific to the urban condition, toward ever more crucial transphysical longings. In sum, man will opt for the self-containment of his habitats, their inward orientation, the cooperative and interdependent nature of the social and cultural texture, high density performance, the imperative of integrity and self-reliance and, finally, the complexity and miniaturization of the milieu. The space city will, therefore, be an unequivocal test of our readiness for the vertigo of a momentous step toward spirit.

I will proceed through the hopeful triad since there is where I stand and since, in so doing, it will be possible to examine the despair triad as well.

1)   THE ESCHATOLOGICAL CONCERN

First, I must critique the lifeboat metaphor and the carrying capacity thesis. I would offer the notion that their weaknesses do not come so much from relativism peculiarly anchored to the consumer ethic (the gross national product mentality), but from the scientific theory on which they stand being quite possibly unscientific, basically a verification of past facts which shies away from expectations that appear unscientific since they are only in the realm of the possible (feasible). If this is so, if the science of the carrying capacity and lifeboat ethic is unscientifically applied, then its use is needlessly vicious. It is the viciousness of inflicting pain and death by the incongruous application of a paradigm.

Let's look at the carrying capacity thesis as it seems to have developed. The first living thing on this planet had, as a necessary support system, the entire existing cosmos, since only the existence of a specific if unknown cosmic balance made possible a specific if unknown solar system balance. This made possible on earth the appearance of a specific organism (one had to be the first). The cosmos in toto was the "territorial imperative" of a bacteria-like organism. No cosmos as such, no bacteria as such.

Even at that moment, or a bit sooner, things were becoming autonomous, that is to say, not purely deterministically generated; life forms were not hopeless prisoners of a totalitarian cosmic dictum. The solar system was coming to life and on earth, for instance, physical balances were affected by physiological counterbalances. Oxygen was freed into the forming atmosphere through the initiative of living organisms, etc.

A first massive implosion of territoriality from cosmos to solar system, specifically, sun-earth-moon, was taking place. So it came to be that the territory of each organism was a proportional fraction of earth bulk to which was added a similarly defined fraction of the sun energy falling upon earth and, in addition, relatively small influences such as moon tides, cosmic radiation, etc.

If one takes a look at the contemporary scene and simplifies the model, one sees that every human being requires the presence and use of a cone of matter (defined by the radius of the earth, with a base measured by a circle upon the biosphere, atmosphere included) of, let's say, approximately one hundred acres. This gigantic mass, to which must be added its share of sun energy, is but an infinitesimal fraction of the original mass necessary for the advent of the first bacteria-like organism—and we begin to feel crowded—but we also begin to appreciate the providential tendency of life toward frugality. Providential, since if it were otherwise we would soon be face to face with the fatal dialectic of a self-parting, expanding universe and a level of consciousness that must abide by the fierce rules of shrinking carrying capacity, face to face with lifeboat ethics, triage, etc. That is to say, without the tendency toward frugality, there would not be the rationale of evolutionarily expanding capacity, extension of reach, and contraction of needs, but rather an ontological wall made of indisputable and ultimate stop signs: a dying sun, the size and resources of the earth, and, consequently, life seen as a short fireworks display of arrogance and opulence.

Where is an even more incredible explosion of frugality in store? It is in the most frugal and crowded mode of all, the brain of man, that powerful cognitions are working out more miracles of contraction and frugality (the Urban Effect in full swing) and, lo and behold, a few hundred thousand years after the invention of divinity, that prophecy of utter economy, the mind conceives a fully lived, extraterrestrial existence. The implosion in the brain creates, at least potentially, an explosion of ecologies, eventually unlimited in number, capable of sustaining and developing life, ad infinitum.

If for a moment we assume that we will make the step of colonizing space and do it without diminishing man, then what do we have? An utterly new relationship with the world of matter. We will literally mine the universe, the solar system at first, rearranging and processing matter into hollow cities of all sizes, types, and populations. The order of the Christian God, "go and multiply," would see an unimaginable degree of realization and the carrying capacity of the cosmos would grow exponentially. With this, the lifeboat theory would be blown to bits since it would serve only that self-righteous society unwilling to get down to tasks and construct new boats, one after the other, on and on forever.

But why such explosion of life? For what purpose? The answer is theological. Before going into it, let's reiterate what would happen to the territorial imperative. With the space venture, the bulk of matter necessary for each person would shrink dramatically from the individual earthly cone, with a corresponding ecological veneer and sun energy, into a bulk on the scale of a home attached to an urban landscape, to which would be added an open space of some acres or a fraction of an acre and some energy from the sun and stars on which the city might depend. In other words, it would be as if the earth (or any other celestial body) were to be peeled off in successive skins,[2] each containing an interiorized landscape (cityscape) of minimal physical bulk: a characterization of the human environs as exponentially frugal. Thousands upon millions of hollow worlds, inner-oriented because of locally produced gravity, would invade the universe from as many points in it as there are conscious centers (similar to earth). Eventually, each galaxy would have the carrying capacity of four thousand million consciences (the earth today) billions of times over, a true explosion of consciousness throughout the physical universe.

What is so desirable in such a model? On the personal level, one

[2] The earth would be the last to be so treated, since the biosphere is original, unique, precious, and beautiful.

could ask if one would choose to be born. Even if the personal answer is no, to negate the birth of others, provided there is carrying capacity, would be rude to say the least. On the ontological level, it would seem clear that it is only with the intensification of reality by the presence and action of life that we might eventually bring compassion and grace to the whole cosmos, the integrated universe.

The theological answer, insofar as life and consciousness can be generalized, implies that:

1) Consciousness is an unbelievably interiorizing stress.
2) Consciousness is an unbelievably complexifying stress.
3) Consciousness is an unbelievably miniaturizing stress.
4) Consciousness is an unbelievably frugalizing stress.
5) Consciousness is an unbelievably animating stress.
6) Consciousness is an unbelievably transcending stress.
7) Consciousness is an unbelievably urbanizing stress.
8) Consciousness is an unbelievably divinizing stress.

It is only half true that there are but potential powers of consciousness; a cursory survey of life's evolution clearly, if coarsely, demonstrates such power. These implications are all versions of the fact that the eschatological imperative is issued from reality as an inescapable command: do unto matter (the mass-energy universe) what you do unto yourself. Make it into conscious matter, into logos. That is, demand and force out of an ephemerally conscious universe that which will ultimately be a child God of infinite conscience, infinite integrity, infinite love.

When the biological has reached dimensional limits—the size of organic molecules—and has not been supplanted by a "better" media—since only that which can plan and operate[3] congruously, intellection, can also put more understanding, design, and will into ever smaller amounts of mass-energy, space-time (miniaturization)—it is the space city, the urbis et orbis in one, which is to be sought as the next step toward logos. This is a statement of feasibility and desirability at the same time. To work against the process is ultimately to work against logos itself and consequently against the spirit. This feasi-

---

[3] That it can also operate incongruously is a well-known fact, therefore, our constant condition of emergency. But what if we were to lose our intellectual capacity?

bility demands implementation. The question remains open . . .
when?

It would be then for the sake of logos that life must free itself
from the earthly prison. And, if it is possible for life to free itself
from the earth, isn't it then a mortal sin not to do so? And isn't the
fact that life could not even conceive of leaving the earth before the
appearance of consciousness, and the fact that thousands of years
ago the first step toward this leaving expressed itself in metaphorical,
religious form, proof of sorts that it is the task of life and specifically
of consciousness to do just so?

From a territoriality of the whole cosmos necessary for the appearance of the first living cell on earth, to the ecological cone necessary today for each creature populating the earth, to the minute territoriality of a space city, we can measure the powerful trend toward
frugality and the concurrent opening of the whole universe to the
spirit. Once upon a time, a whole cosmos for one infinitely puny life;
eons later, intellection grasps at the alchemy of matter and makes it
deliver its latent energy and potential conscience, giving impetus to
the possibility of mining the cosmos, of making a moon into "large
numbers of earths," etc.

The ape, tethered by gravity pulling down toward the center of the
earth, has its territorial imperative by the ecological capacity of the
earth. With the appearance of the human mind, the tether is potentially cut. The ecological capacity is potentially transferred from the
limited earth to the endless universe. For this potentially quasi-
infinite growth of liveliness, two things seem to be indispensable: a
quasi-infinite growth of will and a quasi-infinite growth of reverence.
Given these, divinity is inherent in the future.

There are two final considerations relative to the eschatological
concern:

1) How much or how little we make of liveliness and consciousness-spirit is somewhat irrelevant since no matter what opinion
we have of them, to have an opinion, any opinion, is per se an
identification of ourselves with them. One option we do not have is
to give them up without giving up life itself. The fostering of these elements turns out to be a law of nature which tautologically states
that the ultimate meaning of the ensuing process will not disclose itself before its exhaustion. This late disclosure is not due to secrecy

but to incompleteness. To reveal itself to itself before the end, the Omega condition, would be an anticipation of creation. Religious structures are this anticipation and as such they are an important exercise in futurism. But by necessity, those exercises fall short of target, since the target is not there yet; it will be there only at the end of the process.

2) A word about compatibility. Each generation has its own environmental compatibility, that is to say, a person is hard put to reject those conditions with which he has grown up. But each generation is piggybacked on the preceding one. The individual cycle demands a return to the infancy grounds (reentry into the mother; we call it the father), and for each infancy such grounds are the maturity grounds of the parents (the preceding generation). This is providential since it secures both change and continuity. In fact, it would be difficult, if not impossible, to come up with a better scheme. This dialectic of change versus continuity makes conflict inevitable. It follows that it would be not only unrealistic but downright unjust and cruel to want to thrust the move to space upon the present generation as if it were a pleasure trip or a palatable prospect. But it could be for our grandchildren. The fact remains that, notwithstanding the incompatibility parameter, the parameters of territory, carrying capacity, and environmental development are in constant flux and expansion.

2) THE SPLITTING OF THE HUMAN SPECIES INTO SUBSPECIES

One of the most momentous outcomes of successful space colonization will be the appearance of human mutants who will perform more fittingly, not just in one new environment, but in a variety of new environments. We are the children of our environments.

A most critical area of decision (or nondecision) is, therefore, the genetic pool area, and with it, new conceptions of human values, justice, equity, hierarchy, fairness, etc. Are we able to withstand the thought that quite possibly, perhaps inevitably, human kind might become fractionalized (fractured) into (for instance) living fossils (the earthlings), psychotechno man (cyborgs), or superman (an intellect-

relayed multitude constituting a single creature), similar but on a different ledge of evolution to an insect colony?

Since the future is not a process like the unrolling of a sacred scroll but is instead a process of creation, nothing that we might conjecture or plan will ever turn out to be the future. Therefore, as it is quite possible that we might never leave the earth, it is also quite possible that a polarization on this planet might eventually force upon us some strange variances from the human kind we are now accustomed or resigned to. That is to say, a genetic schism might be not only a consequence of, or peculiar to, space colonization, but could be, in fact, the cause for space colonization.

Isn't what is going on now with the mystique of technology a kind of pilot project for a mutation in the making, which in turn urges man into its space probe? Technological man, the enfant terrible of the twenty-first century, could be the mutant that has yet to find a sound justification for his appearance. Now or soon, as a form, a container filling itself with purpose, he could cause life to extrude itself into a new set of parameters, a new universe authored by consciousness and its prowess in understanding, guiding, transforming, metamorphosing. Are we in for a radiant new creature, or are we in for life's abjection? The question is open and will be open for eons. In fact, from our earthly perspective, from our present, that possible radiant creature would be a monster anyhow, since we could not stand the sight of it. Whatever the case, we cannot escape the future and therefore might as well become conscious of some of its possibilities:

A)   Since it will not make sense to copy the earth's environment "over there," environments more congruous to the space situation will eventually define new morphological characteristics of fitness and response. Our physiological makeup might end its usefulness, but well before such definitive makeup might end its usefulness, well before such definitive and radical dismissal of the organic (see "Mass Transit–Mass Delusion"), we will probably mutate ourselves into cyborgs of sorts, as we do already in the push-button syndrome.

B)   In the meantime, will there be a transformation of the mother-lover-son drive[4] in favor of a scientific intrusion into the immensely chancy but immensely rich genetic pool afforded by the het-

[4] I refer to the Christian hypothesis of the fatherless birth of man presented in the myth of the Virgin.

erosexual mechanism? Might not this powerful and (as yet) unpredictable gene pool be the best, if not the only, insurance policy against any cosmic emergency? Should we then dare to take such a step?

C) What, besides the ability to think, will eventually make spacemen like earthlings? And what if the thinking apparatuses themselves become extravagantly different?

D) Will there be a change of heart about slavery, since sooner or later the notion of superior and inferior might be fostered among genetically different subspecies and peer groups? A benign version of such discrimination would make way for the earth as a living museum, the earthlings and their beautiful earth visited now and then by chartered space fraternities. A benign hypothesis in the restricted sense of doing away with violent confrontation, bloodshed, and genocide . . .

We must beware not to make humility into insularity and eventually into bigotry. If it is true that man is unique, it is also true that he is uniquely isolated and confined, possibly isolated because confined. But what if he were to explode at first into the solar system, then into the Milky Way, would there not then be good reasons for the species to venture into new, unthinkable explorations of the psychosomatic potentials we carry, in view of encounters with other centers of consciousness and grace?

If one has to admit pure terror vis-à-vis the opening of a galactic trapdoor under one's humble but arrogant, venturesome but cowardly, compassionate but bigoted self, one must also be encouraged by the possibly infinite radiance of the future on which such a trapdoor is opened.

3) THE SPACE PROBE IS THE URBAN PROBE

Are we really working at the creation of a Son-God, the masterpiece of evolution, or have we deviated in the process and become the authors of a monster? To get an answer, I think we have to consider the normative mode I call the Urban Effect. The transformation of the cosmos in the direction of the spirit is the Urban Effect. The Urban Effect is an eschatological imperative. As a corollary, divinity is the Urban Effect. Since the Urban Effect is yet at an embryonic stage of development, the city today is not very close to what it will be (ought to be), nor is God close to being the monistic and absolute center of love we (religions) anticipate. But there is an immanent Urban Effect which incarnates a limited divinity, the immanent God[5] (the God of the present).

This choice of terms, Urban Effect, divinity, God, is neither casual nor sensational. It puts an eschatological thrust into the human condition by going at the mainspring of human performance where it becomes social, cultural, civilizing, civic man. Civic man is not an experiment from which life might or will derive some advantages. He is instead the manifestation of the same kind of thrust that throughout evolution has and will keep the living stuff working upon raw matter at the cutting edge of consciousness.

The Urban Effect is the causal stress which forces the production of enclaves of consciousness, starting with the most ephemeral, the original microorganism which appeared on this earth thousands of millions of years ago. These enclaves of consciousness will eventually incorporate all of the universe in ways and expressions as multiple as the worlds involved in the process and the times in which they perform. Then will occur a further synthesis into the oneness of Omega. The frugal (miniaturizing) character of the process insures that the end will not find itself short of means by seeing that the end-means equation will grow exponentially to the final point where the numerator is near infinity and the denominator is near zero. The enclaves of consciousness would eventually join together, thanks to the implosive force of the complexity-miniaturization paradigm which will be enabled by cognition to warp the cosmic laws into divine law. It could be said that it is not so much the case of increasing the amount of spirit-consciousness that might exist scattered throughout the cosmos (the Tao) as the endowment of each particle, but it might be the case instead of desegregation and conjunction of each particle of consciousness with the others by way of the Urban Effect and the creative process which ensues from it. The original atomized spirit, the atoms of consciousness which can be conjectured to be composing the universe, this Alpha $1-10^{80}$ God is prisoner in its own iron

[5] This whole eschatological argument is absurd or blasphemous unless we are able to make a distinction (and keep it constantly in mind) between the potential and the actual.

cage of determinism together with the other 10^{80}–1, and it is one of the 10^{80} [6] deities of the pristine, polytheistic universe.

What is the logical thread that causes the Urban Effect to be the eschatological thrust? It is the common rule that any discipline (the eschatological thrust in the present case) has to foster that which originated the conditions allowing for its birth. If the Urban Effect was the causa prima for the advent of consciousness-spirit, then the enhancement and impregnation of the cosmos by conscience-spirit is dependent on how forcefully the Urban Effect multiplies and reinforces itself throughout the cosmos.

There is a sort of premonitory situation which must be read even though it justly (but unjustly) sends shivers down one's own spine. It is written in the invertebrate, on land and sea, in societies of insects, in slime, mold, slugs, in the various (and infamous) ant or termite colonies, wasp and bee nests. These are aggregates of acting matter, and why not thinking matter comparable perhaps more to the mammal brain and its own specialized hierarchy than to anything else? Gravity itself seems forgotten for the time being, so much is the living matter inner-oriented, totally absorbed in itself, pure living matter, flesh, thinking flesh. These are protoconscious cities, anticipatory, if brutishly so, or urbis where the dependence on matter becomes less and less measured by bulk and more and more measured by arrangement and discrimination, complexity and miniaturization, intensity and transcendence.

If there is an eschatological guide to turn to for assistance in our decisions and actions, and if this guide is predicated on the emergence of the divine via creative genesis, then breaking away from the earth's bondage is indispensable. It is not indispensable in the sense of being also sufficient—in fact, this breakaway could end up being an escape from responsibility and grace—but rather in the sense that there is no access to full divinity without the concrete intrusion of consciousness into all corners of the universe. Call it, if you like, redemption of matter whose sin is not to be as much as it ought to be: spirit. Or call it, as I prefer, the creation of a new and divine universe where each and all things are a radiant and transparent synopsis of each and all for all times and all places.[7] This assertion is not a burn-

---

[6] The number of particles in the universe according to some calculations.

[7] A state where time and space have collapsed and, therefore, a condition of total resurrection (and resurrection is total or it is not).

ing of one's own bridges to (ecologically minded) salvation, it is a reinstatement of the concept that *the bridge between matter and spirit is matter becoming spirit* and the process cannot be halted at any accidental moment, the present.

That the notion of breaking away from the earth is contemplated in most religions shows the anticipatory power of theological thinking. Usually this anticipation is not seen as entailing a physical migration of this life from the planet to other places, but if this is the interpretation, then the anticipation is wanting and the prophecy does not fit the eschatological grid. It would not suffice that the cosmos might sit in adoration around earthly magnets of intellection, as many of them as there might be scattered throughout it (thousands of millions). Intellection must move into the cosmos and consume it into consciousness, make it suffer the intellection of itself and cause it to transcend itself and create the "not yet," the divine.

Reaching for the divine (the work of the spirit) demands this inexhaustible bridge of matter, all matter consuming itself into its own entelechy. This is essentially the imperative of *intensifying the performance of matter* (*mass-energy*), that is to say, it is to cause the Urban Effect to become the universal concern, the rule and not the exception, and, ultimately, cause not so much the City of God but instead and indeed the God-City, the Omega Urbis et Orbis . . . It might indeed be indispensable that our anthropomorphic god be reinvented into God in the likeness of the city, with the massive reservation that both the Urban Effect and the ultimate (entelechy) expression of it in divine terms are inconceivable, unimaginable for our limited conscience and grace. To make a pale metaphor: to think of Omega urbis et orbis as a redeemed Detroit is comparable to the mystification one would experience if presented with a tiny blob of tissue, an embryo, and told that one beheld a beautiful, mature person. The mystification would be even greater if the embryo turned out to be not that of a human but of a fly. Detroit is to the God-City as the embryo of a fly is to the full-grown person. Between the two is the demonism of the evolutionary metamorphosis with its own cul-de-sacs and its own triumphs.

Therefore, what we will weave in space is going to be a series of cities that will add new force, new degrees of eventfulness, new situations to the Urban Effect. One, quick to come to mind, is freedom from the gravity burden (leading to consequent genetic alterations).

Another is the physical interiorization of the environs (and consequent psycho-social-cultural alterations), and another is the crowding syndrome coming to fruition with new force. Crowding in this use
of the term is not the bunching together of people, things, and time,
but the highly selective, discriminating coming together of disparate
and per se less intense elements, in similar but not identical ways, as
within an organism (plant, animal) or associations of organisms:
crowded, living, durational events incredibly full of interdependent
processes responding to the needs and hopes of the organism. Since
crowding is a divine attribute, copresence, cocreation, understanding,
knowledge, reverence, fullness, radiance . . . then the Urban Effect
(the crowding effect) is inexorably present whenever and wherever
there is a thrust toward such a condition of grace.

In summary:

1)   Space migration is on the human agenda.
2)   Is space migration now a responsible act, a diversion, or pure
escapism? A careful scheduling of our means, intellectual, ethical,
and otherwise, might show that the best defense against the squalor
of the lifeboat theory and carrying capacity miscalculations is the ultimate frugality of a life thrust which can and must pervade the
cosmos.
3)   True frugality is the antithesis of mediocrity (see "Relative
Poverty and Frugality"). Therefore, a vivification of the cosmos,
which cannot but be frugal, is bound to move man to a higher ledge
of the evolutionary pyramid.
4)   To this end, there is no escaping the need for a more reverential, urbane, civi-lized sense of the human experiment and, ultimately, the need for the eschatological vision of a universe in the
process of self-divinization, the Urban Effect.

It is in the nature of the progression that sees matter becoming
spirit (the entelechy of itself) under the pressure of the Urban Effect
that the conscious, intellective life on and in the seas will not be (forever) an exception to the rule. The uniqueness of the environment
should be a guarantee of the uniqueness of the modes and structures
adopted and defined there. I see two main dangers:

1)   the exploitation syndrome.
2)   the hedonism syndrome.

The exploitation syndrome, typified by the oil rig, sees the sea as a nuisance, an expensive one, and seeks the shortcuts which will reduce the cost of exploitation by concealing the true price tag. There will be, therefore, for the conservationist the task of digging out the inner costs, disregarded intentionally or in ignorance by the exploiter.

The hedonism syndrome, less capable of environmental evil within certain limits of development, might be, is, de facto, one of the main promoters of resource exploitation since it demands an ever greater variety of support systems, equipment, and logistics, and because it appeals to ever wider markets. But there is a specific potential for evil in the hedonism syndrome which makes it far more insidious. It is the possibility it projects of a culture desperately mediocre, a recessive culture, a genetic retrogression.

To make the point in evolutionary terms, I offer the following parable. Once upon a time, two divine beings came out of the sea and dwelled on the land. *They toiled within an environment which turned out to be harsher than the one they had left.* But through their toil a new radiance emanated from them. They were conscious of their consciousness. They were becoming creating creatures. Then one day, one of the beings fell victim to loss of anima and returned to the sea. He was the ancestor of whales and dolphins. The creature that stayed (fast) on land was the ancestor of man.

In the Eden of the watery universe, hedonism has imprisoned the consciousness of conscience and kept it in a twilight of innocence. In the stormy landscape of stone and soil, of marginal life or exuberant life, an immensely radiant destiny is being woven on the warp of time. It would be tragic if the involvement of contemporary man in the sea world were to be a delayed *return* to innocence, since the outcome would be not innocence but sloth charged at best with guilt, at worst, with irresponsibility (hedonism). It is, therefore, not a return which we must seek but the forceful intervention of the Urban Effect within the ocean ecosystems and the development in them of civilizations that would implement originally, that is to say radically, new expressions of the spirit.

The Urban Effect as the Genesis of the Divine

SYNOPSIS: For three or four thousand millions of years, life has been nipping away at the earth, constructing for itself ever more miraculous abodes. Complexity is explosively affirming its own power to synthesize spirit. The Urban Effect presides over this process of interiorization and sensitization. This genesis of the divine is the tidal wave we are part of and partaker in.

In the last few years religious movements and new churches have been sprouting with fresh vigor in many countries. Perhaps this is an indication that when a society loses its ethical moorings or its sense of grace, a counterbalancing stress develops within it. Unfortunately, there is a great deal of arbitrariness and conceptual poverty in this reaction. The mediocrity of the remedy seems to reflect the mediocrity of the patient. The difficulty is intrinsic to a reaction which has not internalized the dimensions of the problem. We are shortchanging ourselves.

It is in view of this that I find myself compelled to propose an eschatological model which has one necessary premise: *The preeminent nature of the divine is complexity.* Without the presence of complexity there is no possibility of grace in its totality or in its inclusiveness of all and everything. Once one is willing to perceive God, real or hypothetical, present or future, as the epitome of complexity, as an infinitude of consciousness, copresence, relatedness, knowing, understanding, love, and integrity, then one is compelled to look for the divine apart from those conditions which are inimical to or incapable of such infinitude.

The summation of those conditions is to be found in the categories of mass, energy, space, and time. To be made of any of them limits wholeness and might touch upon the absurd. To be made of them is to be defined according to the grid of space, of time, to be fragmented by the granularity or mass-energy. Divinity in its totality has to be independent of mass-energy, independent of space-time. And by independent is meant not a condition of reciprocal exclusion but a condition of consummation of one into the other; if it were a condition of exclusion, there would be the divine and, in parallel with it, that which has been excluded. *In this theological model, mass, energy, space, and time consume themselves in the process of authoring and nurturing the development of the divine.* In the condition of non-total consummation, there is a lack in the perfection of divinity. (If one or more components of a chemical compound is left out, the process is incomplete.) In such case, there is a perfectable divinity, capable of completing the process by consuming the remainder, perfecting itself into the absolute.

What is this consummation? Perhaps there are no alternatives to the nature of consummation. The consummation of mass, energy, space, and time might have to be, perforce, neither out of nor away from but into the entelechy of all. Only in a totally internalizing sweep is the divine achieved, ultimate and totalizing. Ultimate indeed, since a primeval condition, absolute and total, entails the involution of a clean sweep into the original world of mass, energy, space, and time. Think of a TV commercial where, by the reverse action trick, a polished floor is "unswept dirty." This sets the following model: a process of becoming is the consumption of the mass-energy universe through the space-time parameter under the pressure of complexification. The pressure of complexification has its origin in the imperative of survival, in fact, in the imperative of survival and the imperative of transcendence (the true function of survival) of mass, energy, space, and time.[1] Because of this pressure, the becoming is not arbitrary and entropic but is self-disciplined and asentropic, made of progressively more forceful transcendencies (that disincarnation which is the stuff of evolution) of the present into the next present, each yielding the activation of more mass, energy, space, and time into conscience, duration, and spirit.

If there is a point of arrival where such a process has consumed what one might call the media, mass, energy, space, and time, into what one might call the message of the spirit, logos, that is to say, the point where the process of becoming (evolution) reaches the condition of being ultimate and therefore mass-less, energy-less, space-less, time-less, then it might be appropriate, if not necessary, to hypothesize an original, primeval condition, self-same and also deprived of mass, energy, space, and time, a condition of original being, a negation of nonbeing. There is, therefore, in this model a *primeval being preceding mass, energy, space, and time and an ultimate being which is the consummation of mass, energy, space, and time.* The

[1] Therefore, the rosebush and the lizard will survive in the transcendental flight of consciousness away from an eventually dying, consumed solar system.

Alpha being and the Omega being are separated by the process of becoming (evolution). Two beings, one the offspring of the other, yet utterly estranged from one another. *The Alpha being, the Father,* negating nonbeing, empty of significance and full of the potential granules of mass, energy, space, and time, an utterly brutish media on the verge of becoming. *The Omega being, the Son,* significant and radiant, the crucible which exhausts the media in the escalatory process (evolution) of creating itself, the ultimate message.

In its absoluteness, being can neither recognize nor stand otherness. Therefore, there is no way for one being to be coactive and copresent with another being. Once the Alpha being has burst into becoming, becoming is all there is until the consummation of itself, total and absolute, into a new being, the Omega being. The inherent impossibility of the first being touching upon the last being and in so doing acknowledging otherness and partaking of it, is also the inherent nature of creation, the mystery of that which is not yet and that which will originate it. The primeval being is lost to becoming. The *ultimate* being caused by becoming is not (yet). Therefore, *anguish is intrinsic to the process in the double aspect of incompleteness (becoming) and of unknowability* (the mystery of the future which is not yet).[2] Such anguish is also the primer which keeps evolution progressing, transcending step after transcending step from one now into the next, on and on in pursuit of the ultimate.

The thesis is that the process which will eventually dissolve the mystery and abate the anguish is the Urban Effect. Fundamentally, it is that original phenomenon in which two or more particles of physical matter began to interact in ways other than statistical and fatal (the Laws of Physics), that is to say, in ways which are organic or living and eventually instinctive, conscious, self-conscious, mental, cultural, and spiritual. The Urban Effect is the progressive interiorization, urbanization, of the mass-energy universe, initially deploying itself in space-time and eventually recollecting itself, through the transfigurative process of evolution, into spirit. The Urban Effect, in the fullness of its transfigurative action, makes visible and active all those forces and categories which characterize the living and the loving: interdependence, interaction, perception, learning, care, co-

---

[2] But it is in the final condition of Omega being where the comprehension of Omega being is achieved (since Omega being is all-encompassing). It is then that anguish ceases to be. See "Logos as the Omega Seed."

operation, altruism, feedback, synergy, compassion, transcendence, beauty, integrity, intensity, passion, trust . . . At the very beginning when life is only a very dim manifestation of consciousness, the Urban Effect is embryonic and skeletal, and yet astonishing if compared with its physical counterpart, the random-like existence of the mass-energy mode.

The *initial act* of the Urban Effect is the breaking of being into becoming, the first acknowledgment of otherness. It originates the space-time coordinates necessary to unravel the mass-energy latent in the Alpha being. *The final act* is the Urban Effect, at last exhausting space-time in the transcendence of the last mass-energy particle, completing, therefore, the denouement of becoming into the Omega being.

As night follows day, resurrection follows the vanishing of mass, energy, space, and time. The vanishing is total as postulated and all the events of all places and all times are (they have become) coexistent, coactive, coconscious, coordinated. This occurrence secures the totality of the Omega being, since in its utter complexity is contained and integrated all that had once been becoming (mass, energy, space, and time) in its ultimate of total knowing, total presence, total experience, total love. *The Omega being is the totally miniaturized offspring of becoming because it is the mass-less, energy-less, space-less, and time-less ultimate. Therefore, the Urban Effect operates as the escalatory disincarnation of mass, energy, space, and time into the divine, if and when wedded to the escalatory intensification of complexity and miniaturization.* In fact, the Urban Effect, the making of the divine, is a true process of complexification and miniaturization for the simple reason that elementalism and dispersion are ontologically foreign to the nature of the divine. In the presence of elementalism and dispersion and, perforce, their inertia, coaction, interaction, cooperation, knowledge, and love are impeded, limited, and curtailed from their ultimate fullness. They are the media getting in the way (in the sense of being as yet unusable) of the totalized all-inclusive message.

The infinitude of the divine, the Omega God, is postulated on the reduction to naught of both space and time, the devices through which mass-energy media cry out for the spirit which is slowly and painstakingly being generated within its own folds (Mother Nature);

and in generation is consummation (the son consuming the mother, making himself out of her).

There is an eschatological imperative shrouded within the Urban Effect. If, by the nature of the divine, the Urban Effect is submitted to the complexity-miniaturization necessity, then our urban undertakings (an infinitesimal part of the Urban Effect present in the universe) are clearly ordained by the methodology which informs the eschatological process. *They have to sustain and function, clearly and uncompromisingly, for and within the complexity-miniaturization paradigm.* By so doing, spirit extrudes itself from matter by the consumption of it (disincarnation). *Arcology and the second-generation arcology, the Two Suns Arcology, by intent and design try to be congruent with this paradigm.* One could then summarize by outlining the What, the Why, the How, and the Urban Effect:

WHAT
1) Alpha being as the negation of nonbeing.
2) The Alpha being shattered by becoming at the onset of mass, energy, space, and time.
3) Becoming disincarnated (consumption of mass, energy, space, and time) into Omega being, logos. Logos (Omega God) is the resurrectional advent of all becoming.

WHY
The Alpha being of total elementalism and brutishness "longs" for an otherness (total integrity and grace). The becoming is the bridge between Alpha being (the Father) and Omega being (the Son). The incompleteness of the becoming and the unknowability of its ultimate metamorphosis (logos) are the causes for life's anguish.

HOW
The loss of being into becoming triggers the process of complexification-miniaturization which step by step sees mass, energy, space, and time becoming spirit up to the final step (leap) when by the total and final consumption of the media, the Omega being, the message, comes to be.

THE URBAN EFFECT

The process of complexification-miniaturization is the URBAN EF-FECT, the durational process which will eventually precipitate mass-energy-space-time into the mass-less, energy-less, time-less, space-less event of Omega, the resurrectional condition of being.

Mass Transit—Mass Delusion

SYNOPSIS: The flat grid of our cities and the Urban Effect are irreconcilable. Where one is, the other cannot be. The flat grid is the unspoken (and unspeakable) indictment of the flesh, the fracture of the bridge channeling matter into spirit. Ultimately, it consigns consciousness to the protoconsciousness of a computerized will.

What would a blood corpuscle say or do if his longings and his compulsions were divided between a lung 15,000 yards away and a kidney 18,000 yards away? Would his choice make any difference? The poor corpuscle would never make it to either organ, nor could it respond to dozens of other institutions wanting and begging it to join them. Many of our "corpuscles" never make it either. Our corpuscles are ourselves and those inherent rights that a civilization dutifully makes available to its members.

Successful or not in the pursuit of these rights, the masses are highly transient. The delusion, massive and stubborn by the billions of dollars, is inherent in any topographic layout which makes distance the number one obstacle to participation, affiliation, service, help, or information. This topography, the flat topography, fosters the delusion that that which cannot be achieved by shortness and swiftness can be achieved by energy and velocity. That is what kills the corpuscle. In order to succeed, it would have to be many times as powerful (person and automobile) as an individual corpuscle (person) and many times faster (person and automobile). Even more paradoxical is that if the corpuscles were faster and more powerful, the body they would travel in, the city, would necessarily, axiomatically, be destroyed by the savage machines (for singles or groups) which made them so.

The size, the nuisance, and the arrogance of such insane, misbehaving corpuscles, that is to say, the scale of the imposition upon the body and the scale of the body (the city), are incompatible. No matter what medium, single carrier or mass carrier, is interposed between the corpuscle and the organ, between the persona and the institution, the disproportion remains such that one is always the nemesis of the other. It is a disproportion which ingrains itself into the makeup of both the personal and the collective soul of the city.

Mass transit is only a delusion of lesser magnitude than the delusion of the personal carrier. It is cheaper (though it does not pay for itself), less energy-consuming, less preposterous. It still does not face the facts. The facts are that we deal with a finite world, a finite personal life-span, a finite energy endowment for each individual, a finite intelligence, a finite patience, a finite capacity for sufferance, a finite solvency. All those finitudes are under the umbrella (or in the iron fist?) of the mass-energy, gravitational rules. It might be quasi-sane to ask what in the hell we think we're doing. We are furiously destroying life, while shouting with the wind left to us by frustration and pollution, "I am free, I am free at last."

I know what the reaction will be: "Who the hell does he think he is telling everyone what fools they are?" For one thing, history has repeatedly proven that it is often the reasoning of one confronting the reasoning of many that is the key to better answers. Additionally, and more importantly, the assumption that the many are the great majority, that everyone is on the other side of the fence, is untrue. The opposite is true on two counts:

1)   Of all man's present and past, only a small minority belongs body and soul to the Los Angeles syndrome.

2)   Of all of animal life, none (not one animal organism or association of organisms in extrabiological structures, beehives, anthills, etc.) belongs to the Los Angeles syndrome. Only a small minority of human beings, a puny minority of nonvegetal life, is Los Angeles-oriented.

Then the transient masses given to the ethos of gigantism are relatively small; the mass delusion is a minority delusion. What this says is that quite possibly I am speaking for the relative as well as the absolute majority. The problem is that I am addressing myself to a minority which happens to see things differently.

Why the ethos of gigantism? It is the ethos exemplified in the analogy at the beginning of this paper, the corpuscles having to equip themselves with an engine bigger than themselves in order to pursue distant goals. But the nemesis of gigantism is that it is self-escalatory. The bigger combine (person plus mechanism) demands more space (50–60 percent of the city surface). Thus, the system is expanded. The expansion of the system foments the enlargement and multiplication of the combine. Then the never-ending series of cycles of expansion is seeded genetically in the gigantic body to become its ethos. A flight over Los Angeles will show what I mean. All of them, even the little towns, are gigantic spreads of square miles upon square miles of repetitive encasements of people. Since every one of those people had and has only a small part to play in the encasement and since habit makes for acquiescence, those people, us, tend to believe that such dogmatic encasement is freedom. To suggest that the dogma is the negation of freedom is tantamount to apostasy. We are (or seem) determined to embrace the dogmatism of the two-dimension grid. And since, at this point, we are where we are forced to be (different options do not exist), an even stronger argument is made for the contention that one must be practical, meaning that even though we might be dead wrong, the best thing we can do is to make wrongness "even better," wronger.

The plain truth might be the unwillingness to really feel the massiveness of the problem, its intrusion into all facets of life, and the rejection of the responsibility for both atonement and redemptive action. If one divorces oneself from responsibility for a certain situation, one finds a thousand excuses not to feel guilt or to do anything about it. Our actions either reveal reverence for life and ourselves within it or they do not. The bully, the sophist, the opportunist, and the hypocrite are, in the final analysis, powerless to score anything of importance for the human condition. Believe it or not, this is where the bulk of the debate of mass transit versus single movers shows itself for what it is, an exercise in futility. Both solutions reveal an absence of perception of the reverential nature, in fact, the theological nature of a true resolution. This reverential vacuum is the scourge of practical man and it is what causes him to be eternally late for his appointment with destiny.

The pessimism expressed here is not toward our capacity to develop into better selves. It is a negative view of the trust we put in the practical turn of mind, since I firmly believe that behind practicality most often lurks the unreality of renunciation, copping out, as the saying goes. Nothing makes copping out sweeter than self-engendered righteousness: belonging to the well-adjusted, responsible, proven majority of a minority. A cursory look at history and prehistory does quick justice to such a prejudice. The well-adjusted majority has two nemeses:

1)   Fossilization in a matrix encasing each expression of each of its members, and

2) Death at the hand of physical, biological, or mental adversaries or an alliance of them.

What is the rationale demanding a theological framework for a logistical problem? Quite simply, the inextricable copresence of information-understanding-response with life itself. Where one is absent, the other is illusory. But the capacity for perception of information-understanding-response is based ultimately on the logistical carriers the system can utilize: psychological, mental, social, cultural, or physical, or any mix of them. Cut the flow and you cut life. Strangle the flow and you strangle the consciousness of the immanent.

Taking the city as one of the many and most recent manifestations of the highly cooperative nature of living stuff, one can then name the first city, that cooperative or community where more than two particles of matter become interdependently locked and synergistically responsive to one another. The locking and responsiveness established the import and nature of the logistics of consciousness, the form that would make possible the function, consciousness, which would appear eons later.

Given the decision center, the brain which developed from a prototypical invention, the nerve fiber, throughout evolution the problem has been how to get the information there swiftly and undistorted, and then, how to get the response out, swiftly, measured, and pertinent. Nowhere was speed or bulkiness part of the scene. They could not be, since their nature is brutally inimical to the delicate balance of the unfolding event.

The city has evolved into myriads of miraculous organisms, each successfully winning this logistical battle through swiftness and measure in a crescendo of complexity which no mechanical instrument, computer included, can match. Now the latecomer, one split thousandth of the last second of the last minute of the last hour of the twenty-four-hour crescendo of life, the Los Angeles syndrome, negates all those things, saying, "I'll show you the way, the better way, the true way . . . the rubber wheel way."

A true delusion of grandeur, where the gigantic is seen as the grand design of the human intellect, a "flat" human intellect, as the case demonstrates well. Any realist who has even a purely cursory acquaintance with the laws of their modynamics and the equation of energy input can instantly diagnose the pathology of gigantism: waste. Since for the city the essential parameter is life, such waste expresses directly, and brutally, life's waste. Given a giant, as any small or big Los Angeles is, gigantic instruments are necessary to keep some spark of life in the flat body. Gigantic instruments are exactly what life has successfully avoided throughout its own evolution. Smallness and discreteness have been the characteristics of the instruments (organs) selectively constructed by the living stuff. In the inorganic field, the gigantic and the small, proportioned to their respective performances, are exemplified by the automobile and its kingdom, the elevator and its shaft. Within the cityscape, one goes for destruction and absurdity, the other goes for the swift and the proper. There is no black magic in this, simply the magic, in the case of the elevator, of the well-measured response to a certain need. The automobile signifies the bloated, irrational, self-defeating trend toward a human condition which translates into physical terms as the entropic quiescence to inertia, an inertia paradoxically pursued through the consumption (transfer) of physical energy (gasoline included) and human energy at a synergy threshold less than zero. It goes without saying that the replacement for the car is not so much the elevator as it is our own legs.

Since the rewards, the ends, for such consumption (consumerism?) are becoming smaller and smaller, and since it cannot be otherwise because they are inversely proportional to the "elephantization" of the instruments (the means), punishments keep developing in import and impact (from laborious parking to paralysis of flow, for instance). In the biological context, the punishments are apparent in a body that has trespassed beyond the reasonable limits of its own containment envelope. In the urban context, the punishments are ripened by gigantism where a polarization in horizontal directions is developed. An ineffectual direction, rejected by all manifestation of the animal kingdom. This is the flat city, a poor giant, a poor flattened giant, the most absurd of any conceivable structure whose purpose is to sustain the development of a transvegetal, conscious, willful, acculturating, and personalizing life.

It is, therefore, not just probable but fatal that no interconnecting modes of flow, be they personal or collective, will give results that might warrant the investment they require. The only answer, if the giant is kept as a mystical body, is to renounce in massive terms most of our direct interpersonal and interinstitutional contacts and give ourselves to more and more remote linkages. This is a decision in the making and it is a momentous decision. Somewhere, in its future, the flesh will be discarded in favor of nonphysiological structures. What of the soul when the flesh is dead?

Move data and ideagrams instead of moving matter, flesh included. It sounds good, and for many sides of life it is the right path. But for the full development of a sentient, compassionate species it might demonstrate itself, and too late, as utterly deficient in depth and substance. And then, on a less intangible plane, what about a meal by teletype, a swim by letter, an orgasm by phone, etc., or is it a Vietnam by audiovisual, ten years of it! The flesh, to life's advantage, resists abstraction.

Even if all the events which do not necessitate the transference of matter were to occur remotely, and even if we were to accept the naught of total electronic (de)sensitization, the bulk of the logistical problem would remain unaffected, especially if we keep in mind that we are already massively dependent on the telephone, telegraph, mail, radio, TV, and a fairly good network of energy, transportation, electricity, gas, etc.

The options are fairly restricted, if not desperate. They play into the hands of the worst enemies of civilization: desensitization and segregation. The effects, as we all know, do not stop at physical disruption. They impinge upon the delicate inner world of the psyche and intellectual action. They brutalize psychosomatic man indiscriminately, independent of place, time, caste, blood, religion, or economic status.

One effect of this brutalization is that the actor loses the capacity to understanding that he/she is the victim of a condition that would otherwise be unacceptable (incompatible). The victimizer achieves the ultimate in victimization: render the victim dumb to his own mistreatment. If one has not had the experience of diverse situations, one cannot truly conceive of other possibilities. It is easy to see how hopeless the situation becomes for those persons born and raised under such a "bad star." In a society where learning is overwhelmingly consigned to symbol systems, from the written word to the electronic message, at the expense of the firsthand experience which environmental perception and direct contact offer, a very legitimate question comes up: Do we need our bodies? Do we need our bodies because they are both an instrument for consciousness and a source of true emotion and joy, or are we enslaved to a flesh we might better get rid of, since it is a hindrance to the marvelous computer-like brain for which direct electrical impulses are far more clear and superior than the painstaking journey of information through those conveyors and transformers we call our senses?

The question is neither idle nor farfetched. In the long run and in view of scientific coherence, the idea of moving information instead of moving mass demands that the linkage between event and brain (the decision center) be most direct. Hence the intrusive nature of the organs of perception (flesh) and the desirability of bypass. Then, if the body ceases to be more than just a support system for the brain, let's get a better one . . . There are all conditions or situations where the disposal of the body is temporarily achieved and they are not peculiar to our technological society. The student sealed off from the outdoors by a windowless glass intent on "learning" about nature, the absentminded professor, mathematician, or logician absorbed in their work, carry their bodies around as impediments. In the holy man, a kind of holy man at least, the body is not only ignored but chastised, punished, because it is the impediment limiting one's own deliverance into God, that pure spirit which the information technician finds in the noiseless vacuum of the electronic yes-no switchboard of the ideal brain, the fleshless supercomputer of future times.

If it is assumed that humankind is given on the leash of gravity to a world which is preponderantly two-dimensional, and understanding the delusory character of both modes of transportation, single carrier or multiple carrier (mass transit systems), that is to say, given the grid of the American town which is assumed to be an asset, and since the inescapable sin is the inescapable gigantism (the pathological dysfunction) of any flat system, then it is axiomatic that the technology of information will eventually find it necessary to dismantle man, the flesh-and-mind animal, to recompose him into an efficient machine of will.

Will the desires of such a machine have a superior capacity for creation, or will its desires, its longings, be bent toward the utter tranquility of a dead universe? Would a willful automobile keep running or would the unremitting pressure of entropy bearing on each of its particles, molecular, atomic, and subatomic, have the upper hand (upper steel claw) and leave the automobile preempted of will, preempted by the statistical fate (unwill) of statistical machinery?

That is to say, does a purely electronic conscience[1] stand for a transconscience or does such electronic conscience stand for the intrusion, in the most fiendish way, of determinism into the world of consciousness so painfully developed by the escalation of sensitization? Does not the flat city stand squarely as one of the moorings for the development of such electronic consciousness?

Is this reasoning faulty because it is intrinsically incoherent or irrational or because it is an extreme though logical extrapolation of a trend? I think only the second objection is worth considering. Or is it? Even the most momentous transformations are, for the better part of their development, hidden among the numerous components of routines which vary only slightly from day to day. The advent of language is a good instance. From grunts and squeaks to a Sophocles tragedy is a lengthy if unarrestable progression of enrichment, discrimination, definition, and metamorphosis in both physiological and psychological terms.

To stay closer to the subject, it would be hard to pinpoint a day, a year, or even a decade which marks the transformation of a physically pedestrian species into a substantially rubber-wheel species (the West). The transformation has been gradual, unpredictable, undetectable if one were to take a few samples separated by a few days or a few months. All of that notwithstanding, the carless society of sixty or so years ago has become the car-dependent society of today. The impact has been, and even the car mystics would agree, cataclysmic.

What I am proposing here is that this momentous transformation (in two to three generations' time) was nothing less than a first but critical step in the direction of isolation (segregation) of the individual, whose reconnection with the world has to be via remote, abstract communication devices. Quite a nemesis for man, via the automobile, that invention whose original aim had been the opening up of the world to everyone.

For an individual as sketched above, the flesh becomes a hindrance in due time, since only a gross technology, a reactionary technology, could accept the ineffective communication of events (no events) via the TV tube-organ of sight-brain-mental processing. Technology will bypass both TV tube (and its technology) and eye-

[1] Not just the present technology of information but whatever the future has in store that intentionally or not will bypass the senses and, therefore, the psychosomatic organism.

sight (and its biotechnology) to plunge its sharpening probes into the convolutions of the brain, in the righteous assumption that very soon that blob of flesh will be archived in the museums of anthropology with the rest and the remains of the human body.

Since the getting-there machine, the automobile, cannot get me there reasonably, since the bus or the subway can do only a slightly better job, that is, can get a selection of me through a selection of routes to a selection of places in a selected time slot, then I turn to the electron, the minibulk, mass transit representative of me, and I make it into my informer and messenger . . .

BUT WAIT ONE MOMENT. AM I NOT A BUNDLE OF ELECTRONS MYSELF, ANYHOW? THEN WAIT, WAIT. LET'S REARRANGE MY ELECTRONIC PATRIMONY INTO A MORE EFFICIENT SYSTEM, THERE . . . WHAT? THE BABY IS CRYING . . . THAT WON'T DO. A DEFICIENCY TO BE CORRECTED. THE COUPLE WHAT? THE COUPLE IS DANCING? THE WILL OF A WHIM . . . AMEND AMEND . . . WHAT? THE LADY IS AGING? FORGET IT. THE LADY IS ETERNAL. THE CYBORG LADY IS ETERNAL. WHAT? ETERNALLY WHIMPERING? HOW NOSTALGIC, HOW STUPID. THERE, THERE. SMILE, SMILE, DAMN YOU, DAMN LADY, DAMN BUNCH OF WHIRLS. THE HELL WITH YOU . . . THERE, THERE. LOOK, THERE IS FATHER . . . GET TO IT, GET WITH IT . . . FATHER! FATHER! MY GOD, FATHER IS MY GOD AND MY GOD . . . MY GOD IS DUST, AN IMMENSE WHIRL OF DUST AMONG INFINITE WHIRLS OF DUST.

BLOOD, BLOOD BE MY GOD . . . SOMEWHERE THERE MUST BE BLOOD, A DROP OF IT, A DROP OF GOD. LET'S BEGIN ALL OVER AGAIN . . . I REVERE THEE. THEREFORE, I MUST TRANSFIGURE THEE . . . EVOLUTION BEGINS AGAIN. CAN IT?

4

———

Relative Poverty
and Frugality

SYNOPSIS: There is a feeling that frugality is a graying of existence, a retreat, a renunciation. On the contrary, frugality is the opposite of mediocrity which is, by definition, wasting life. The truly frugal is the truly integrative and essentializing. Frugality ultimately shows the physical universe to be the mediocre universe, and takes as its imperative that life "goes and multiplies" throughout the cosmos and does transfigure it.

The attempt of this essay is to show relative poverty not as an expedient toward a certain goal but as the brick and mortar for the construction of a condition of equity and transcendence through a lean ecological-theological congruence. The subject of frugality rises from the observation that ignorance is the lock on the door that needs opening. Since no one ever ceases to be ignorant, the presumption of knowing the right key is, per se, fraught with danger. Be that as it may, one can identify two sources of ignorance: ignorance for lack of experimental processes, and ignorance from the inability to profit from experiential processes. Every process is experiential but the experience does not necessarily identify with the subject matter. (In reading about Victoria Falls, one "experiences" the experience of the writer, not Victoria Falls.) The first case of ignorance is part of the existential context of youth; the second is part of the more or less limited "sensitivity" of all age groups. Parenthetically, since growing up is the process of consciously and unconsciously applying cumulative experiences, the learning-doing process, it is in the nature of things that at the beginning (and all situations are, in part, beginning situations) youth can only turn to a *vicarious* and *mimetic* modus operandi based on trust, trust in those who have had some learning-doing experience. Watch the little sister acting out her elder sister, the sons and daughters playing grown-ups . . . For most of what we do, this modus operandi does not change throughout life. Only in what we "specialize in" do we transfer some of this trust from others to ourselves.

Ignorance is the lock on the door to frugality not so much for the poor who cannot do better, but for the person who has opted for it intentionally. This person must know, viscerally, the rationale for the choice, since not to know is to be ignorant of the issue and consequently blind to the condition of man. To put it bluntly, *frugality must come from synthesis, not from ignorance or quiescence or weakness.*

Synthesis is a conclusive action in the process of discrimination and elimination by which a few essentials are established as the moorings for one's existence. It is a divesting of the physical and transphysical self as much as it is an encompassing of both within one's own specificity so that the garment of frugality can mold itself more intimately to both the tangible and the intangible self. If it were otherwise, if indigence, for instance, were to be the context of frugality, then one would but stand as a synopsis of the least human of the human condition, the condition of wretchedness where the mind cannot work since the body is dying. The body is dying when somatic man is ignored on the poor assumption that once the flesh is fed with the right protein, one can forthwith turn on the psyche anchored to it.

The intent of relative poverty is not to suffer and do penance for the sins of man or specifically for the sins of avarice, gluttony, and covetousness. It is instead to glorify life through the lean, conscious exercise of one's energies in the face of odds which, when understood, cannot but show themselves as overwhelming. It is, at its best, a performance saturated with the tragic sense of life itself, a sense full of seminal particles, a sense that can give reason and scope to sufferance, that immense towering ogre of all history, drowned in cruelty but also suffused with beauty. To perform in the tragic sense of life is not, one must be clear, a morose and bleak prospect. It is a conscious development of the self along a path littered with things that must be ignored, a path irksome with the unexpected, the mystifying, the barbaric, the blasphemous, the malicious . . .

With all of that, and in spite of all of that, one's spirit can construct a not-so-ephemeral counterreality, the intent of which is grace and deliverance, a deliverance that is future-oriented, a creation constructed on the warp of the unknown which gives an oracular (demonic) tinge to its appeals. If this grace is suffocated by wealth which mistakenly thinks it can buy deliverance, then those occasional buffers, which are necessarily part of the countenance of one's life, become the indispensable crutches for a life gone astray in the pursuit of happiness, a pursuit which is made ephemeral by the fragility of the scaffolding employed to reach it, the inner fragility of an all-insured, all-granted happiness via affluence. To the fragility which is innate in coupling, if not identifying, inner grace with hoarding and the power to maintain it, is clearly added the precariousness, in both physical and moral terms, of such a condition vis-à-vis the indigence of most of humanity. We are thus faced with a double sin: a sin against one's own spiritual worth and a sin against the needs of the species of which our own spirit is part and parcel. The intentional condition of relative poverty is not the seal of sainthood but has its rationale in the human condition, when such condition is perceived and understood in some depth and when deeds follow upon the path of understanding. That some or most politicians, economists, and managers might see the frugal way as the suicidal way simply shows what the materialistic turn of mind does to man. While it is certainly true that the application of frugality would play havoc for a while with the Western system, the "consumerism societies," it is also true that such societies have not lifted the spirit of man one iota above the quiet and not-so-quiet greed which conspicuously characterizes them, a greed by now endemically infecting that part of mankind which has been touched by the technological revolution. It might well be that this historical phase of the species has to pass through the quagmire of greed to taste firsthand the bitter sterility of such a condition. Only after that may man freely choose to move into the future with less technological redundance and more inner conviction.

One of the convincing aspects of arcology is that it stands, in parallel with the individual, private, frugal ethos, for an equally frugal, public, universal condition. Environmentally, it does for society what frugality does individually for the person. Naturally, the visitation of grace upon arcological, frugal man is far from automatic. But what is automatic is that as a direct consequence of one's willful abdication of affluence-opulence, the wealth of the earth is given a chance for more equitable distribution. A forced abdication of opulence would only mean that for the time being someone or some society is quarantined in the indigent's station, that station where revolt and vendetta mount their pressure. If, on the other hand, abdication meant withdrawal from society and its productive cycles, applying the tenet that "what I cannot get for myself I will not produce for anyone else," then one deprives man of those tools and those products that need to be produced so that the strength they bring to man can be equitably shared.[1] One can hear the laughter or the bone-rattling indignation of a successful society looking at the picture of itself as the good Samaritan, as if I were proposing some sort of mass philanthropy making the world into a limbo. I am really suggesting instead a civilization which in a conscious, lean exercise of its energies and knowledge has fewer false gods to indulge in. To such end, some steps seem necessary:

1) Free oneself from the hypocrisy of equality.
2) See and feel that the freedom to be equally mediocre is a sorry state.
3) Understand that mimesis and vicariousness are the indispensable ways by which the anguish of the species, its sufferance, can be contained (the norm) within bearable boundaries when it cannot be transfigured (the exception) into grace.

Why do I think I am on target with these rather oblique statements? Willing or not, we are in the theological realm, in that reality where the individual is, for the sake of himself and his progeny, subordinated to something which is more than the sum of all components of life. Pierre Teilhard de Chardin, speaking of sufferance, compares mankind to a tree whose branches bear different loads and are in different health conditions (see point 1). All branches are part of the tree's integrity, they all have part in its development; all branches, and specifically the weakest, partake of the glory of the tree. They partake of it, but they are not equally responsible for and expressive of it. If they were, one could suggest the following paradox: The pruning gardener—God?—works on a pair of twin trees; on one He trims off the weak limbs and on the other He cuts off the stronger limbs. Good sense would say that the first tree has been well conditioned for further development in terms of inner structural design and that the other tree has been maimed. Carry the analogy too far and you play into the hands of the God's-chosen-people ethos. Yet, to ignore the unevenness in the components of the system is to

---

[1] In a humanized family of man, the United States could double its productivity and export two thirds of such wealth to other societies by a willful vow of relative poverty. This might become a must. In Christian terms that is what ought to be, and concomitantly, that is also what ecologically, in survival terms, must be. It is not pure coincidence that theology and ecology come to be one indivisible process.

be blind, hypocritical, or perversely pious. For the human tree, the point is not whether to cut or not to cut the weak branches but to acknowledge that the truly compassionate way is to see that the weak branches, which are making their contribution according to their strength, are vicariously joyful in the reflection and mimesis of what the stronger branches do for the tree (see point 3). To stay a while longer with the analogy, but now defining the tree as the bearer of fruits indispensable to the betterment of man, and seeing man standing under the tree as short in stature if tall in hunger, only a human pyramid will put the fruits within reach. The pyramid will go up according to physical laws and acrobatic skills. The most limber and best-conditioned individuals will have the joy of picking the fruits (and will, for an instant, rejoice in the life current). They will then toss the fruits down to the less fortunate, the vicarious enjoyers. One of the assignments of civilization is, of course, the construction of scaffoldings which will afford anyone the thrill of picking the fruits. But it will never happen that everyone will find the interest or the courage or perseverance to pick the fruits. For most, it will be a case of getting fed on a diluted version of the burning flame-fruit. (I must make clear that nowhere in the pyramid do I see the sign of mediocrity. I see only the signs of individual limitations.)

Leaving the analogies, one can look at societies and their histories. Men and women can equally or, better, equitably enjoy the reality they bring forth in the measure and terms which their inner worth can afford to them. We enjoy or suffer, which are the same, in the measure of the reflection of what we are in what we behold or do, not one iota more or less. We are instruments which can produce only those sounds made possible by the sophistication of our makeup. If it might seem unjust to say that a wired washtub cannot do for a violin concerto, since it is more fair to see all of us as violins, we might want to consider that: 1) we are not just passive instruments but rather the active players of ourselves, thence what we play of ourselves we make ourselves into: 2) as violins we might be well made or poorly made. The quality of the instrument is a genetic fact, as yet beyond our control. Consequently, the quality of the sound, if we so want to characterize it, will be a significant parameter of our performance; but the substance of the music is of our making and only of our making . . . or is it? *It is not so much of our making as it is of our choice.* The Beethovens and the Debussys play music of their making on wired washtubs or on Stradivariuses. The professional players choose from the repertory that which suits them to perform. Both the professional player and the listener *vicariously* enjoy with the composer the music he has made himself into, and by a process of *mimesis,* doing on our own what someone else has originally done, we even cocreate or recreate fragments or figments of it.

We are all pupils of someone who most of the time we do not know and we do not need to know. Each of us is, in fact, the pupil of literally thousands of teachers, our fellow travelers on the journey from beginning to end, our contemporaries or our ancestors. In such a situation, the most damaging thing one could do to oneself, or that society could foster, would be to go after the emptiest of all music in sympathy for impiety. This is to seek mediocrity and to sanctify it with the consumer ethos which maintains that the buyer can purchase only what the producer makes, to which the producer retorts that the nature of the product is a direct result of the market (consumer) demand. This is the most dangerous thing democracy has had to cope with and in the Western world it has coped with it poorly. If the elitist societies of the past, Western and Eastern, have something to show, it is that "freedom" has not been identified with mediocrity. In fact, it was a tenet in those societies that only the exceptional were or had the right to be free. By "exceptional" was meant privileged, a distortion which doomed all of them to extinction, but that position was normative then, since social justice was at best a remote concept.

Can anyone say that the price for nonmediocrity has been too high? What we can say is that if the democracy of mediocrity ("mediocracy" as coined by Frank Lloyd Wright) is the ultimate in freedom, freedom has been a mirage and a poor mirage at that. Its true name is license, the institutionalization of mediocrity by the stamp of approval from the authority and tyranny of the vicarious and mimetic Joneses (see point 3).

The point is that mediocrity and frugality do not mix. They can only coexist. They do not mix since *frugality is quintessential and mediocrity is quiescent.* It is only by the reduction of mediocrity that frugality can prevail. *A mediocre society is by definition a wasteful society, since it is a society which is incapable of that leanness of thought and action that is characteristic of the frugal condition.*

It should be somewhat clear that contrition and penance do not necessarily fall into the framework of frugality, as it should be clear that they are not excluded from such a scheme as a matter of dogma. The latter point is a necessary corollary because in the Western world it has become axiomatic that both contrition and penance are the residue of barbaric and obscure moments of history. In the meanwhile, the psychoanalyst, with his own contrition-penance syndromes, has in those same moments a field day. Contrition and penance come upon the soul consciously, or, if the society forbids it, unconsciously; but they have to come upon it, since the soul is the testing ground for our sense of rightness, while the world and the persona are saturated with wrongness.

Wiser societies have not put up such a (technologically) solid wall between themselves and their anima. Indeed, for some of them it is often in the extreme opposite direction, which makes for uniformity. So much is given to contrition and penance as to bring about mortification and a sullen acceptance of punishment. At one extreme is, thus, the self-righteousness of ignorance, arrogance, and contempt, the true garments of mediocrity, which is sometimes clad in gentle apparel but most often in its armored opulence; and at the other end is a meekness blurring into the total helplessness of abjection.

It emerges that frugality as synthesis and quintessence, far from being in the lukewarm center of the line connecting the two extremes, propels itself equally away from them both into an asyntropic flight toward the spirit.

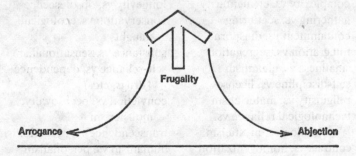

It is naturally easy to imitate any mold, including the mold of frugality. It is up to those who seek to be part of the arcology experiment to examine their own consciences and seek guidance from the flame, tenuous or roaring, they treasure there. The experiment might demand a lifetime test, since the aim of it is the transformation and possibly the transfiguration of contemporary man. This transformation is the most utopian aspect of the experiment as it necessitates a durational collapse of tradition into a brief one-generation time span. The establishment of a tradition is something that can hardly occur within a lapse of time as short as that. That notwithstanding, if we cannot approximate such a condition, we have a poor chance of succeeding.

Another difficulty inherent in this proposition is that the goal of establishing a tradition is the least fashionable thing to propose in a time when the most popular slogan is "set yourself free, break out of all traditions." The fact that the slogan is absurd does not make it less attractive. In fact, it is attractive because it is absurd and the best way to be absurd is to abide by absurd slogans. It is indeed so attractive as to be propounded by the most established (and absurd) of all establishments, Madison Avenue. Purchase this or that and you will be an "original," unique among (millions of identical) uniques. But then, we would not be in what we are in if our aim was to sway dutifully to the tune of the day.

A glance at the unfashionable position of arcology and its fashionable opposite:

frugality vs. affluence	cooperation vs. confrontation
quality vs. quantity	use vs. ownership
complexity vs. elementarity	longevity vs. obsolescence
gathering vs. scattering	conservation vs. ecological
containment vs. diaspora	naught
integration vs. segregation	substance vs. sensationalism
smallness vs. gigantism	self-reliance vs. dependence
self-discipline vs. license	(drugs, etc.)
religiosity vs. materialism	conviction vs. peer loyalty,
technological reliance vs.	mobsterism
technological mysticism	transcendence vs. reductionism
contrast vs. homogenization	humanism vs. personalism
authority vs. power	universalism vs. nationalism

To return to the theological component, in my view true religiousness states and bases its action on the belief that it is more probable that the whole of the universe will animate itself than it is probable that that part of the universe which is animated will die. In view of the present as we know it, such a statement will appear as the emptiest of all boasts. It is, notwithstanding that, the only proposition which reduces evil to naught since a fully animated universe signifies that the living has achieved that degree of pervasiveness and sacramentality which automatically precludes a parallel existence of nonlife, that is to say, fate (evil as the absence of destiny). Thus, fate has transubstantiated itself into destiny, has found a destination. At the end of such journey, the laws of mass-energy would have ended their reality (usefulness), since the whole of mass-energy would have transcended itself into logos. But then this transcendence is not a hypothesis or a future possibility, it is a daily occurrence. We, the humankind, are matter transcended into spirit, a spirit as yet raw, fragmented, dark, violent, and excess-prone.

The utopia of sectarian religion is the assumption that such a condition existed once, "at the beginning was the word," and that for unexplained, inexplicable reasons, such total plentitude had to be broken: imperfection as the offspring of perfection. Since this is an immense fall from grace, in fact an absurdity (the only true impossible), the causal entity for such a fall must always be singled out as the most damnable of all possible realities, Lucifer, the Devil. Only the invention of the Devil could begin to justify the invention and existence of God, since those actions to God had to be the attributes of an evil spirit. But the Devil cannot be a son of God gone mad, he can only be the son of a mad or impotent God. The Devil is that bottomless bag where one can find an explanation for everything that faith cannot reflect upon its own God. If my theological, ecological analysis is correct, the bag is even more capacious than the religious soul is capable of imagining. The bag is the universe in toto from which must be subtracted the perfectable speck of nothingness we call the living. "The Devil made me do it" means that what is bearing upon me outside and inside of myself is causing me not to be master of myself. I am a tiny god while at the same time I am in immense turmoil of brutishness, spanning immense spaces for infinite times. Therefore, the Devil not only possesses me (I am not lost within it), but I am the Devil, which has somewhere in a remote corner of itself a tiny speck of divinity speaking, shouting out his (my) anguish. My relative sacredness is still the relative concreteness of a sigh in a caldron full of boiling sulfur.

Relativism says that *even* the maggot is holiness in the flesh, the paragon being not those living things upon which the maggot feeds, but rather that same matter which the maggot is minus the living flame which is the maggot's makeup. The maggot, therefore, is either sublime ecstasy of matter made flesh or it is a dumb pile of isolated subatomic particles given to randomness. This is a measure of the anguish which Lucifer, the universal maggot, is prey to: a Prometheus whose most sublime thought is to reach that platform of being where the devouring of dead flesh is pure ecstasy, the ecstasy of perpetuating one instant longer the remote possibility of the divine through the sufferance of the evolutionary ladder. To my understanding, Lucifer is not then a fallen angel who has lost grace, but a maggot in search of a condition of grace which will offer possibility for its own evolutionary progeny. We, the supermaggot, niched somewhere on the evolutionary ladder, still in very close proximity to our Father, the maggot God, must have a taste for the sublime flesh, the food of consciousness, and for the responsibility it carries with it.

The frugal want to make sure that the ties to the maggot God are strong in the context of the past but constantly cut and dissolved in the context of the future. We are as acrobats at the tip-top of the living pyramid and the apple we reach for is the apple we can create while resisting the call of the immense sea of nirvana, the once all-powerful, all-inclusive, proto-living universe.

The lust for life is not to be found in maggot-like ecstasy, the unselective gluttony of the mediocre, stated and willed. It is to be experienced as an emergence from the Red Sea of life and of man's sufferance, cleansed of all those deposits which are the end product of acquiescence to the call of our maggot ancestry, the sediment of mediocrity. There are moments of history when gluttony is impossible. The temptations remaining, the possibility of their satisfaction is remote. Those moments are in many ways precious and catalytic. They set the condition where necessity might translate itself into virtue. At that conjunction, the individual has to be the persona prima in the melee, missile and target in one, a flying target seeking the heat of the thick of things because there lies the possibility of a magic leap into an unknown, higher grace.

Piety and frugality are not the same thing. Piety has a ring of resignation to it which frugality cannot endorse. Since the true anguish of life is that which hurls itself upon indifference, seeding each speck of matter as if the present battle against unresponsiveness were the conclusive one, that makes each moment the magic moment, the key to deliverance and creation. In this unlimited naïveté, the world is always new, as if the beholder were acquainting himself with it for the first time. That is the state of being for creation. The frugal is a state where the tragic sense of life, this acknowledged anguish, is the bread and wine for that hunger by which consciousness is possessed in its emergence. We are not butterflies sapping the sweet nectar of reality. We are still a divine metamorphosis of the hungry maggot capable of transforming rotten flesh into grace, the dead into the living.

A vow of relative poverty is a conscious acknowledgment, within a socioeconomic structure which equates happiness with affluence, that we are the battleground where life confronts nonlife and that we choose to be responsible for its eventual transcendence. If this vow lacks the fire portrayed by the cenobite and the wretched, penitent seekers of God, it does possess, to say it once more, the belief that the flesh is part of the divine spirit. It is, in fact, the original tabernacle of it. It is earth saturated with expectation, the expectation of a grace beyond conjecture.

Arcosanti as Intent

SYNOPSIS: This is perhaps, as has been suggested, a humorless statement. I would say that the spicing of humor is essential if and when the chosen ingredients are appropriate. This statement attempts to define at least some of the ingredients of Arcosanti. It goes without saying that Arcosanti had better be able to smile, giggle, and laugh at itself.

1) It is not a commune or a utopia.	1) It is anti-utopian by design and content.
2) It does not support the contention of communes or utopias that individuals or groups can break away from society and achieve fulfillment.	2) It favors the notion that investigation and experimentation, within defined time lapses, can produce new and useful patterns for society.
3) It is not given to the notion of the Garden of Eden.	3) It is a town faced with the challenges of life.
4) It does not believe the millennium is at hand.	4) It believes in a quasi-infinite journey into the uncreated.
5) It does not believe in paradise on earth nor does it see its task as the pursuit of such an imaginary condition.	5) It believes in an eventual grace far beyond our times (all times) and sees the human task as the indefatigable effort toward such grace.
6) It is not a group or a place where enlightenment and happiness are achieved because truth has been reached, as if truth were something defined a priori and available for discovery and use.	6) It is a group and a place attempting and coordinating things in a different way so as to better serve the family of man, not because truth has been discovered but because a greater coherence can be established between the longings of man and the mystery of the universe.
7) It does not want to position itself at the fringe of immanence as the ashram	7) It would like to be at the cutting edge of the groping process in which humanity

of salvation among the wreckage of humanity.

8) It cannot endorse the notion that the human species has fallen from grace and works toward redemption through good deeds or through the annihilation into which nirvana delivers us.

9) It does not endorse the lifeboat paradigm, nor does it endorse the notion that it is pointless to build rafts or luxury liners until the passengers are dissected, reconstructed, and made socially acceptable.

10) As it does not believe in the possibility of total fulfillment now, so it does not believe in the anointed people who attempt to impersonate the truth.

11) It does not believe in self-righteousness or self-pity, especially when most of humankind is on the verge of indigence and famine.

12) It does not endorse the notion that all men are created equal (as if cloned from a God-given prototype).

13) It does not believe in the reductionist paradigm

creates itself by being apprentice and master in one.

8) It does endorse the miraculous nature of the evolutionary process and its quasi-infinite perfectibility, leading to the total reenactment of itself in the final resurrectional condition (Omega).

9) It sees itself as an indispensable raft, the construction of which is imperative, even though acknowledging that the passengers and their society can and will be less than perfect. The raft would be the vehicle of continuous transcendence.

10) It acknowledges the immensity of the task ahead which dwarfs the achievements of the past and sees as pointless or opportunistic the notion of God's chosen people.

11) It believes in self-responsibility and in the recognition that we are and we do a fraction of that which we could be and could do.

12) It endorses the notion that the individual is born with his own original, specific, irrepeatable characteristics.

13) It believes that life, supported by science and

and its mechanistic implications.

14) It does not believe that the behavioral sciences can fully describe life and guide man toward fulfillment.

15) It is not simply oriented toward steady-state and stewardship as the means to achieve harmony between oneself and nature within a somewhat unchanging universe.

16) It does not endorse the notion that in life simplification is for the better, the bias of both "return to nature" and technology.

17) It is not antiscientific, antitechnological, or anticultural, but it disavows the substitution of culture by technology.

18) It cannot accept the notion that fire is natural and atomic fire is unnatural, or that we are bound forever by modes which are natural to the exclusion of modes which are unnatural.

19) It does not believe in instant civilization or any other instant thing, including instant knowledge, instant grace, instant wisdom, or instant acculturation.

20) It does not endorse the notion that the child is a

technology, is a creational process, an esthetic process.

14) It believes that life consists of the art of living, and as such transcends the territory of science.

15) It is oriented toward transcendence: the creation of ever-new relationships between the inanimate and the animate, in favor of the latter, to the end of a fully conscious universe.

16) It does endorse the notion that it is the nature of life to seek ever more complex and conscious relationships.

17) It favors the notion that science and technology are instruments for the development of culture and for the transcendence of the existing into the new.

18) It accepts the notion that eventually the living stuff of the universe will go beyond any danger signs, since the pursuit is of the total and ultimate, and, therefore, comprehends all and everything.

19) It does believe in development by personal toil and commitment to the necessity of growing into a better self through minute, experimental steps.

20) It sees the esthetic as the process by which the

natural artist because it does not endorse the idea that art is effortless and spontaneous.

21) It has no sympathy for the deceiving notion that everyone is an original creator.

22) It does not see "doing one's own thing" as very relevant for either the individual or the human family.

23) It does not support the easy, quick, and fraudulent way out of mediocrity.

24) It does not believe that the pursuit of happiness is a valid goal, or that, given the human condition, it is attainable in anyone's lifetime.

25) It cannot endorse intolerance, greed, violence, arrogance.

26) It is not pessimistic or cynical, neither is it gullible or market-oriented.

27) It does not endorse opulent ways, the consumerist, insurance-mortgage ethos, or the transference of self-responsibility to others.

28) It has no use for the "us" and "them" notion, nor for

fundamental anguish of the human condition is transfigured into the esthetic experience.

21) It endorses the notion that we can all be artists by mimesis and through vicariousness and gregariousness.

22) It does see as imperative that "one's own thing" becomes our own thing, not by mob action, but, by transcendence of the ego into the self, the human self.

23) It is for an existentially difficult and protracted, in fact, indefinitely protracted, way in.

24) It believes that the pursuit of worthiness illuminates the tragic nature of life with radiant moments of joy which are the anticipation of a possible, future fulfillment.

25) It must try to affirm tolerance, generosity, nonviolence, reverence.

26) It is optimistic and passionate, seeing quality as a quantitative measure of spirit.

27) It endorses the frugal ways and sees the consumerist, insurance-mortgage ethos as ultimately demeaning to the person, a postponement of commitment.

28) It advocates the concept that at times a small group

the mob elitism of mediocrity.

has to come out and beat new paths for the sake of all of us.

29) It cannot endorse the power of coercion and its consequences.

29) It endorses authority based on knowledge, the power of persuasion, and their consequences.

30) It does not endorse a Bill of Rights, any Bill of Rights per se.

30) It endorses a Bill of Rights and a Bill of Duties as two inseparable halves of one whole.

31) It cannot sympathize with the Woodstock syndrome—the conversion by edict and mob fulfillment.

31) It endorses patient, disciplined seeking of understanding within the contradictions of the human condition.

32) It is not a countercultural, sectarian, or religious establishment, or a Zen Center, a meditation center, or a neomonastic center.

32) It intends to be a working model, a prototype, that might be influential in transforming the environmental, social, and cultural character of the present.

33) It does not deem as momentous that the mind can bend a spoon or that willpower can alter the heartbeat.

33) It does deem momentous that life transforms matter into flesh, into mind, into spirit (of which spoon-bending is a manifestation).

34) It does not see religion as revealed truth nor does it see the holy books as documents of divine intervention into mismanaged human affairs.

34) It sees religion as myth-making, and anticipatory-modeling and the holy books as collections of human wisdom (or unwisdom) and compassionate teaching.

35) It does not endorse the tribal syndrome, the return to nature, the withdrawal of man from society, or pseudoconservationist ethics.

35) It endorses the Urban Effect and the eschatology of the transformation of the physical into the living, the social, the cultural, and the spiritual.

36) It does not identify with any church or any denomination, old or new, eastern or western, or with the limiting confines they might define for reality.

36) It does endorse the concept that through the evolutionary process, the miracle of life and spirit will pervade and consume the universe.

37) It does not believe in the benign or just Father-God expectant of a penitent or resigned humankind.

37) It believes in the possibility of a divine radiant God-in-the-making, whom life creates out of itself.

38) It does not believe in revelation and in its revealing god.

38) It believes in creation, which is the evolutionary process.

39) It does not believe in the distributive justice of a divine Father, resurrection of the dead, or in salvation.

39) It does believe that if the evolutionary process carries on to its conclusion, a state of total recall will be reached in which resurrection will be immensely revelational.

40) It does not believe that man is unchangeable, that is to say, has reached the apex of his potential.

40) It believes that man is an embryonic creature who might eventually develop into unimaginable grace.

41) It does not endorse the idea that success is the only and indispensable proof of worthiness and grace, or that being recognized by the present is a sanction of one's worth.

41) It sees success in the often ambiguous light of something that by being ripe for its own time might ultimately fail its appointment with destiny and fall short of future expectations.

42) It does not endorse a condition which fails to recognize a hierarchy of values, performances, meaning, substance, and responsibilities.

42) It supports the condition where movement along a hierarchy of responsibilities and performances might become the normal experimental process of growth for any person so inclined.

43) Since the gap separating armchair wisdom from

43) It endorses instead the idea that in most cases

sweating performance is a chasm, it does not see much value in the "I told you so" syndrome or in pontification in the absence of responsibility.

self-righteousness is a diaphragm concealing from the ego its own loss of anima.

44) It does not see the past as sacred and worthy of return, nor does it see the present as the wreckage of such a sacred past.

44) It sees the past as nothing short of a miracle and yet a very deficient one. It sees the present as demanding more commitment to all-pervading grace.

45) It does not go along with the idea that the urban context is built for a known society, if for no other reason than that the known society of today is not, and better not be, cannot be, the society of next year and next.

45) It assumes that only an environment which is constructed for an ideal and, in many ways, unknowable society, will not shortchange the society which eventually inhabits it.

46) It does not identify the process of construction with the experience of the constructed and working town.

46) It distinguishes the process of construction from the experiencing of the town, since only the functioning instrument will be able to perform its own task.

Arcomedia

SYNOPSIS: Information, interpretation, and expression find a friend and an enemy in electronic technology. It is urgent that the awesome power of light and sound be reintegrated within the environmental existential context which originates them. The learning process will then be enhanced.

One can say that the genealogy from the sun to the spirit is the subject matter of evolution. Consideration of this generation of consciousness within the folds of matter, this transformation of the raw and savage power of the sun into the biosphere and homosphere of the earth, is not to be seen as the cult of a cosmic furnace but as the homage and investigation in awe and bewilderment of the order of a physical cosmos capable of generating within itself a consciousness of itself. The homage is to the deed which the spirit of life is about to perform, the actualization by metamorphosis of mass-energy into a transuniverse which I choose to call esthetic. This homage is the act of worship. As this transformation of matter into form, this esthetogenesis, is achieved only by the force of compassionate man transforming nature, the true act of worship is the esthetic act by which man moves another step toward grace. The ontological, theological, and esthetic are the funnel, the wind and the pollen, in the participatory act of creation of the universe of the spirit.

Can one physically define a circumstance made of space and structure where one is moved closer to the awe preceding creation? Only creation can beget creation. Therefore, there is dread of setting up a pedestal which is the negation of the sculpture it will support, a sterile Arcomedia.

This is, then, not another attempt at making a harmonious environment for man to stroll about, nor a simulation machine for things which do not exist any longer (Walt Disney), nor a house of worship such as a church, a synagogue, or a mosque, nor a laboratory for the alchemy of technology, nor, last of all, a museum where things are brought to be viewed and dissected. It is intended as an esthetically conceived framework that will contain, harbor, shelter, host, display, and chastise the efforts of individuals or groups who are trying to wedge themselves into the spatial-temporal-oral-sensory existential immanence of reality in order to wrest away from the mineral another parcel of matter to imbue it with the quivering of consciousness.

This active filtering device is a means and an aim in itself. It is the solicitor of genetic straining in pursuit of becoming and it is the fruit of those same genes. It is, therefore, not just the hardware for creation but a creature begetting others. If it were what it ought to be, it would be the bridge spanning the gulf between wishfulness and deed. Taking the wish as the face value of the deed, the program is then very clear: the genesis of the instrument, Arcomedia, is of the same nature as the genesis which the instrument will partake in producing. This genesis is an esthetogenesis, the extension of anthropogenesis into ever more rarefied realms of matter-energy. Arcomedia is not an instrument for survival but an organism fertile with creations other than its original one.

That is why it is not a museum or an art therapy center. It is not a place of worship as such, but a place where awe is objectified into sensory events. It is also not a house of God, but a God-maker. The blasphemy is only in the degree of presumption and not in the presumption per se. Is it presumptuous to assume that we are more God-like than a pile of rubble?

If consciousness means to be of the process, then just strolling about in and on the body of the self-making God, a promenading passivity, is the true blasphemy. Concurrently, the characterization as an amusement park or fictional-simulation environment is inappropriate, not because it might be incapable of sustaining such things, but because it stands for what it is and does, not for what it might fake.

The scientist, the priest, and the artist focus from three different directions on truth, justice, love, and creation, the intellect is made sensuous flesh to add to the in vitro analysis of the flesh components, the somatic, sensitive synthesis of responses to its own maker, or cause, or midwife, the sun, the astronomical furnace related to the earth so as to be the sustenance of what it had been, itself the prior originator, life.

The matter-of-factness of our relationship with the environment, this interface of no interface between the I and the it which routinely briefs the mind and the body on the context of the moment, the response of the I to the incoming assault of the it and its negative predisposition toward the delicate balancing act of the I. This routine of being sensorially plugged in to nature can and ought to be brought to the light of consciousness frequently and, if only in flashes, empowered with the joyfulness of discovery and participation. The person who, predisposed toward the discovery of truth in science, lovingly and sensuously opens himself or herself to the vivifying truth of religion which empowers it, in the tension and anguish of the moment constructs-creates the esthetic. Arcomedia, the etherealized topography, would lend its structure and form to the moment of creation.

The difference between a school and Arcomedia stems from the difference between the learning of a certain skill and the application of it. Conceding that it is in the application of something that an idea or a sign is sharpened and rounded, the fundamental difference remains that in the learning process as such, the focus of action is on learning itself, that is to say, there is no focus to work toward other than the apprehension of a certain aptness. On the other hand, the use of an apprehended idea or skill must have a focus and scope which transcends them. Therefore, for instance, the net and sharp separation between the context in which the master performs and that in which the apprentice learns.

The process of learning, both per se and abstractly, is the appropriation-internalization of an otherness. The process of creating is the transcendence of the enriched self giving a new parameter of reality to otherness. The anguish appears not in the appropriative stage of the process, as in the recipience-passivity of the student being just the process of self-augmenting and informing, but in the anticipatory stages preceding, without any guarantee of success, transcendence and creation. It is there on the testing ground of the soul that the ambiguities of both the I and the it come to do battle and to bring anxiety. The seams that good sense and logic had sewn, optimistically or expediently, to bind the strands of information into the bag of knowledge begin to give way as creation bursts from the rationality of a position to the transrationality of a becoming which is incommensurable with its matrix.

Learning and discovery (scientific work) are more germane than learning and creating, in agreement with the proven fact that the most fruitful period in the scientist's life is the twenties and thirties. Discovering is, after all, a more original way of learning. The discoverer is a pioneer in learning, the first to climb a certain mountain. The mountain will be rediscovered time and time again by the student who finds paths, ladders, ropes, and signs which are the props and information easing his task of apprehension. The same props and information can dull the experience, the toll of nonoriginality. This tax is the ennui of learning and its presence is not the fault of the object-matter but of the subject-student when and for whom discovery has been lost to drudgery.

The discoverer (inventor?) of a paradigm is the explorer seeing some of his own conjecture confirmed by the solidity of a landscape. The consumer of the same paradigm is the settler whose anxiety is not of the order of true or false, but of easy or hard. For creation, both anxieties, true or false, hard or easy, do not come to grips with existential anguish. The what (truth-false) and the how (easy-hard) are superseded by the why on which the esthetic metamorphosis comes about. Nor should the why constantly asked by science be confused with the why with which philosophy battles. The why of science refers to an accepted if unfathomable reality, the why of philosophy to one's willingness to accept and abide by a possibly unfathomable reality. One is about knowledge of what is (epistemology), the other is about acceptance of what ought to be (ontology-eschatology).

Creation is the offspring that the manipulation of the two whys is able to transact. On one hand, what they are is not what they can become: on the other, just because they are, they must transcend themselves into an as yet nonactive metamorphosis. Discovery is understanding. Invention is coordination-manipulation. Creation is metamorphosis. Arcomedia, optimally, is the staging for metamorphosis, a metamorphosis itself of some power, so as not to contradict at the outset the aim of the effort. Which is, by the way, the common ill of places of learning (campuses) or of work (the studio loft, the warehouse, the basement, etc.), places of pettiness, of ostentation, of sterility, of squalor, of dereliction, of dehumanization, of naught.

It is also neither a Woodstock nor an Apollo launching pad. A Woodstock is where the soul is mired by the mind lying itself into mindlessness, where the effacement of conflict is the wiping out of the person, where even survival cannot risk a fourth day, where simplicity is elemental parasitism, where the tribe raped of its structure is only the mob. The Apollo scenario is where raw technology is rampant technology, where intelligence is pitted against conscience, where the complicated and brain-bugging coordinations mystify the complexity of man's mind, where materials and energies are waspishly single-minded and thrown into a time-space venture. Here the sap of life is made too much like a superfuel to run in the involute plumbing of rockets, not in the evolute arteries of the flesh. Woodstock is life residual. Apollo is life interstitial.

As the ecological status quo is taken to task by the frenzy of the western Homo Faber and some ecologist, philistine, or less bright than expected, dwells on the egalitarianism of man, animals, and trees, the human biological tonnage—to speak only of the physical bulk—is steamrolling ever more land mainly for the dormitories of the affluent nations. The self-righteous ecologist-pietist, Woodstocked or Apollonian, is tuning out through the simplistic way of the tribe, be it ape-naked (Woodstock) or electrocastrated (Apollo). The furiously disciplined megamachine of nature could hardly believe her eyes, if she had any (and indeed she has them, three billion pairs). Soon the ecologist-pietist, more sentient, future-oriented, conscious in his fantasies of the low-keyed harmony between man and nature, should put his ear to the deafening howling of mineral nature, upset once and ever since by the disturbing, unbalancing, arrogant jellies coalescing in primeval seas and early lagoons. How dare they . . . the mineral says and says again.

Original and Radical?

The most common mistake about my work is the belief that some years of introspection have produced a take-it-or-leave-it package solution to the urban problem. Rather, I am proposing a methodology and at the same time trying to illustrate it. The methodology is original and radical in the literal sense. It is original by being "of and with the origin," and radical in the parallel sense of being "of the roots." It is not original or radical if those terms are defined in the vernacular, because it is the oldest, the most used, and the most rooted of all methodologies applied to life. To grasp and to accept this methodology, one needs to be free of the Adam and Eve syndrome, that is to say, free from the historian's mental block that makes one stop at the gate of prehistory on the tenuous contention that what preceded man was and is devoid of pedagogical, experiential, or methodological importance for him and therefore cannot disclose anything as to the possible future of man, his mind, his society, his culture. An unoriginal and unradical stance, untenable vis-à-vis contemporary science, unable to fit into the evolutionary momentum, this static historicism is hard put to explain how matter becomes thought and spirit, how a fiery ball of mass-energy, lost in a corner of a run-of-the-mill galaxy, has transformed and transfigured itself into the earth of today.

If this incredible development is seen metaphorically as a cooperative effort of myriad upon myriad of workers constructing their collective home by putting rectangular brick above rectangular brick (the methodology), and if among the immense number has appeared now and then a queer character with extravagant round bricks which are unsuccessfully and disruptively thrown together and end in heaps of rubble (the mutants that have failed), then I find my niche among the myriad, the advocates of rectangular brick, the builders of the structure, not among the strange ones, the going-for-broke, opulent technocrats of all ages. The myriad is the rank and file, beginning with the first, original, and radical simple cells and proceeding up through the successful mutations of all species, vegetal and animal, through the Garden of Eden into the demonic universe of the mind, all along the pain-filled bridge making matter into spirit.

It is when the historian wants to be pragmatic that the historian becomes pathetic. His round bricks keep making a fool of him by allowing him some battle victories in the losing war of incongruence. He becomes, with the great technocrats, the staunch advocate of a better quality of wrongness, the true face of the pollution slough and its entropic backsliding away from the spirit.

As with any honest methodology, the original-radical methodology proposes a necessity not a sufficiency. It does not suffice because efficiency is not sufficiently endowed to be an end in itself. It is plainly a good instrument for the fostering of the construction of the bridge between matter and spirit.

To the next question, "Do we need a methodology?", there is a pretty stark answer. We *are* a methodology, successfully developing itself into an aim. We are free agents inasmuch as we have methodologically invented ourselves from the first ambiguous living cells into what we are, quasi God-like automatons, free within the most subtle portion of ourselves, the mind, to prognosticate, indeed, to plan, for a less coercive future.

This methodology can deliver life, as it has done for eons upon eons, to survival and beyond. Therefore it is within its guidelines that we will rediscover man as a truly compassionate animal. The methodology is the process by which the early, vague interiorizations of physical bundles, the first living creatures, grow in number, complexity, compactness, and power along the evolutionary ladder until the person, the civilization, and the culture come to be and become a routine event. This interiorization shall not stop, if life will not stop. It shall grow, if life will keep evolving. The arcology at its minimum best is but a mechanism necessary, but not sufficient, for such continuous interiorization of the world of mass-energy. It is part of the nuts-and-bolts pragmatism of matter becoming spirit, of hunger being overcome, of deprivation being cared for, of life becoming personhood. It is of the species, all the species staying on course, the course that has a future because it constructs the future by congruently and willfully making horse sense (the rectangular brick) or what it does instrumentally, thus freeing the spirit for ends unforeseeable because they are as yet uncreated.

5

Sacred Spaces

SYNOPSIS: We, as sensitized matter, perform the miracle of sanctifying that which we behold, but we also mismanage our power when we work in our "equipment yards" where reverence is conspicuously absent. The sacred space is where reverence constructs the future more and better than where reverence sings nostalgia for the past. The Gothic masterpiece is as much a successful challenge to the stony and brute nature of physical reality as it is a hymn to the Father-God.

Why is it a general premise that space per se becomes sacred space as soon as it is perceived? It is because perception implies consciousness of some sort, and since consciousness is a manifestation of sensitivity (the sensitization of matter), it follows that whatever might be the sacredness of matter, more sacredness impregnates the humblest parcel of living stuff than can be found in a whole galaxy from which life has been subtracted. The perception of matter makes it glow with the vicarious sacredness of consciousness. Space, time, structure . . . all are a quivering emergence when touched by the sentient stuff of the living.

If the steadfastness of life and the habit we have of being part of it explain the callousness we demonstrate toward life's constantly miraculous nature, they also suggest the immensity of the spiritual, sentient phenomenon which can take for granted the most improbable of things, consciousness itself and, what is more, its constant unfolding. Therefore, we are materially a walking, eating, sleeping, doing, struggling sacredness among the sacredness of the vegetal and animal kingdoms, a tiny tidal wave of sacredness pressing against the immensely large and relatively inert reality of mass-energy which composes the cosmos.

Our level of reality is one in which a certain saturation of sacredness is taken for granted and forgotten as routine. When we speak, then, about sacred places, we speak of a sacredness beyond the routine. The difference might be of proportion or relativity. That is to say, the conscious achievement of a sacred place is to be perceived as literally drowned within the unconscious sacredness of the living phenomenon. (Desegregation is tied to such perception.)

One might ask the worth of building sacred spaces if they are both redundant and puny. The question, in another form, has been with man for a long time: "Why do we need to pinpoint a center of God-like power when every manifestation of life is a centered manifestation of such power? Why God beside life, or inside life? Why not God's life or life-God?"

The answer might be simpler than we expect. It might be that in the most intimate folds of life there is and ever more will be an insatiable thirst for comprehensiveness of things, emotions, understanding, wisdom, and reality. The epitome of comprehensiveness is the concept of deity. So much so that we are willing to lose ourselves in it if in exchange we are conceded even a brief glance at its glory. The pursuit of comprehensiveness develops more and more subtle instruments of interiorization. The vivification of inert matter plunges consciously into the evolutionary tide and puts energies and knowledge at its service.

The mystic experience, the saintly life, and martyrdom are roads or superhighways toward the experience of a densified reality. Drug addiction is (probably) a shortcut ending at the feet of idols, since, contrary to paths which project into the future and the spirit, it looks backward toward the unified experience of earlier events and duller, simpler perceptions—the nirvana syndrome.

The religious road to full sacredness is a noble attempt to make do without the real thing. This is because the religious context is that of simulation inasmuch as theology works at causing the hypothesis of God to become a reality. Since the theological effort is working on a possibility, it has to simulate such possibility. As we do not have a God yet, and we cannot really do without one, we construct a structure that stands for a hypothesis of sacredness: the theological structure. In fact, if one separates the theological structure from the God it is aimed at, one could almost speak of it as a simulation of a simulation.

An alternative to the sacredness attempted via theological simulation is the sacredness achieved via esthetogenesis. To convey the difference between the two, one could say that for the theological way the future is conceptually designed as the progressive identification of life with God, with the mystifying inversion of the whole historical schedule so that the declared intention is the reentering of the flock into the divine corral, not, as evolution would indicate, the progressive creation of both flock and divine corral. In this mix-up of discovery with creation is to be found the confusion about theology and the esthetic. In its clarification, one can find what distinguishes one from the other. If theology is a structure in quest of a content, the esthetic is a form that defines the content. The first is an invention, the invention of God, and an attempt to anticipate and simulate the performance of such invention. The second is a creation (a fragment) and as such, within the extreme limits of the fragment, is a particle itself of the mystical body.

A sacred space, to fulfill its aim, should be that environment where shrouding the conceptual and simulative structure of religion is the concrete radiance of the esthetic creation, a corporeal fragment of divinity. Why is it that the temple is rarely a sacred space? Because the sacred space literally has to be the battlefield where the translation from simulation of a hypothesis into the actual historical construction takes place. Therefore, it is not a pure space, a noncontaminated place, but the phalanstery where the improbable affirms itself and makes itself bit by suffering bit into God. Once the anguish innate in the improbable nature of life and in the even more hypothetical creation of the Omega God is glossed over by the bartering of a society in quest of the golden egg, the genesis of sacredness is stifled and the esthetic creation does not occur. Therefore, a weak structure of theology (theoecology—see "The Theology of the Sun") is surrounded, shrouded, by an even weaker esthetocompassionate form.

And if the temple rarely succeeds in being a sacred space, the marketplace is even more ill-equipped for access to sacredness. Think of the bank or the gas station. In one, the most abstract of all commodities is made into an icon, deified. In the other, the riches accumulated by the genesis of God, the high distillation and concentration of the sun's energy, are collected to be burned on the altar of another idol of contemporary man, the automobile.

Where is it then that sacred space has a chance to reveal itself? In the city, the totality of it, where finally, if only as a seed promising the tree, the comprehensiveness demanded by consciousness begins to show itself, where instruments and symbols, energies and containers, devices and events, physics and metaphysics can focus into a premonition of sacredness and in the dynamics necessary to the unending quest for the Omega condition.

Is there a contradiction between the necessity of a critical mass, the city, in order to have the sacred, and the art object which I tend to see as a fragment of such sacredness? Not in the absolute sense, if one clearly sees that the esthetic genesis is somehow the interiorization by the artist of the condition of emergency inherent in the critical mass (its improbability, for instance) and the intrinsic anguish which pervades it, and the ability of the artist to transfigure such a condition of emergency: anguish into an objectified emergence, the work of art. In a sense, the city is the suffering implicit in the actualization of the theological simulation, while the work of art is a fragment of what such simulation is ultimately seeking. The esthetocompassionate city is the synthesis of both, the Civitas Dei. In a way, the artist must think of the city, even if he only carves a twig, because the charge of his anguish must be commensurate, must be the same, as the charge of anguish which impinges on mankind.

If it is true that little anguish yields a weak artist, the opposite, great anguish, great artist, does not necessarily hold. In fact, if this were true, each ounce of anguish would translate into one measure of harmony and, therefore, anguish would become simply a passport to paradise, something one signed up for at a bureaucratic theological archive. But the true unforgiving nature of anguish is its pervasiveness and imperviousness, and only rarely can its armor be pierced to pour out a radiant metamorphosis. What great anguish might give access to, aside from esthetic genesis, is either mental illness or sanctity, that synopsis of the hypothetical, future Omega God.

By fragments of God, the esthetic act, and by the sufferance of an implemented simulation falling short of target (since it is the fate of simulation to mistake the fake for the real), matter makes itself more and more sensitized, and the bridge between matter and spirit is reinforced by new fibers of consciousness, knowledge and grace. To sustain the journey, now and then comes the blinding light of the saintly or the martyred, a synopsis of God within a synopsis of sufferance.

The presence of the theological, the structure in quest of a content, and the presence of the esthetic, a form defining a content, can or ought to combine in the most favorable occasion for sacred space.

If we keep in mind that for the theologian the content must be the living content of the immanent God, we cannot avoid what seems to be a mandatory condition: the object must be the container of such immanent God, who is most densely and robustly constituted where humankind is the participant. We are dealing with the Civitas Dei, the new Jerusalem, in a process of emergence, an esthetogenesis.

To my knowledge, the Civitas Dei can be conceived only within the arcological methodology, the sine qua non in the definition of sacred space. This would not be so if the arcological methodology coincided with the theoecological methodology. How can one escape the tautological merry-go-round? It might not be possible since the worth of the equipment, life, depends on its success, and the success of life will in turn define its worth. The value of utopia has to be found where it ceases to be utopia because it has become reality. Reality can have a future only if it is able to make the future, the next utopia, into reality.

Perhaps the tautological trap is set with the acceptance that whether life succeeds or not, God will still be there. Therefore, we need not demonstrate the existence of divinity by the presence of life and then turn around and demonstrate the worth of life by the immanence of divinity, as one does by endorsing the reality of the Omega God.

If this reasoning is not necessary to achieve sacred spaces, it is necessary to explain to ourselves why sacred spaces are so rare and why they escape rationalization. They demonstrate what they are by being what they attempt to demonstrate. They are forms whose meaning, the content, is the form itself. They do not have to perform. They are the performance of the immanent God. By way of clarification, one can take another manifestation of Homo Faber, the bulldozer. The bulldozer is a structure whose form is present only in the performance of the machine. The idle bulldozer is a nothing. In the instrumental world there is the thing and the performance of it. In the noninstrumental world this distinction vanishes. The media and the message coincide not in McLuhan magic but in sacredness.

The dynamics of one, thermodynamics, are useful devices in the creation of the other, the dynamics of the spirit; the dynamics of the photosynthetic process are useful in the production of the vegetal world whose entelechy will find its path toward the spirit via the duration intensification of evolution. Then the process from matter into spirit, the sacred, has its origin in the instrumental pool, the physical universe, and its aim in the Omega God where all of it, the universe-media, is etherealized into the Omega God-message. The TV tube is, therefore, a media which will convey messages, good and bad, pertinent or idle, strong or weak. The truly sacred space is a media-message of the sacred immanence of the Omega God.

Architecture as Information

SYNOPSIS: Consciousness is like a membrane interposed between the inner mystery and the outer mystery. The quality of the membrane, our conscience and our doing, is directly dependent on the intensity and the appeal of both mysteries. The environment, the outer mystery in its proximity to ourselves, is then the most powerful conscience-maker (life-maker). Evolution testifies to that. Architecture as environment is the man-made conscience-maker.

THE MEDIA AND THE MESSAGE

This paper is about information and not communication because the subject matter, the man-made environment, is a situation where McLuhan's slogan "the media is the message" applies. Considering a TV set on one side and an edifice or group of edifices and the spaces between them on the other, I would say that only remotely does the TV set, media, stand for the program, the message, it conveys. That is to say, there is not, notwithstanding McLuhan, an unbreakable relationship between the media and the message. Vietnam would have been with us even if the only electronic conveyor of messages had been the radio. For the edifice, or man-made environment, it is a different story. There the media, the physical structures, are more than mediators between an event and the perceptual system, the person. The mediator becomes the actor, that is to say, it is actually information in and of itself instead of being a remote presence, a conveyor, like the wire in the telephone, the transistor in the radio, or the picture tube in the TV set.

A communication system may be prevented from being an information system by its nonmediatory character. To perceive the taste of an apple is to taste an apple. The apple is then a communication system which is also an information source. An attempt to perceive the taste of an apple through an hour-long TV special would clarify the incapacity of the medium, TV, to be specifically more than a communication device. As such, it can deliver only that which can be abstracted from the nature of any event and conveyed through the mechanism as information. For the TV, this nature must be visual, not tactile, tastable, or olfactory. It is aural (through the auxiliary of the sound system) and visual by definition. Therefore, TV is a versatile communication system when an event can be dissected and the abstracts of such dissection can be delivered through either of the two communication channels of sound or sight. TV is, however, remote by the nature of the process of dissection, abstraction, and construction. A manipulative, interpretative confounding information noise. In a phrase: a remote way of bringing an event to witness. Moreover, since the visual and oral are only two elements of any event, even the visual-oral communication of visual-oral elements suffers crippling limitations from the viewpoint of information. Vietnam again made the point. For ten years or so, the audiovisual reporting of events did not convey the brutishness and savagery of a cultured society. Ugly pictures and ugly sounds do not, cannot, compete with the direct information which is the sufferance, participatory and sacrificial, in a durational process.

As any other technological device, TV is abstractional and simplifying. Abstractional, because everything that comes through the tube and the loudspeaker has to be abstracted to be channeled into them. Simplifying, because the channeling process itself can only be accomplished by a reduction of multiplicity-complexity into singularity-simplicity.

If we move now to the other example under consideration, the edifice or group of edifices and their interspaces, we see a different situation. What they communicate is also what they are. That is to say, they are a media that cannot avoid intruding as a message. The intrusion is necessary participation in the events that they contain, shelter, influence, instigate, chastise, and imprint. It helps little to say that in some measure this is also true of the TV. The influence of a communication system cannot obscure the distinction between communication and information which clearly tells us that TV is itself a new set of information which happens also to be a communication channel. The ideal TV set is that common denominator-homogenizer that by total self-effacement becomes the magic communication, a mirror of things for which the mirror is totally irrelevant—offering no consolation or resurrection, for instance, for the dying who are projected on the screen. Again, the TV as a communication device is irrelevant to the taste of an apple; it might be relevant to the understanding of the apple, it is not ever relevant to the nature of the apple. If it were, it would imply that the apple could only be real with the advent of TV. It must be said that a certain event or chain of events can fully become reality only when their staging and content are concretely copresent and acting one upon the other, as is true in the environmental field. The ideal man-made environment is a powerful presence which itself acts upon the actors it shelters. Thus, although it has purpose as a communication system, it has an even greater purpose as an information context.

MAN AND HIS ANCESTRY

Contemporary man technologizes himself to death and then rushes to those sacred places and spaces where he can remotely observe a different man through some of the physical things he has left behind (or ahead). The different man, his ancestor, is the man of toil, slavery, heroism, idolatry, and faith. For each contemporary wanderer going into the wilderness, there are a thousand pilgrims going to the places of man. Even at this young evolutionary stage of the human species, the return to man is stronger than the return to nature. Already at this very early age of civilization there is, between man and pristine nature, the man of history whose call is at times nothing more than the crumbling stones and miserable shards of some historic and prehistoric garbage heaps. (One can say that, in most instances, cities would grow vertically above successive layers of litter and waste, the by-products of civilized man.) Beyond the ruins of his continuing hubris, documented in the remains of his cities, man has been reaching for surman in an effort to hold at bay and tame the fury of the nonliving universe. He must remind himself that since life is the exception to the rule, the rule being nonlife in the physical universe, he is perched precariously on a tenuous limb surrounded by nothingness. His gods care, or so he thinks, for his tottering through the construction of the history of his being. Contemporary man avidly seeks the remaining documents which will communicate to him information on such construction.

On this journey through history, the journey contemporary man seeks to reexperience in his pilgrimages, man manipulates the physical world and produces all sorts of wares, small and large, private and public, lasting and ephemeral, humble and flamboyant, functional and symbolic. Those physical things make up the nest where his children learn what is normal or not, what is peer-grooming or not, what is customary or not, what is useful or not, what is respectable or not. The adult or the child-adult molds himself by molding the physical environment, and his matrix closely fits the physical matrix he inherited and the one he himself is altering by his being and doing.

THE PHYSICAL CONTINUUM

This physical world is the world of objectified information in which we are immersed as on an all-enveloping continuum, a continuum sensitive to our responses as much as we are sensitive to its challenges. This sensitive continuum is only that cortex of the physical universe which is closed to man and it does not contradict the maximal indifference or hostility of the total universe toward life. It might help to see the importance of this if we can understand or remember that information does not necessarily have a one-to-one relationship of words and concept to brain and attention but is tied to the ebb and flow of the continuum that permeates, even if only skin-deep, the surface of the earth. We are, as any living thing is, under a constant assault of information, a limited part of which is verbalized and abstracted to reinforce the importance of this enveloping, environmental sensitization (or occasionally desensitization).

SENSUAL MAN

One might want to reinforce this observation by adding that the most valid recollections of past information do not come via conceptualizations but via odors, taste, sounds, light, settings . . . Most of us have felt the poignant quasi-reincarnation of a past moment, triggered by a familiar (and perhaps not too pleasant) smell. An olfactory datum triggers an avalanche of information, well forgotten but neatly stored away in the helix of memory. In fact, what comes upon us is not objective information but the subjective emotion which shrouded a past event.

The physical milieu, then, is a formidable teacher, a significant molder of ourselves, the sensuous receivers-intensifiers-transformers-transmitters. It does not simply inform us, it reaffirms our identity by the coordination and mediation of our being with our becoming. Therefore, the state of being, solicited by the information load of the physical milieu, is constantly stressed in the dynamics of becoming.

That, by the way, is why we all agree on the evil nature of the squalid environment where the cruelty of man is made forceful by the brutality of bricks and wood, stone and asphalt, litter and bareness, all organized to make bleak spaces anticipatory of bleak lives.

There are two ways in which we transform nature, producing a totally man-ordered environment and, therefore, causing ourselves to be globally informed in specifically environmental ways that are not customarily called natural.

MAN, THE FARMER

One way is agriculture. Immense sections of every continent, excluding perhaps Latin America, Australia, and Siberia, are physically restructured so as to present a surface which is only remotely similar to what it was in the past. To understand the scale of the transformation, one could try to imagine Europe as it might have been before the appearance of large human settlements (a cross between the Amazonian forest and the Wyoming prairies?) compared to the Europe of today.

If one looks for mass information in its compelling and lasting results, one cannot fail to see the difference and the respective impact of the two modes: the early wilderness and the tamed landscape. In both cases, it is a kind of information whose pervasiveness itself makes it difficult to be conscious of, as the liquid medium of water goes unnoticed by the fish. Although it is responsible for their morphology and existence, so it is for the information envelope which invests and molds man from his ancestral childhood, man the hunter, or man the farmer. It is the sine qua non of his existence and his relatedness with nature, a relatedness so tightly woven between the two as to work as much on the instinctual as on the intellectual areas of consciousness. What some of the theorists on environment versus the theorists on genetic determination of human behavior seem to forget is that the genetic is in itself an environmentally defined category whose time beat happens to be far more extended than the commonly used time measure for environmental influence. On this score, one cannot let go unnoticed the stark fact that a slightly different cosmic coordinate of earth mass, distance from the sun, rotation and revolution length, and the nature of the sun itself would mean a *very* different kind of life and a *very* different kind of man. *In evolutionary terms the environmental information is truly the maker (and the breaker).*

THE CITY BUILDER

A similar discourse could be conducted on the second way by which man transforms nature, the construction of his habitat and the places that contain and shelter the institutions of life, work, exchange, socialization, culture, worship, etc. It could be a similar discourse, if it were not for the fact that there is in this second way a special kind of intensity and the definite appearance of the manmade, the nonorganic reordering of mass-energy. In a true sense, in this second way it is as if each stone and brick, chunk of mortar, splinter of wood, iron, or bronze were imbued with the light and heat of the struggle man puts up in the face of nature stubbornly welded to her own entropic ways. Man, ever so determined to break the entropic locks, is willing to exude sweat and blood to force upon them the miracle of a metamorphosis. In historic terms, this metamorphosis is supported and documented by the successive waves of civilizations at whose hubs are the tribal enclaves, the villages, the towns, the cities, and the metropolises.

THE INNOCENT APE

It is therefore one of the most obscurantist moments of a culture when such culture makes a Woodstock a historical moment. There, to be specific, the dwindling into nothing or, worse, into the squalor (the sea of litter and garbage left) of the environment, both natural and human, is taken as a gate to human recognition and interaction. We deal here, needless to say, with the true nonplace of utopia. In that kind of naught, psychosomatic man is made naked and defenseless. One could hardly imagine the depth of desperation that the multitude of Woodstock would plunge into if on their return to "this world" nothing would be found of man's environment, and in its place only the best of the Garden of Eden (optimistically to make for the easy survival of the naked ape, man). The loss would be felt, perhaps not down into the bone's marrow of the man-animal but surely into the concealed pit where consciousness niches itself. And the meaning of the loss would be that suddenly a whole universe of information, an immense kinetic library, this most comprehensive information machine painstakingly constructed by generations of men and women would have been wiped out, leaving man with not much more than his eyes to cry and his ears to hear the cries of others. It would suffice if this essay did no more than alert the reader that the loss of the man-made physical world, with all its intolerance, its bad and savage corners, would be the equivalent of man's fall from grace.

ARCHITECTURE AS INFORMATION

In its broader significance, architecture embraces virtually all of the nondisposable, noninstant, and relatively nonobsolete world. Architecture is the alterations made upon nature by the organic, the psychological, the mental, the components of man's consciousness where the social-cultural stresses operate within and emanate out of the human kind. Architecture, again in its broader scope, is not only a shelter for communication and information institutions, a medium, but is also strongly and directly, at times overbearingly, mass information itself. A message, a multiplication of messages which, besides having in the context of the city a character as pervasive as agriculture, also has the intensity and the concentration peculiar to the action of consciousness upon its own flesh, so to speak, almost as if the folding over of the cerebral cortex would correspond to a folding over of layer upon layer of significance, the significance one can perceive in the most successful cityscapes. Naturally, such architecture is not simply the architecture of buildings but the architecture of environments, the cityscape mentioned above. One cannot even begin to enumerate the number and the specific identity of the most famous examples of cityscapes. A few at random: Babylon, Chichén Itzá, Jerusalem, Karnak, Athens, Angkor Wat, Peking, Lhasa, Algiers, Carthage, Rome, Amsterdam, Istanbul, Venice, Florence, Paris, London, Leningrad, Calcutta, New York, New Orleans, San Francisco, etc. And there is the even more numerous group of smaller cities and then the small towns, villages, and enclaves. For each of them there is a unique ethos that reflects the spirit of the inhabitants. History has been made and changed by them. What of the future? At the end of this paper I will briefly present arcology as what I see to be the only methodology which by intent faces the most critical areas in our contemporary world.

INNER MAN, OUTER INFORMATION

It seems that in a historical period when populations migrate massively into urban settlements, the quality and promises of urban life itself are spiraling down to very low common denominators. The phenomenon is nowhere else more apparent than in the United States where the urban ethos has never had the chance to become significant. Industrialization, which has been a mover in the urbanization of man, has been very unkind to the city and unkind to man himself. Inner man finds himself edged out of context in most of our contemporary scenes. A lot of communication is in the air and in different kinds of communication modes but diminishing dosages of it seem to pluck the chords of inner man. This might be the fundamental, and perhaps the only, resistance to the concept of architecture as information as expressed by the contention that what really counts is the inner man (see Woodstock). And, if we stop at information instead of looking at where and how information extends into knowledge, it might be difficult to reject such a contention. But then the opposite could appear to be true also: since (inner) knowledge must be constructed with bricks of information, of which architecture is part. The physical environment is the source of at least some of such information. The trouble there is that if the environment is devoid of information, knowledge will be handicapped. To avoid such a situation, the information "coming from outside" ought to encapsulate in itself knowledge, indeed, more than that, encapsulate in itself a power of persuasion which is the consequence of a power of creation. If such is the case, then knowledge and creation do exist outside of inner man and they are the constituents of the best, most total information *he can make himself with,* then architecture is one of the true communication-information and knowledge assets that man has.

If the objection of inner man to the outer values seems to be at least temporarily broken, how does architecture remain a legitimate source of environmental information? Evidently by being valid, that is to say, relevant or, more pointedly, reverent.

A true experience is suffered information. There is a price tag attached to any learning process: time, effort, difficulty, danger, emotional load, etc. Therefore, there is a definite religious side to learning which must be reflected by the sources learning springs from: a reverential fitness within the larger reality, the building within the town, the town within nature. This, though simple to state and possibly to understand, is enormously difficult to achieve. It ultimately demands a whole range of accomplishments capable of contradicting one another and yet remaining coherently copresent, an achievement possible only in the context of a strong human-social-cultural ethos.

THE ENVIRONMENT SAYS WHAT SOCIETY DOES

It is then only logical that the pauperization of our soul and the soul of our society coincide with the pauperization of the environment. One is the cause and reflection of the other. Therefore, escape from the vicious circle that runs environmental squalor into spiritual squalor and fosters new degradation of the environment proposes the necessity of a radical shake-up, a breaking up of more things than one would like, so as to break the vicious circle and also break the reductionist bearing and the incantation of technology.

The reductionist bearing says that the cause-effect chain is unbreakable and there is not much we can do outside of a crudely deterministic reality in which man is fatally made over by forces that do not care for the tender fibers of his constitution. An example of this thinking is the slave labor of children and adults at the beginning of the industrial era whose justification was the efficiency of the rudimentary cybernetic of the man-machine combination.

The incantation of technology is the quasi-unbelievable trust the technocrat puts in technology for the solution of problems whose substance and meaning have left technology behind long ago: problems of ethics, theology, esthetics.

To stay out of the technological mystique without having to refute the usefulness of technology demands a better grasp of the learning process. What does make information come alive, so to speak, is that kind of processing which transforms it from an outer element into an inner energizer. The bread of information becomes the flesh of knowledge, that is to say, a parcel of the environment is interiorized.

This interiorization of the outer is the necessary step for reaching the hidden aims life has in the so-called inanimate world, appropriating some of its components (mass-energy) and energizing them to the point where they themselves begin to emanate a spiritual light. The spirit moves mountains but only in the factual sense of transforming (metamorphosing) such mountains into the surmatter which is the stuff with which the spirit can support itself. For example, fertilizer products, which are made by the progressive removal of a ridge rich in minerals needed for plant growth, go into the making of grains and vegetables. These in turn feed animals, or man directly. There is then man's mind (and spirit) transforming the ridge into more of itself, the spirit. Another example is the marble of a quarry transformed into a temple; here the energizing does not entail a transformation of matter into flesh. In both cases, it is right to say that what counts is what is inside ourselves. This inside is the lens which has the capacity to concentrate the spherical input of the outer into the self, its center, the knowledge center. It is an appropriation of that which is beyond the membrane-skin of our organic self by way of its interiorized and interiorizing power. The vibrant environment (the second way) is that environment which the self interiorizes. The process, ultimately both ways, sees information become flesh and blood, knowledge, and conceptual (though not necessarily conscious) knowledge, something closer to an instinctual wisdom.

INSTANT SOCIETIES AND DURATIONAL SOCIETIES

At this point, it is necessary to understand that interiorization is a duration process, which is why there is an intrinsic fault in the concept of instant societies made up of instant things to use instantly and throw away. Consumerism is possibly not the best characterization of an ethos that is really more sympathetic toward throwaway than consumption. Consumption characterizes a process of wearing to the bone, or the last thread, a specific thing, tool, or garment, container or content. Kleenex, the instant handkerchief, stands as a simple but clear symbol of the throwaway society. Kleenex, stored in the box, can find its way to the garbage heap by the instant intermediary of a nose blow. But interiorization is a process which cannot occur in short flashes surrounded by the blackness and bleakness of naught. Therefore, when the assimilative, transformative process dwindles into a game of warehousing raw data in the brain, real growth becomes impossible. As it takes a certain amount of biological time to transform bread into flesh, so it takes a definite psychosomatic time to perceive, digest, and make knowledge out of environmental input. The instant thing, whatever it is, is below the threshold of interiorization. It simply bounces against and away from the sphere of the self which under such bombardment will slowly wither into the stone of ego.

It is indeed one of the potential assets of an informative environment, this offering to the self of more and better elements for self-transcendence. It is in the environment that the self finds pleasure and the enticement to reach further and further, to appropriate, acknowledge, and finally interiorize ever larger spheres of reality. By this process, the territory of the self can extend to the border of the man-made environment, the city for instance, but (and here a whole new connection between matter and spirit enters into play) since it is a territory of knowledge, it sees as unnecessary, indeed burdensome, physically holding or owning that which is in fact his/hers, inasmuch as it has been perceived, grasped, understood, and made into knowledge. At such point, when ownership becomes a burden, the authority of knowledge, which should be the only legitimate authority, can have an edge upon power, which most of the time is, covertly or not, the naked force made available to the most aggressive, cunning, and greedy, the possessive.

KNOWLEDGE AND OWNERSHIP

This is the reason why the real power of information-knowledge in the long run will give the lie to most of the notions relating to the territorial imperative and its appendix, the view that ownership is sanctioned by God and therefore is to be held as a sacred right of man. It would appear that on this score man has stepped backward below the animal level. On the animal level hoarding is seldom practiced and territoriality is more imagined by the scientist than enforced by the animal since his territory is a field open for all sorts of activities by other competitive species, vegetal and animal.

It is a rush judgment since it does not take into account that man, as the maker par excellence, has introduced into the world a whole new reality that can be divided into two parts.

First: that part of the man-made which is so directly involved in the life and routine of the person as to be identified with it. It would be futile, for instance, if not stupid, to say that *my* shoes or *my* glasses do not belong to me.

Second: the institutionalized life of those things which foster the development of homo sapiens. The institutionalized life is anchored to and sheltered by the hardware it needs in order to perform, the largest and most comprehensive item being nothing else but the city itself, including its specific character as this or that industrial center, vacation center, etc.

The question then arises: Who and what is responsible for making and running this second part, who will coordinate the institutions, the marketplace, the industrial plant, the library, the restaurant, the bank, the church, the school, and all the other complex machines for creation? One answer, not necessarily the best, is the person or group having a specific holding and hoarding of power. Private property might well belong in a series of intermediate steps between a world where the responsibility for the necessary institutions of society is consigned to the father-king and a world where such responsibility becomes a more intrinsic part of a theoecological process, whose guiding track is purely and simply, but sublimely, difficult, the reverence for life. A totally reverential humankind would find it difficult to grasp the meaning of ownership, since there would be no meaning one could attach to it any longer other than a reminiscence binding needs, anxieties, fear, and insecurity to greed and intolerance. If this appears as a politicization of the question, it might be wise to remember that the polis is the place where the instrument of politics takes root and that, for this reason, the policies that make for the running of the polis and the nation are idle whenever the three-dimensional, physical, gravity-loaded, and durationally real polis, the environmental polis of information-learning, is in disrepair or does squalidly buffer society from the aggression of climate, weather, functional breakdown, foreigners, enemies, and bureaucrats.

REVERENCE AND THE PEDAGOGY OF THE ENVIRONMENT

On another occasion I put the question of the environment this way: If we take care of our environment because such care is imposed by edict, the result might be order in appearance, death in substance. If we take care of only that portion of our environment which we own, the environment will be like a sea of litter and dread dotted with small island utopias whose segregated order is the true origin of chaos. This is a pretty close description of the urban-suburban situation today. If we take care of the environment because we have a sense of reverence toward it, then the reverential fire will make the environment glow with the embers of the spirit.

What makes this diversion pertinent to the environment as information is that once the environment is accepted as bona fide information and germinal knowledge, there still remains the issue of seeing that fraudulence is not introduced with the package. In general terms, one could contend that a direct consequence of a sanctified concept of private property is a pauperization of the environmental pedagogy. Under such narrow, untheological, and unecological constrictions, the environment becomes the locus where things are hoarded around increasingly withering selves at the expense of the person and society to the point where the selves are not much more than petrified egos and the physical landscape of society is reduced to the dread of suburbia. At such a stage the environmental pedagogy reaches its lowest form; it becomes a fraudulent arcadia, parasitically grafted to the dwindling resources of the earth.

KNOWLEDGE AND POWER

There is no way to overstate this unless we make knowledge a purely cunning instrument for self-assertion. Then we incur the unbreakable contradiction of knowledge becoming, as it has in all ages, the shelter for all sorts of falsehood necessary to hold steady the machine of power. What we exhibit is what we are, and we exhibit poor knowledge by putting sacredness where it does not belong, in the holding power sanctioned by an ambiguous social contract. To say that, nevertheless, the dimness of suburbia contains the strong light of self-determination might be less true than convincing. Idolatries are powerfully fostered among the democracy which has taken residence in suburbia; not least are the legitimatized idolatries ritualized in church parlors or in drive-in temples, the idolatry of quiet greed which has crept through and around the illusion of an innocent or bland life.

One reaction to environmental fraud is naturally, as pointed out above, the Woodstock naught and commune nostalgia where in crude ways the past condition and ideal of (animal) innocence is sought. The illusion is short-lived and it ought not to bring regret or breast-beating in sorrow, since we should be able to understand that natural man of today is a different creature from natural man or protoman of the Garden of Eden and, therefore, the pedagogic impact of neo-nature caused by man is different from the pedagogic impact of pristine nature surrounding, nurturing, and harassing Adam and Eve (attached now to the electronic breast of rock).

If education is to make ourselves see, to be seers, then the physiological, perceptual functions of sight and sound and smell and touch are at least as important a part of the pedagogical process. The child is made to see by the parents and the teacher in long years of guidance. Or is it truer to say that the blindness of parents and teachers is the gravest handicap the child runs into in his efforts as a potential seer? What is it that makes the squalid environment a punishing environment? Fundamentally, the power it has to force blindness (and dumbness) upon the individual who cannot escape it. It is a simple mechanism for survival aided by the degenerative process of organs not used. We learn not to see (and feel) even when we look (and hear). This psychological blindness-dumbness destroys the source of environmental information. The spring dries up since the retina and the ear have been disconnected from the mind. Blindness is endemic in a mesmerized society, condemned to live in cruelly bleak environs. The stark fact is that the physical environment which for more and more people is becoming the urban-suburban environment is, or should be, a powerful information-knowledge source. It ought to be also an uplifting, engrossing asset for us, the people living in it, if it will perfect and foster an ethos which reverentially goes about the business of survival as if it were instead and indeed the true art of living.

KNOWLEDGE AND SACREDNESS

To make an example, what has sometimes been called a temple of learning, the university, suffers ultimately from unwarranted limitations, since it is a walled-in machine for information. It is instead the city, as the temple of life, or the Civitas Dei, which is to become the ultimate source of true knowledge. But this is a cryptic discourse unless we unabashedly acknowledge the sacred nature of the living and the necessarily sacred nature of the learning process. By a not-too-long series of relays, one reaches the theoecological imperative. This says that since ecological dynamics have brought the earth from its dumb state, a fiery agglomeration of matter eons ago, into a body whose skin, by man's mediation, is in the process of taking conscience of itself, the whole ecological process is the pragmatic development of that sensitization which is none other than the etherealization of matter into spirit. Why is this a sacramental phenomenon?

THEOECOLOGY

Since sensitization is necessarily a phenomenon of sufferance, the sufferance of an experience attempting an ultimately compassionate exploit, to transform the natural into the loving, it has a sacramental thrust which makes the ecological development a theological evolution. Then the places and spaces which are part and parcel of those dynamics become the business of sacredness. The good city is a sacred locus. It is the Civitas Dei. It is that complex machine for information which by the nonexpedient ways of design also becomes knowledge in itself, where the media has finally, if only within limits, sublimated itself into the message, a large interiority reverentially turned to the handling of particulae sacrae, the polis dwellers. This is the city as an open classroom, open to all ages so as to let energies and wisdom make and cause life to be an ever-stronger radiance.

If the real conditions one finds in the city of today, any city, are a far cry from all of this, the discrepancy is to be seen as a gap between what ought to be and what is. On the other hand, note that the cityscape has established throughout history a sound record, indeed the indispensable record of man's quest for the spirit. Nor is this idle talk, and the best demonstration is the previously mentioned pilgrimage, uninterrupted and massive, of the cynical society of today to the remainder and still operative centers of the past. Man avidly seeks out of the bricks and stones that past with which man has labored. We will be the damndest of fools if we forget that the force-fed information of some academics, the electronic included, has great and often damaging limitations, and if at the same time we go on ignoring the subtle and lasting way by which the environment constructed by man is by its own nature the most available and enviable tool: the true mass-information and communication media-message.

If we care for it, the rewards will be clear and unequivocal; not the least would be the reduction of urban violence and vandalism. Since ownership is a poor substitute for knowledge, it is in the optimum environment for learning where the resentment against those things that others hold and one is deprived of is destined to show its precariousness via precisely the perceived and felt precariousness of hoarding. From this acknowledgment to the metamorphosis of resentment-vandalism into reverence, the path might be difficult but it is, in any case, the only one man has access to.

TECHNOLOGY AND KNOWLEDGE

Something should be said about the role, or the intrusion, of what goes under the name of technology in the environmental learning machine, the city.

1) Extrabiological technology, the technology of the man-invented and man-produced, finds its effectiveness in its innate bent toward oversimplification. Western technology owes its success to the analytical mind and to the innocent dogma that all things can be reduced to black and white terms. The result is a simple-minded ethos sustained by hordes of complicated equipment, each single-mindedly running its own metronomic life cycle for and against the master will. One of the things that disqualifies the technologist in city planning is this innate propensity for analysis and oversimplification. The person

who can break down and investigate the pieces seldom has the capacity or interest to construct and synthesize, let alone to metamorphize. The combined results of technological oversimplifications point to an environment which at best appeals to the naked, psychosomatically blind, dumb, nonsensual mind which is by training deprived of the durational dimension. It is the instant environment I am talking about, designed under the cloak of obsolescence.

2) If and when the technologies of logistics, transportation, delivery, and retrieval serving a system, an urban settlement for instance, become too cumbersome, the system is surely sick. Servogigantism is a pathological condition. Therefore, beware, for instance, of the automobile mode. It is a killer. It is the killer of the city as a radiant information-learning milieu. The servosystems must be self-effacing so as to let society express itself. As they are now, the only expression we see is the brutal, squalid expression of a hopeless logistical megamachine running man to distraction and destruction.

If I seem to crave a romantic nostalgia, I am giving the wrong impression. I favor a more subtle technology, a self-effacing technology, in accordance with the psychosomatic laws of efficiency and harmony. Consider the human body and see how beautifully concealed is the fury of the physiological robot keeping up with the avalanche of things introduced by the improbable next moment. Consider then a car-ridden city and see the enormity of the logistical breakdown of our technology of information via integration. Not only is the individual isolated within his pollution machine but the machine is the fulcrum of a whole series of divisive, brutalizing, wasteful, energy-burning, noisy, segregational objects ranging from the superloop to the four gas stations on a crossroad, from the endless parking lot to the endless ribbon of semiparked cars on the traffic-jammed highway, etc. Since the aim is not to come up with aimlessly complicated hardware but with that kind of hardware that facilitates a complex perception-action, the complex environment only rarely coincides with the environment bulging with costly, complicated mechanisms and gadgetries.

Fritz Lang's film *Metropolis* well illustrated the magnitude of a technological Frankenstein monumentally bearing down on those specks of passion, or spent passions, called "people." Self-effacing technology, the truly efficient technology, forcefully if not automatically signals good tidings and is, in any case, the necessary step toward the liberation of the spirit from the reservoirs of mass-energy.

APOLLO CAPSULE AND KNOWLEDGE

That is why, not contradictorily, we could look upon the Apollo capsule as the seed of a cathedral. It is the seed around which life has consciously and unequivocally, in this instance dogmatically, begun its journey into the extrabiological technology of complexification, after a long history of analysis-simplification operating on and for the destiny of man. With the Apollo groping, the sacred, which is the conscious and the passionate, the complex, begins—even if involuntarily and only tangentially—to put down roots outside of itself, indeed, outside of this world and into the miniaturized hardware of the capsule. Capsule and man, if yet distinguishable, are not separable. Since the evolutionary mileage to be traveled is infinite in space-time terms, the Apollo capsule is almost totally deprived as yet of a rich and unpredictable environmental impact. It is a naked contraption for survival. But then, what was the new-formed earth of a long time ago? It was a classroom stripped down to the bare geological bones, empty of pupils and teacher, a silent mass of media incapable, as yet, of any message.

ANGUISH AND KNOWLEDGE

The environment which is capable of truly informing is that environment which has durational dimension. Durational dimension is sufferance dimension, the common human experience that ultimately what surrounds and contains us is beyond our grasp, as what makes us do and be what we are is beyond our grasp. This anxiety is the dimension of sufferance necessary for the conception and construction of the places where we live. Without it we simply disavow life and miss getting at the core of it where splendor and darkness mingle. It is also the dimension that, when present, gives the environment that surcharge of information which triggers the process of understanding and identification. The emotional impact that a landscape or cityscape has upon a person is a combination of the exhilaration of understanding and at the same time the anguish of realizing the massiveness of the unknown that such an environment makes tangible. Several coincidences comprise the magic of a good environment. It is this magic which breaks through the barrier of the thickest hide and forces a swelling of the ego, even if for a few moments, into a matrix which transcends it into the self, and through the self breaks into the communion of universal consciousness. The lightning of perception and its moment of knowledge measures the length, in durational beats, passed in constructing the magic of the instant. In different measures of intensity all good environments operate transcendentally on the ego and therefore are information-communication, knowledge, and re-creation in one.

In contrast, we can take the harshness of the Las Vegas strip. Nothing there is willing to show as positive, either duration or the sufferance of process. It is purely a two-dimensional and fraudulent promise of an instant of happiness, an orphan's shout into a post-geological wilderness.

SPECIALIZATION

In a world where durational development seems to make special fields of understanding more and more necessary, that is to say, since specialization and analysis seem to be necessary and irreversible processes, two parallel events might be indispensable:

1) Each one of us must come to feel in the most tangible, touchable way that he/she is part of an immense creature whose ideal nature is to be conscious of all its parts and, therefore, can treat each and all of them as particulae sacrae.

2) That unless we can put our trust, as particles, into other particles which partake in the making of such creature, particles which we know mainly by proxy, we will be in for one catastrophe after the other. Naturally, the burden is on each of us to be worthy of the trust others must put on our deeds.

This is, of course, what we have been doing all along, with more or less grace, but always with the illusion that eventually omniscience and omnipotence would become the legitimate characteristics of each one of us. Religious creeds encouraged and encourage such hope against hope. Needless to say, it is part of the anguish of the human species to know better, to be more humble.[1] But to be truly humble takes the unlimited ambition of being a truly conscious, participatory particula sacra of something whose totality is larger than the sum of its parts. And it can only be so if the sum becomes an integration, a knowledge-creation process, an evolution of matter into spirit on the bridge of matter becoming spirit.

ARCOLOGY

It is therefore an understating of our predicament to say that the future is very uncertain since we might see the advent of either a technological nemesis or a spiritual genesis. In attempting to forecast a spiritual genesis I have adopted the term arcology—architecture and ecology. It is an attempt to focus on the city all the major problems of contemporary man: population, limited land, limited resources, limited energy, limited food-production, segregation, pollution, bureaucratization, technological mindlessness, waste, greed, cultural deprivation, and spiritual naught. The arcological methodology has something very central to offer for the solution of all these problems. It is my contention that the arcological commitment is a necessary if not sufficient step toward a new conception and implementation of reality. To put it briefly, by a *contraction* and greater *sophistication* of the physical side of man-made reality (equipment, machines, services, utilities, etc.) a greater complexity and greater understanding and knowledge are made possible. This in turn could trigger greater spiritual depth in the actions of man and society.

Contraction is in the sense of a progression of miniaturization-efficiency so as to achieve more with less. *Sophistication* is in the direction of the above and in the sense of eliminating the enormous extravagance and irrelevance we have constructed around the magic of the machine and the gadget.[2] A stroll through a shopping center will quickly show how unreal the world of affluent man is within the context of a family of man besieged by hunger, poverty, coercion, illness, ignorance, etc. But there is an even more fundamental reason for this unreality. It is in the intrinsic spiritual poverty denounced by

[1] Written before the resurrection model. See "Logos as the Omega Seed."
[2] It is by the presence of the two elements, contraction and sophistication, that one can anticipate the advent of interiorization, the alter ego of conscience.

such massive surfeit. Research has indicated that the "housewife" has 140,000 optional items with which to survive happily in that no-man's-land called the kitchen. Many people strive to do their best to go through the full catalog by direct experience. For this mental dimness we are all responsible and all paying dearly, and at last, not incidentally but coincidentally, we put ourselves where we find ourselves now, in the energy bottleneck. The magic word is, needless to say, frugality, frugality which is not to be found in segregation of spaces, functions, institutions, activities, productivities, bloods, castes, religions, etc., but in integration of them in a truly interactive condition, a condition that can only be found in the city . . .

If the city is to be what it is meant to be, the most comprehensive structure for learning, the function of which is a growing understanding guiding man toward a greater sensibility and, consequently, creativity, then nothing is more urgent for man's destiny than this focusing of his efforts on the transformation of his communities into ecologically oriented cityscapes, those media that have consumed themselves into messages. Since this new orientation has a spiritual-sacramental undertone, the ecological orientation becomes a theological reality, a theoecological thrust. We come full circle, then, where communication as mass-media finds reason to exist because the information caused by it is momentous to the masses, us. They are, that is to say, saturated and quivering with the imponderable, the mysterious . . . the divine?!

Tall Buildings and Gigantism

Gigantism is a pathological condition which destroys the morphological congruence of an organism. It does not refer to absolute size but to the relationship between size and performance. An ant two inches long suffers from gigantism. A whale suffering from gigantism would be a whale of a whale, bigger than any healthy whale. The outsized animal is the gigantic animal.

For many of the things man does, there is a relationship between object and size. Hand tools are, in general, very much size-defined. A 25-pound hand shovel is gigantic, a one-gallon teacup is gigantic. On the other side of normal size is dwarfism: the mini-shovel, the mini-toothbrush, the mini-teacup. All of them, because of either gigantism or dwarfism, are pathological tools. But as the size of the hand shovel is measured by the muscular capacity of man, the steam shovel is geared in size to the per hour tonnage capacity. The latter machine is better defined as a giant machine than a gigantic machine. The adjective "gigantic" is used to define a dysfunction in a system that got too big for its own good performance.

The tall building is often a structure that got too big, indeed, too tall for the good of man. It has much too often become a gigantic warehouse for white-collar workers to which some or many frills are added or applied to unruffle the feathers of noisy if ineffectual social-minded birds. Because of the dysfunction inherent in tall buildings as they are designed today, many of the complaints against them are more than justified. They point at the abstract content and at the sterile ethos that is characteristic of the efficiency-technocratic mind, a truly mindless kind of brain which acts lobotomized.

The fault of the segregative, single-function tall building would be similar to the fault of a liver which doubled its size and at the same time limited the variety and subtlety of its activities, were it not for the fact that the cells of the tall building, this inflated liver, are self-conscious, personalized, free-agent cells, the people acting in it.

The reason for such double ineptitude is to be found in the functional-morphological break between the organ, the tall building, and organism, the town. The anthropomorphic metaphor might not be original, but it remains eloquent and legitimate. The tall building is a gigantic organ unfit to serve a normal-size organism. It is, furthermore, an organ unfit to serve a gigantic organism which is also unfit for life. Even if both the gigantic organ and the organism were reciprocally well proportioned, they would be unfit since such scale is disproportionate to a balanced relationship between their morphology and their performance.

The hitch is simply and essentially that one cannot design and build tall buildings outside of a highly structured context, not because one cannot conceive of a tree outside the forest, but for the far more stringent reason that the limb cannot be designed apart from the trunk. The town or the city is the true organic unit, the tree in this metaphor, indivisible, and when divided, incomprehensible and indefensible. The tall building per se is pure limbo. It is ontologically, economically, and politically a pure speculation. If we do not move from mutilation into fullness, we must sooner or later confess to impotence because of incompetence.

The tall building is indeed more valid as a premonition, a preparation for things to come than it is valid per se as a working system of a technological society. As a working structure, it is plagued by the demeaning tempo of its own limited functions. As a limb it is too isolated, too specialized, and too big; as a premonition of a full organism it is too timid and too small. It is, furthermore, most often a two-dimensional structure which, seen from the point of view of physical logistics, is handicapped by its own functional and structural fragility. It is a scaffolded, bureaucratic machine, benevolently called an administrative-organizational structure, made efficient by the truistic economy of the vertical juxtaposition of functions. Only when the tall building transforms itself into the city will the tall building become part of the tree in the forest or the meadow and not remain an inept limb incapable of really giving life its due.

This transformation demands a radical reconsideration of premises and procedures, and touches upon social, cultural, political, and economic structures. Without such radicalization the tall building remains an unfulfilled hypothesis suspended in technocratic abstraction as another vivid example of a better quality of wrongness.

Ecology as Theology

SYNOPSIS: Practical man is constantly bruised in his encounters with reality since reality is not practical but real. The scars left by those encounters litter the past and will eventually bury contemporary man because by giving to Caesar so much (everything) nothing is left for God. We need to reconnect matter to spirit, Caesar to grace, since we are an unbreakable mix of matter and spirit.

If a model of reality is a device by which knowledge enacts itself, then the validity of the model, its truth, is proportional to the effectiveness it demonstrates in the pragmatism of enactment. If Euclidean geometry had not been useful to the technological enactment of the last two millennia of man's inventions, then the Euclidean model of reality would have been true to a lesser degree or, at a limit point, it would have been absurd. This is an indigestible notion for the so-called pure scientist for two reasons. The first has to do with the possible abstractness of the scientist's mental process which renders him/her incapable of making the connection between the statistical and the willful or between matter and spirit, since according to them the willful treads on non-scientific ground. The second reason might have to do with the anticipatory gap separating a model from the context of the present, a context incapable as yet of verifying the pragmatism or truth of the model and consequently a context that views the model as useless if not meaningless.

In the first instance, the scientist's model of reality is intrinsically deprived of substance, the substance that makes life as real as, or more so than, stone and fire. His model is therefore a game in words, symbols, numbers, categories . . .

In the second instance lies a case in point about the anguish inherent in the living phenomenon inasmuch as the liveliest part of such phenomenon is a prefuture, a cantilever on the future, and is as such liable to remain utopian, to be lost in the folds of a history engaged in other models. Not only might the model be lost, but its potential offspring may also not see the light of day.

If the hand shovel idea-model had been lost in such a way, the steam shovel model would probably not have appeared. Even if it had appeared, the work accomplished by the enactment of the hand shovel model would have been lost. It would have remained utopian.

Therefore, each model has its own historical moment of truth and unless the model comes to fruition in such time slots, the truth of the model is lost since its pragmatism (effectiveness) had no chance to develop.

The model developed in the thesis of the Omega God identifies the evolutionary (ecological) unfolding of reality with a theological development. That is to say, a God is being slowly and painfully created, a potentially monotheistic divinity is developing out of the utterly polytheistic reservoir of mass-energy and conscience. Of the many components in this process, humankind is a pivotal element. For the sake and development of this pivotal element there are postbiological inventions, postbiological technologies, which are necessary and indispensable instruments to further evolutionary inroads.

The ecological city, arcology, is one such instrument. It is a complex instrument, a medium which is also a message, tangibly and pragmatically part of the transpersonal nature of life which is also theological. Ultimately, in fact, arcology will be stone made into spirit, not simply a mechanism of economic, political, and logistical expediency. It has to be spirit moving mountains, not so much because of physical manipulation of mountains (mining, etc.), but because of an inner flame elicited within the stone itself by design and grace . . . the process of esthetogenesis.

Then there would be a constitutional tie between theology and arcology. *Theology is a genesis* and *arcology stands for a truly human landscape fostering such genesis.* In other words, to better explain the model, one can say that psychosomatic man, the whole man, can be called theoarcological man.

Theology is genesis because whatever in the universe points to an increment of consciousness also points to the further development of a sacramental, divine strand within such universe. (In "The Two Suns," an attempt is made to characterize the theological model as the progressive fulfillment of a skeletally invented god, the filling of a form-idea with a content-evolution, a true genesis of God.)

Arcology is a human landscape because this immensely difficult and hubris-endangered genesis of the immanent God of the present (all presents) is to be a powerhouse where, by the virtue of such genesis, both the tangible (mass-energy) and the intangible (spirit) are inextricably coactive. Within the complex containers of the physiological are also the containers of the social and cultural which act together in the making of the individual as much as in the making of human societies.

For such an undertaking, this totality of life and consciousness emerging from the mass-energy framework, a house is thus in order, a house that can cater to its needs, an ecological architecture, whatever that may mean or imply in the different stages of its evolution. The invention of the idea-city is the invention of the house in question. The word arcology (architecture and ecology) is used to indicate *one of its objectives:* the imploded organization of the physical into a sophisticated instrument capable of *serving* and *expressing* the transpersonal consciousness of the society, a cultural-theological-creative genesis. *Serving,* inasmuch as it gives to such society the physical structures for its action; *expressing,* inasmuch as such physical structures are, for better or worse, representative or, in more germinal situations, anticipatory of its ethos.

Of arcology as a human landscape, one could say that if, in the genesis of humankind, both matter and spirit are present on a continuum, then today any instant in the durational process (or any other day of history or prehistory) documents the more or less specific and successful coordination of matter (soma) in such a way as to cause matter to transcend itself. The inner light of coordinated matter is the spirit (psyche), specifically a coordination of the physical into specific and successful systems whose innermost light is the spirit.

But assume, as it is assumed here, that humankind is more than the sum of its individual components, persons, and that this sum needs a locus and a consciousness (a soma and psyche). Since one locus and one consciousness would imply a fulfilled model (see "Religion as Simulation") of the human experiment, it is more realistic to expect that fragments of locus-consciousness will be the pluralistic foci for this reality, the reality where the person is more than itself. Typical and most dynamic of those foci throughout history has been the city. I call the city which the future might see, arcology, for the purpose of reminding us that the good city is an architecture of ecology, in necessary human terms. Needless to say, this simple fact bears radical fruits, bitter fruits for the individual who believes the world is his own private hunting ground, exhilarating fruits for the individual who believes that there is such a thing as a theological component to his/her significance.

Indeed, after a brush with the theological dilemmas, one would state firmly that if a theological component is the backbone of the evolutionary phenomenon, then arcology (the city) is a necessity in the process of becoming a virtue. The mystic might argue that if one precludes the possibility of achieving the spiritual condition via non-material roads one bestows too much importance on matter. In debating such a notion one ought to consider that if and when what we call matter is rejected as a basic, necessary, indispensable component of spirit, then one is faced with the unavoidable senselessness of an evolutionary tide tragically (or foolishly) involved in the transformation of the material into the immaterial. If there is no theological back, arcology is simply a necessity dictated by the laws of mass-energy. This might be the golden trap, as William Irwin Thompson describes it:

Evolution moves against the direction of entropy; as matter moves toward more probable states of maximum molecular disorder, life moves toward increasingly more improbable states of maximum molecular organization. More and more is packed into less and less, until the miniaturization process reaches its greatest level of what Teilhard calls "complexification" in the compactness of the human brain. The simplicity of its size and shape belies the dazzling complexity of its interior. For Soleri this process of complexification linked with miniaturization is the lesson the city planner should take away from the study of nature. In evolution, simplicity is always linked to complexity: while huge dinosaurs lumber into extinction, tiny mammals chatter in the trees. Soleri would say it is much the same with our cities now. The huge megalopolitan beasts are sprawling all over the earth; in terms of thermodynamics, they are spreading their energy equitably through space and approaching the heat-death of entropy. They destroy the earth, turn farmland into parking lots, and waste enormous amounts of time and energy transporting people, goods, and services over their expanses. They so fill their ecological niche that they destroy it, and thus become caught in their own evolutionary dead end.

Soleri's answer is urban implosion rather than explosion. The city should contract and intensify, but in order to hold its information in negentropic form, it should imitate evolution and complexify itself through intense miniaturization. A city of

600,000 should become a single, recycling, organic arcology. The people would not live crowded in ghettos but on the outer skin of a towering arcology that faced toward a nature that was once again natural. Thus the surface of an arcology would be a "membrane and not a wall." Inside the arcology, along its central spinal axis, would be not the natural but the civic space. Here society would turn inward for the concerns of man and culture.[1]

But then, if the theological backbone is only imaginary, everything has the same worth; both necessity and virtue become the empty frames of a mindless reality.

[1] *Passages About Earth* (New York: Harper & Row, 1975), pp. 35–36.

6

The Technological Frankenstein and the (Delphic) Oracle

SYNOPSIS: The "technology" which constructs organisms (biotechnology) is a complexification thrust. The technology produced by the mind of man is a simplification thrust. The second is either subservient to the first or its nemesis. Since in the absence of technology the evolution of consciousness would be subject to limitations inherent in the flesh which reflect upon the mind, the denouement rests on handling the oracular (mob-oriented) pronouncements of the technological Frankenstein in ways which "force" (with its help) the spirit from matter.

We should pay more attention to the old saying, "Make virtue out of necessity." If the "necessary" bottlenecks we are setting up for ourselves are not producing "theological" virtue, we may have only two other alternatives: the obscurantism of a massive social-economic-political breakdown, or the perfectionism of the technological Frankenstein. The technological Frankenstein is not the consumer technology of today but the "controlled survival" technology which is in the making. The controlled survival technology is the one advocated by the lifeboat model where the grimness of the means preempts any possible transcendence.

Leaving obscurantism aside, not because it is the least probable future but because its novelty would be in the shifting of the centers of power and the shrinking of the elite into smaller enclaves of greed, one way of seeing the difference between the technological future and the controlled survival technology is to consider the bivalence of necessity and virtue vis-à-vis life. Virtue without necessity is meaningless, having neither a legitimate origin in stress nor a radiant becoming in creation. It is at most the virtue of the "virtuous," the steady state of recycling the self smoothly among the smooth recycling of otherness. Without resolution into virtue, necessity is and remains a fact without transcendent characteristics. The fact is that facts do not make reality but only sustain it. From this point of view, one could say that history is the flow of the real functioning as the yeast of life whose dough or ingredients include "fact particulates": all the granules of organized mass-energy swept away by the storm of the spirit into a premonitory image of a theological synthesis. The technological Frankenstein is the technology of the factual universe.

What is the factor that makes such technology a real possibility without even demanding the prodding of malice? It is the one predominant tendency of technology to simple-mindedly cosmogenize, to go through a chain of transformations in every technical process where an initial stage in which a "personal" need prompts a domestic device—the hot iron, the washboard, the cold box, the winged bicycle—is followed by the successive transformations of such domestic inventions into more and more "sophisticated" versions. Then, later but certainly not finally, the hot iron becomes the pressing machine (or etherealizes by the introduction of permanent-press fabric), the washboard becomes the super washer-dryer, the cold box becomes the refrigerator and the refrigerated food-packet, the winged bicycle becomes the space probe, etc. The device is taken away from the hand of the maker and is thrust into a "cosmic coordinate" of a sort, from the particular to the general, from the personal to the impersonal. The more technology serves man, the more remote its modes and niceties. Therefore, it is not anymore the smart and slightly peculiar neighbor who is envied for his cold beverages but the consumer society which forces the voluptuousness of an ice-cold Coca-Cola on everyone; not the rumored heavier-than-air hops of two brother mechanics but the take-it-or-leave-it global newsreel via sky probe, etc. The consequence of such cosmogenizing is a remoteness which tends to present individuals not with processes but with facts and the end-products of processes: the factual universe mentioned above.

How evil is remoteness? A school of thought states that remoteness is man's enemy. It says that things at hand are the only concern of the just man, that alienation is the unavoidable consequence of remoteness. It is a soothing song too often sung by opportunists or fools. It is really an animal fancy of postanimal man. What is at hand is nothing but a prefuture. As such, it is the nonformed in quest of a form. To point at the blind spot might suffice to suggest that there is an inner remoteness which is as frightful as the most distant of all alienation. This is the biological remoteness of our bodies. Is this a believable proposition? For one thing, if it were not for such remoteness we would not be shocked by injuries or by illness. We would be sufficiently familiar with ourselves to take for granted the vulnerability of the flesh. But indeed our physiological innards are enormously foreign to our consciousness. They are a factual though remote reality, and indeed they must be remote so as not to paralyze the whole organism. If remoteness is necessary vis-à-vis the inner, could it not also be true that remoteness might be necessary vis-à-vis the outer? Consciousness would then be a focusing of perceptions on a few elements selected by the discriminating force of an organism; a focusing immersed in an ocean of remoteness, a personal noosphere of light enveloping a sphere of remoteness and working as a membrane of radiance separating such inner sphere of remoteness from the outer sphere of remoteness, the cosmos. The inner sphere is remote and asyntropic; the outer sphere, preponderantly remote and entropic. This noosphere, as the alchemist, works at the metamorphosis of this or that part of the outer into new envelopes of radiance.

If our existence can be described as the reality of a membrane of consciousness interposed between two universes equally unknowable (the inner universe is complex, durational, imploded; the outer universe, spatiotemporal, expanding), then the degree of consciousness inherent in the sensitized membrane depends upon the flow, quality, and quantity of information traversing through and apprehended by the membrane. This situation entails the desirability of an environment surrounding the membrane as rich as circumstances allow, and it is entirely up to the membrane, us, to see that such richness is made, nurtured, maintained, accrued, and transfigured for the sake of the beholder.

Since encapsulated by two "mysteries," pressured, in fact, by one working around the other, the inner remoteness and the outer remoteness, the performance of consciousness of this individual noosphere is ultimately of an oracular nature, ambiguous and divinatory. The power of the oracle is in grasping the enormity of the power of remoteness and in developing the capacity to use some of such power without being annihilated by the inertial mass of the whole of it. Intrinsic to this oracular power is, consequently, the anguish of the obscurity of both the inner mechanisms (physiopsychological) and the outer elements: physical, from atom to galaxies; biological, from virus to man; social, from cell association to city to God; and cultural, from Adam and Eve to esthetogenesis. To attempt to know all and to be "tuned in" to the whole damn thing is not only a futile exercise. It is a suicidal one, since by excessive dilution it leaves consciousness below the threshold of radiance and the individual blurs into nirvana (the condition of nonbeing).

The ambiguous-divinatory working of consciousness is not in the freewheeling mode concocted by the Protestant individualist who "has made it," for the simple reason that the two mysteries, the outer and the inner, are stern wardens to the conscience.[1] But neither is it the decomposition of the sphere of radiance into the double sea of remoteness, since such diffusion is a renunciation of the responsibility of God-making which is the truth of such radiance. The ambiguous-divinatory working of consciousness is not hindered but is supported by the rigor of its own necessities. It is in this rigor that on occasion such necessities resolve into virtues, not least, the virtue of metamorphosis, i.e., creation. "The best spirit comes from the greatest torque" and how could it be different? De-stress life and you have nonlife. (Joy is an all-consuming stress only touched upon in few and far apart occasions by anyone.)

Controlled survival technology (C.S.T.) parcels out to each monad, each person, that kind and amount of environmental energy, information, and interaction computed by the Calvinist computer which "knows," via simulation, the future. It has done away with the oracular, that imperative "God-making" of consciousness which is sandwiched, so to speak, between the inner mystery remoteness and the outer mystery remoteness. Since both mysteries have been refuted by the reductionist-dogmatism of C.S.T., since the anguish inherent in the mysteries of life has been boxed away, the future is dependent upon the "rational" acceptance of all the nuts and bolts components of the C.S.T. megamachine. The truth is that each of those nuts and bolts has an appendix attached to it. It happens to be a metaphysical appendix, a bundle of mystery and anguish, a person, or shreds of a person. Therefore, the true play, as seen by the seer, would not be the triumphant parade of a glorious machine emerging into a better self while plunging into the future of futures, but rather a bleeding monster in steel, plastics, and energy, each particle of which brutally, if justly, lubricates its own interfaces with the "had been" entelechy of mass-energy, the spirit. Simplification via supertechnology is a frightening possibility; the supersimplification via piousness is a future-termination. The first cannot make virtue out of necessity (the multifaceted and convergent earth crisis) since its virtue is the unlim-

[1] Therefore, we have the presence on the stage of life of the continuum of routine (see the maintenance loops in "The Theology of the Sun") and the disciplined execution of acts in certain sequences (brushing after meals, for instance).

ited power of determinism. The second cannot make virtue out of necessity since what it recognizes as necessity is an insular, provincial, segregated fragment of the theoecological imperative. Therefore, the resulting virtue is the lukewarm virtue of marginal existence.

To ride the technological Frankenstein is to be meat for the meat grinder. To retreat from the manipulation of mass-energy is to fall into a state of somnambulism but still to be sustained by life's manipulation of mass-energy. It might be difficult at this point to introduce the idea that virtue lies only in the power peculiar to creation. Difficult but not devious, since the road which is neither C.S.T. nor that of a fossilized species is the ascending road into creation, the transtechnological road of the spirit. The creation road is not the abused "being creative" dribbled out by many pedagogues short in reach and long in opportunism. Being creative "en masse" is principally an adaptive conditioning where the harshness of reality is blurred by different degrees of self or induced deception. An acceptable deception perhaps, inasmuch as the double remoteness mentioned before is not a small burden to carry. The creation road still remains that which can only be walked "en masse" vicariously, but at the same time, and not contradictorily, can only be constructed collectively. In the most comprehensive terms, the whole of life is but one creature which includes the most humble of its particles and is always engaged in its transformation.

True humility is the gate through which vicariousness itself becomes fused into the act of creation, since the humble person fuses himself back into the whole living creature. The humble and the meek are, thus, of the Kingdom of God, not at a certain future time but at the self-creating "now" of the theoecological immanence. The creation road is oracular since it is the ambiguous-divinatory transformation of the anguish inherent in the state of remoteness-mystery into the esthetic fragment. But its first act is always adherence to the imperative of manipulating mass-energy for the sake of conscious life. It is therefore committed to the technological process which is responsible for the advent of life in the first place and consequently the advent of consciousness: a biotechnology now moving into technology for the attempt at the transtechnology of the spirit.

The technological Frankenstein is then a quasi-copresent existence which life has to keep constantly at bay. An inkling of its presence can even be traced within the technology of the biological. There is a robot-like savagery in the unbending drive of the organic to carry its own matrix successfully through the tests crowding the road to survival. Cinematography has made visual the voracious drive of the insect: many science fiction movies are geared to the fascination created by the vision of gigantic robot-insects overpowering less "beastly" characters. The most vivid portrayal of such is the enlargement of insects themselves in action. We do not need to fake robots. We have them in the flesh. Our inner remoteness contains a no-less-savage degree of robotization. It is within the Buddha, the Christ, Ophelia, the Virgin Mary, et al. It is the biotechnological robot, a fragment of the parental technological Frankenstein on whose performance our consciousness, our conscience, our "freedom," our compassion are constructed. This immensely complex, vulnerable, but harshly determined mechanism is as remote to our knowledge as the immensely vast cosmos, and it is quite possible that if one of the mysteries were to be understood, it would be the outer one, the mystery external to the biological envelope of the organism, sooner than it would be the unraveling of the inner mystery.

If necessity is going to be our only creed, we will necessarily be given to idolatry. The idol will be the controlled survival technology. This does not entail the obfuscation of the intelligence. Quite the contrary. It might be the refinement of it to a degree not quite conceivable now. But it will necessarily be the obfuscation of the spirit since pure rationalization deals only with the robot in ourselves and with the "outer," consequently mortifying that intangible which is the robot's justification. For instance, of the "mechanism" named Wolfgang Amadeus Mozart, the robot has passed away, and, as robots go, it was nothing outside of the norm. But its master, Mozart's spirit, and the sounds he made into creations are at work molding into other "mechanisms" the thirst for the spirit.

The emergency, the condition intrinsic to life, is thus of a double nature: the kind which might be labeled as instrumental, *"How* can the momentum of life be sustained by the physical media?" and the kind which might be labeled as theological, *"How* can the sustained momentum find within itself the substance that will make it transcend itself, create?" If the second kind is starved into the bizarre (see the frenzy of contemporary "art"), the first will be the successful technological Frankenstein. The frills festooned around it will be made of the shredded spirit of life such frenzy represents. But if the first kind is refused, the momentum will in time dissipate itself into the frigid righteousness of a collective, just suicide. The lust for life must find the stern discipline of nature, protohuman and human, which go together in the definition of necessity, that right energizer which will transfigure necessity itself into the virtue of creation. This could seem an extraordinary demand to put on man, and indeed it is, but it is also the norm since the extraordinary is life itself and extraordinary demands have pressed from life extraordinary responses on a continuum of about 3,000 millions of years. There is no exaggeration in saying that anything animated is truly extraordinary.

But the technological Frankenstein of controlled survival technology has its own hold on the oracular. The computer, not as what it is today but as the technocrat[2] dreams of it, is the oracle of mythical times. In the Delphic oracle, the collective unconscious (Jung) was applying, while seeking, the archetypal rules in a quasi-statistical fashion. As forms in search of a content, those archetypes could find significance only in the essential absolute of the form itself made concrete in the esthetic object, a specific living tragedy, for instance. Since the oracle was not bent on deeds but on prophecies, it was statistically computerizing the next event. Its derisive grimace was to be explained by the "empty" threats of its prophecies, empty up to the moment when they reached the ears of the hero telling him he was after the impossible and making it impossible by simply telling him so. Beyond that moment the prophecies would fulfill themselves through and because of the hero's "sinful" nature. His sins would then be the cause and the atonement for his misdeeds and for the inhumanity of the oracle (the computerized statistician). Both oracle and computer work fatally as statistical simulators[3] and both are culpable of noncomprehension of the compassionate second-nature of the living. But since such second-nature is still an infant, or an "enfant terrible," both the oracle and the computer lack input from the repository of unlimited wisdom. They, therefore, fall back on the repository of "unlimited" chance, statistically structured. The hero is again doomed.

The "mystique" of the oracle-computer is irresistible, and it must be resisted. "It is right" and must be shown wrong. It is powerful, and must be stilled. It is totalitarian and must be bridled. It is in the

[2] The technocratic theologian.
[3] Fate (out of one's hands) in contraposition of destiny (one's own doing).

nature of the robot that contains us, ourselves, and must be transcended. Transcendence, not atonement, is the key to the emergence from totalitarian-mediocrity into authority.

The nature of the inner oracle is to be sought in the difference between its drive, the drive of the self (not the ego), and the statistical drive of the collective unconscious (the Delphic oracle), the drive of controlled survival technology.[4] The biological robot that contains us has tendencies sympathetic to the drives of the collective unconscious. It is one of the cogs of the big machine. The inner oracle is the germ of transcendence but is potent only when it can disentangle itself from the cacophony of the collective unconscious. Such disentanglement is the first step away from the totalitarianism of the collective unconscious toward its refinement into a constructing consciousness seeking future archetypes which do not conform to the dictums of older archetypes worn down and away by the durational currents of evolution.

[4] The best kind of maintenance is in the implementation guided by statistical information.

The Mediocrity of Intolerance

SYNOPSIS: It is paradoxical that a certain dosage of wisdom is necessary to become wise, the paradox of youth having to go about knowing. It is misleading and cruel on the part of the "teacher" to consign the world to the student on the terms that we are all created equal, that we are all innately good, that we are all creative. The consequence of such bland innocence is mediocrity and intolerance. When experience is a dirty word, the password becomes: "Do your own thing, the sooner the better."

A person is not born mediocre, but of all the traps reality puts on the path of life, the trap of mediocrity is the most frequent and the most prevalent. Rejection of a humble attitude toward the experience of growth—an experience which includes the good and the bad, the beautiful and the ugly encountered by our fathers and mothers—is a sure path to mediocrity. A mediocrity of the most rigid kind, as it is made not only of the stuff of arrogance but also of the stuff of intolerance and is locked away from compassion and is locked off from knowledge. It is important to note that such a trap increases the hold of fate on a person. This closing of an individual in the deterministic cage is antithetical to the handling of one's own destiny by dealing with the fatal, deterministic, entropic blows of life. This is so for the simple reason that arrogance and intolerance are willful states of ignorance and therefore mediocre. Such a state is binding to the senses and blinding to the mind. It is a desensitizing condition given to the fire of resentment and, with time and favorable conditions, the crushing fury of hatred (i.e., the Nazi ethos).

It is tragic to see the impetuousness of youth turn into a petrifier of itself on the spurious assumption that one has "got it all" at the outset and all that is left to do is to hammer oneself and one's brother/sister into that scheme of reference. Conservatism at such an early, green, untempered, uninformed, ignorant stage cannot but be reactionary, entropic, brutally pollutant to the life of the spirit, the life that truly shrouds, comprehensively and compassionately, all of us, the deprived, the blue-white-transparent-collar workers, the unemployed, the poor, the rich, the famined, the victims and victimizers, wise and arrogant, gentle and intolerant. One should try to begin one's own life history as a container healthy and as beautifully open as can be, genetically adaptive and able to build upon itself while filling up to capacity. As the container grows, its capacity does likewise, but the filling content (the information load from the outer) does not line up to the growing brim on what one might call a congruous schedule. Thus, as the container enlarges, the content enriches to the point where it must overflow. This overflow is a restitution, a payment of debt in new and original coins of information transformed into knowledge and possibly creation. If this were the mode, then, for instance, the challenge of the idea that an idea can withstand challenge could be given a truly open hearing. That is to say, an idea would be challenged only after it had been understood and it could not be challenged at all if such understanding were not reached. This is the old, old story of the crime done to ideas—assassination—perpetrated by people, clubs, corporations, governments, parties, etc., and it should be most repellent to the anti-establishment young.

Is the young person of today, strongly opinionated and in truth a very poor listener, better off than the meek, "gullible," ready-to-be-molded young person of tradition? Simply not. He is self-righteous, self-pitying, perhaps hypocritically sensitive to the suffering of others, but most of all, he has cast himself in an ironclad bigotry that often will destroy in him the learning, assimilative, volitional temper. Very little comes through which is not of a familiar ring, a very restricted breadth of understanding for the simple if contextual reason of being a beginner in the game. With a whole universe to learn from, with the wealth of means available for such learning, with the stern demands of durational time parceling growth at an exhilarating pace, with generosity exuding from the marrow of our bones, with so much to understand and revere, with so much existential hardship tangible and desperate, how cowardly can our junketing for self-gratification be? Such a sight in the young gives one a slight sense of existential nausea.

But in such a setting we find ourselves, if we let ourselves be caged by a limited set of values whose originators are, by this specific quality of originator, of an uncommon temper. One set of values is substituted for another: impatience instead of patience, arrogance for humility, mistrust for trust, cynicism for questioning, license for tradition, information for learning, insularity for universality, mood for discipline, change for growth, etc. Much of it is purely conceptual, as it has not had the time to become contextual and so has the stiffness of a newborn calf, the flimsiness of a house of cards, the presumption of an unrepentant self-esteem.

The critical assumption is, in fact, well hidden in the simplistic folds of presumption, arrogance, and ignorance. "As I am, the only true concern for me is me as I am." A specific fragment of youth on a grab binge. This is ignorance of the dynamics of becoming, of the slow, eventful, open, growing up. This mistrust of anyone above thirty, a classic statement of cannibalistic cynicism, is a tight corset on the soul and stunts its growth.

If one is so full of oneself because of the minimal information and experiences collected in a short lifetime and if one becomes magnetized and polarized by the magic of the mob and the sweetness of consensus, one fills with contempt and fury and shuts tight the door on any information knocking at it that does not conform to a spare (bigoted) frame of understanding. What occurs is substitution of the frame of reference, certainly imperfect, of a society of hundreds of successive generations' traditions with a frame of reference of a society one half or so generation in length, based only on the studiously weak assumption that truth has suddenly exploded within the collective heart of the generation of the sixties, chosen out of the thousands past and millions future.

Two institutions have supported and fed this diffuse state of the psyche. First, a number of intellectuals, neighbors of Spiro pseudo-intellectuals, professors, instructors, and counselors who, out of generosity, conviction, opportunism, pessimism, cynicism, or ignorance, have blown on the fire of youth and made use of its penchant for prankishness and turbulence. (Some of these exploits, panty raids and the like, often contain more wisdom than we are willing to concede.) With a poorly radicalized indignation toward the blunders of the past, and with a few skeletal models, the pounding and forming of a brittle conscience based on not-so-original molds has come to destroy past idols and institute a new mythology as saturated with conformity as the one almost gluttonously torn to shreds.

The other institution is the electronic onslaught in its double and inseparable form of linear information and nonlinear, nonconceptual information. News and images—sounds, to put it roughly—directed at soma and soul almost indiscriminately, massively, and, at least on the news side, abstractly (information not experience). It is a mix of relatively low quality: emotional, moral, economic, politic, and cultural, manipulated bits sold as hard information. Furthermore, and more seriously for the morality involved, it is often of a content that savagely and absurdly denounces the medium. The "song" reaching the person by way of sophisticated artifices, marked if not stigmatized by the same and executed through them, is an apology of primitive man, the pure, sincere, unimpaired, free, spontaneous, generous animal just outside the gates of Eden. The inner fraud cannot forever stay bottled in the retorts of techno-dollar-nouveau-barbarism-rich labs. But it is seemingly there now, as the rawhide of the young soul vibrates and reaches into the collectivized and superficial ethos of the tribe, no questions asked, no indictment dared. There is then the Dionysian and pretty gross melting in the pot of sounds and images (with pot plus drugs) and the array of indigestible, avalanching information, contradictory, fearful, irrelevant, malicious, unbelievable, disconnected, fractionalized, urging at both the guts and the temples of an arrogantly disposed youth, verbally engaged in vostra culpa mea grazia (your fault for the grace of me), destructive and hopelessly lost in garbled and utopian tirades.

Might it be of some merit to offer the idea of a withdrawal methodology, seeking to remove the person from the group into a "quiet" environment to feed on relatively little but "fertile" information, sequential and linear, given time and favorable conditions for assimilation-maturation? Though such a program might seem fairly static and incongruous with the dynamism of the information generation, it would be, possibly, a reconciliation of those dynamics which are often pure passive randomness of exterior origin, with inner dynamics, of which physiological growth is a miraculous example.

Today, self-pity and presumption are hooked to a frame of reference too shaky for comfort. And shaky it must be, as the learning process in the young has just begun and is in dire danger of being stunted by a prematurely slammed door and therefore becoming too exclusive and segregative. This confusion, the self-righteousness and scantiness of lived experience, of growing up, is the hotbed of arrogance and intolerance even if it is often hidden by a vest of gentleness and candor.

An apology of routine might be in order here since the fine art of living cannot be perceived and performed until the virtue of routine is also perceived. But the appreciation of routine comes hard to youth since time is of the essence in the ritualization of the most simple acts of which most of our lives are made. A culture is the embodiment of life routinized, and of the transcendence that will be exuded by its fitness to the human condition.

A Better Quality of Wrongness?

SYNOPSIS: Feasibility and desirability are often incompatible. A technocratic society has an irresistible penchant toward feasibility which always couples with the market feasibility, "Will it sell? We'll see to it that it does." The ethos of such society becomes dangerously mediocre, and mediocrity wears poorly with evolution. A better quality of wrongness is the passport to obsolescence and death.

(The Gross National-International Pollution)

What is the major frustration of Western man? The ability to do so much and achieve so little. The ability to manipulate so much matter, consume so much energy, and watch his own spirit wither away. Homo Faber triumphant, homo sapiens humiliated. It is, in the largest frame of reference, as if vindictive matter were set upon the destruction of the spirit. Even the political animal feels the malaise. He at least, though seldom, speaks of quality above quantity. He means that all the paraphernalia with which we surround ourselves should be better made, longer lasting, more attractive. He says that we must move from a gross gross national product to a refined gross national product of ever more massive proportions. But this might just be the advocacy of learning how to do better the wrong things, *a better quality of wrongness*. It is like wrapping a sin inside a disaster. (And there, by the way, lies some of the ambiguity of the Nader crusade.)

Must man's well-being be provided by *this* mountain of things and power or *that better* mountain of things and power? Or, is his well-being dependent on a better grasp of his participatory position in the physical and metaphysical environment, and, consequently, on his desire and capacity to act within it? Is there something to the idea that our manufactured world, this tidal wave of cunningly manipulated matter, this endless list of labor-saving devices or so-called labor-saving devices and playthings, this physical opulence, might in the long run be not a blessing but a curse?

If it is true that we, the human species among the other species, are the bridge between matter and spirit, it might stand to reason that the backpack of manipulated matter we load ourselves with can only be so heavy if we want to continue with the construction of such a bridge. A better quality of wrongness gives man an even worse handicap. It is the most massive kind of pollution, environmental and mental, we can give ourselves. It could be termed an entropic back-pack, not only carried willingly on our backs but paid for willingly by our daily toil.

We came to agree quite a while ago that the most valuable characteristic of man is his own nonspecialization. We are generalists and one of our concerns should be to keep open as many options on the future as we can. It seems, however, that we have become addicted to the specialization of dependence. Every one of our acts is dependent on a chain of instrument-energy performances which become bulkier and more unique, not in singularity, because the pride of democracy is in number, but in specialization. Even in trivia like toothbrushing or meat cutting, we advance far into the realm of umbilical cords and connections, conditioning a simple, direct act on and with a remote and polluting power source.

The more inclusive an undertaking, the greater its potential for good and evil. If such undertaking belongs to wrongness, all that it covers will contribute to more of the same wrongness. Let's consider, for example, earth-moving equipment. Each new generation of bull-dozers, scrapers, excavators, or trenachers is an improved, more beautiful group of equipment able to move more tonnage per unit of cost and energy-time. One would deduce that this is where etherealization is fostered. Unfortunately, as wrongness of purpose is the overriding force, the greater the efficiency, the greater the evil.

Our independence seems to be conditioned, glued in fact, to an ever-increasing dependence. The glue that defrauds of a clear consciousness of this dependence is money. As long as we can depend on the ability of money to keep our dependency solvent, we call ourselves independent. But it is one of the characteristics of money to keep open those cycles that do not produce immediate reward, and that is how we set up a future full of punishment. Unfortunately, reality, of which we and nature are part, does not recognize symbols. It recognizes only the dynamics which stand or fall on the foundation of the laws of mass-energy, thermodynamics, biology, etc., and the rigor of its bookkeeping is unforgiving. That is why we find ourselves living in a kind of utopian, unreal world. Our future-oriented makeup, the cantilever out from the mind, the intrinsic ability of man to plan which should insure the fullness of such future, is overloaded with a ballast of poor quality of wrongness now being challenged not by a leaner conscience but by a more self-righteous one. The qualitative upbeat will not restore the balance in favor of the spirit. It will simply put another buffer around it, another fraudulent diaphragm between dependent man and the collapse of civilization.

The cause of the collapse is the incongruence of a spirited phenomenon, man, with his unwillingness to equip himself with an effective, lean, frugal technology. It is incongruent with the limited context of the earth, with the critical dosage of physics versus metaphysics required for the best cooperation of the instrument and its master. Physics is technological know-how. Metaphysics is the reverential world of master-man.

The ecological crisis is really the crisis of the spirit and, in a way, such crises had to be expected. It is the wastefulness inherent in any pioneering venture which has lost view of its aims. Any prototype is a triumph of whatness at the expense of howness, when the effort is in the direction of desirability. It is the opposite, a triumph of howness at the expense of whatness, when such prototype is in the direction of feasibility. Much of the technological revolution went toward feasibility nurtured by and nurturing greed in a most elegant circle, while desirability became only incidental (when not purely accidental). We suffer for it now and it will take time to improve things, but things will not improve if we go on unrepentant with the arrogant goal of a better quality of wrongness.

A better quality of wrongness would have won the Vietnam war for the States, and God knows how good we were at it. Better quality wrongness would in general give more buying power to every man, woman, and child above poverty level with no telling how majestic the suicide of society would be. Better quality wrongness would give another turn of the screw for the rich to get richer and the poor to get poorer as it would make greed more rewarding. Better quality wrongness would make our economic imperialism absolute where it is now in danger of being obsolete. In general, a better quality of wrongness will be the most direct and secure road to obscurantism by way of opulence-insolvency. We have been adamant about economic insolvency. That is the pride of hard-nosed practical man. We are finding out that ecological, that is to say global, insolvency is making the future precarious. Reality is bypassing practical man. The tragedy is that reality is headless if man is not the tip of its thrust.

There is no realism whatsoever in our struggle for an environmental future if we do not conceptualize our predicament radically enough. At the root of the dilemma is the sorcery of ours, the ability and proficiency we have for doing the wrong thing, mass-producing wrongness. Optimal marketability stands for the most massive kind of pollution-entropy. In its bulk, it implicates the physical and in its sinfulness it implicates the metaphysical. With this proficiency in wrongness, we are confronted by the coincidence of two enemies of life: entropy and pollution. Entropy, which is the pollution of life, is also the nemesis of the living environment. To grasp such a relationship is to see the futility of our antipollution, proenvironment contentions. They concern themselves only with the fringes of the existential dilemma, not with the meat of it. Nor can we act effectively on those fringes if we do not realize that they are fringes. To state it once more, pollution is not the by-products or wastes of our technological cycles. It is too often the technological cycle itself and the hardware it produces. Greed easily joins entropy and pollution, as nothing fosters greed more than the open market of free enterprise where open and free are pseudonyms for monopolized and coerced.

This massive production of antilife is nothing else but the materialization of that which wants to move even further on the path of etherealization: the spirit of man. It has an inner nemesis which stipulates that more goes where the most is already: the western enclaves and only the affluent in these enclaves. It also has an outer nemesis which is the predisposition to a global catastrophe where innocent and guilty will perish indiscriminately. Practicality is not the key to a resolution. Practicality has brought about the crisis and it will ever more engulf life in the morass of nonlife. The key is in the reality of evolutionary coherence, which states that more is more only when, consequent to a quantum jump, it can be achieved with less, which is to say, when spirit has overtaken another province of matter. This happens and can happen only by the power of complexity when life becomes richer by imploding itself into a new organism able to sustain itself with less of itself and less of the outer.

How perfectly this quantum jump fits the global crisis of today can be immediately seen. Only by cutting drastically the demands we impose on the planet can we imagine a hopeful future. Such hope would be destroyed if the cutting would entail a degradation of life. But just as so many times before in the evolutionary process, when necessity becomes a virtue, life becomes better than itself. Necessity is frugality which can only find unequivocal ground on equity. The virtue is an intensity of life never reached before. The methodology for this miracle, as for the myriads of preceding miracles, is the miniaturization process. Pragmatism fails man if he cannot see the starkness and the necessity of this methodology.

Let's just say that the living is a phenomenon of communication of information which gives access to knowledge, that immaterial stuff which allows, through evolutionary stages, a response to become a conscience. This is the secret of the identity of complexity and conscience, therefore, the virtue of miniaturization. Here lies the possibility of a quantum jump, the gate capable of carrying affluence into grace so as to make it ecologically and ethically fit. This is the electrifying sense of the methodology of life showing us the straight connection between matter and spirit. Taking matter as outerness, each particle of matter is exterior to all others and interacts with them statistically. Taking spirit as innerness, a sort of polarization of the same particles makes them participatory beyond the statistical rules. It is, in simple terms, as if at a certain point a mechanical process would find itself incapable of fulfilling its own deterministic aims because too many digits have appeared. At that critical stage, process ceases, determinism breaks down, and life begins. With it the outer imposition of determinism itself retreats into the environment to become one half of life's maker, the environment, the other half now being the organism in its inner self. Consciousness then appears as an interiorized universe, as maker and creator of a new universe of the spirit. *This interiorization process is at the threshold of making the cityscape, now only the exterior environment of the city dweller, into an interiority, the interiorized context of the transorganism the city will become. This is a quantum jump and cannot come about if complexity-miniaturization is not forcefully operating.*

The key unlocking one by one the doors on the universe of consciousness is the limitless capacity of the organic phenomenon to move from the most elementary organization of matter, so elementary as to be ambiguous (a virus for instance), to the compound miracle of man and his mind by the instrumentality of complexity and miniaturization. It is as if beyond a critical level of complexity, mass-energy metamorphoses into organic psychism. Inherent in the metamorphosis is the relative minuteness of the organism, that is to say, its absolute miniaturization. For this most pragmatic of all extant things, the universe of the spirit, the better quality of wrongness is pure unadulterated pollution. It is entropy grinding away at the core of life itself. The inability to grasp this hardest of all hard facts stultifies all our undertakings and puts life itself in jeopardy. An adoption of this proven methodology (three billion or so years of development) would not only strike at the core of our problems but would transfigure the earth into a more and more spirited phenomenon.

Taking our cities as one of the more critical aspects of the environmental-spiritual crisis, one could say that if a benevolent God were to take things in hand, he would have two archangels hovering above. The first archangel would siphon off from the city all that which is punishing man, all that which is dead and entropically oriented—a depollution of the organism of the city. The most massive element of such pollution is the automobile cancer, now intimately and dogmatically fused with even the most private events of our society. With it would be taken out the myriads of pollutant futilities that, confronted with the dread facing most of mankind, do not speak kindly of our souls. This depollution, an asentropic surgery, would leave voids throughout our cityscape. This is where the second archangel, the archangel of reverence, could come in and restructure the city into something far smaller, far swifter, frugal, ecologically fitting and humanly alive, solvent, mindful, hopeful, and reverential, *an environmental fragment of a better quality of rightness*. The arcological commitment is one step in that direction.

Nominal Freedom, Contextual Coercion

SYNOPSIS: De facto coercion is routinely accepted as part of the social contract to which we belong. Within such de facto coercion we cut our niche of freedom, seldom questioning the legitimacy or equity of the law of the land (real estate regulations, restrictions, etc.). The price tag of freedom is expressed by the license (sanctioned or not) one gets away with. It is a poor brand of freedom, subservient to the rules of the "free" market.

To Those Nations Still Immune to the Automobile Curse

With all the honesty and candor Western man can muster, he can't escape his contradictory position of exploiter and benefactor (medicine, agriculture, communication, qualified technology), he must avoid indulgence in the black magic of can do–must do. Feasibility seldom coincides with desirability. As exploiter, the only road to atonement, if not redemption, is to pay personally for the wrongdoing before self-righteousness makes him expect the rest of the world to follow suit. That such voluntary contrition might handicap him vis-à-vis the developing countries is a necessary element in their catching-up process. It is a moral imperative. It is right and rational that Zambian smokestacks be dirtier than Pittsburgh's *if* this has to be part of the price for the development of Zambia.

But in the environmental context, giving the worldwide question of equity all the merit and effort due it, the solutions we offer to the problems we face as a species still fundamentally beg the questions. One of the clearest instances of a nonanswered question having consequences of the most pervasive and negative nature is the automobile-pollution-destruction equation. That the automobile as now used is the single most destructive invention for the undoing of urban life, and ultimately our whole civilization, is at best only hinted at. That in the automobile the force of pollution as an entropic undoer of life is most highly concentrated and most powerful is also not seriously considered. In hypocritical rage the battle is waged on the amount of pollutants emitted by the exhaust pipe, as if to kill the dragon (the true pollution) a mask on his snout would do the job. This is as honest as trying to cure a moribund organism infected with bug-sized viruses, a herd of 200 million in rolling stock and all the paraphernalia belonging to them, by filtering the breath of their broken-down lungs.

Will we ever regain our senses and see what is so plainly and pervasively ordering us around for what it is: the cancer of entropy welcomed by us, life, within the folds of life itself? It is, in this case, the sum of all the protean modes of the car: the car itself and the colossal road network, especially inside the cities (it chills the blood to watch Russia plunging recklessly into the car era), the oil refineries, the energy depletion, the oil tankers and pipelines, trains and trucks, the oil wars, the Detroits, the car strips, the parking lots and garages, the gas stations, the insurance companies, the moneylenders, the medical bills, the broken lives, the mystic shows, the segregated topographies, the junkyards, the toil for naught, and, most critical and crippling of all, the physical structure of the cities themselves. All of it for what? Listen to this, all of it is for the specific and official purpose of bringing people and things to the threshold of their performance, that is to say, to the point at which they can begin to do and to be what they want to be and to do. Can anyone sane and free subscribe to such madness? The answer is no. Or the answer is we are neither sane nor free. As a footnote, it has to be said that the automobile can be defeated only in those places where it physically cannot get in—the environment that has no place for highways, roads, and streets: the roadless, three-dimensional city. It is pure fantasy to believe otherwise.

I do not speak metaphysics. I speak the pragmatism of the spirit, that is to say, I speak mass-energy in the process of making itself into spirit. That happens to be the extant reality, the only one available to man, the only truly human one. I speak bootstrap physics, physics that by its bootstraps pulls itself beyond itself: the mineral ecology of this earth at the beginning of its evolution transforming itself into the noosphere of today, the current human ecology. If the politician and the economist, the technologist and the behaviorist, the doctor and the scholar speak of something else, that is our mutual hard luck. Man and the living world are the bridge between matter and spirit. Man is, in fact, matter becoming spirit. The whole of this world is now engaged in this most momentous genesis: mineral, vegetal, animal, and human kingdoms in a converging and well-documented effort four billion years young. One should not trust a planner or a leader who does not subscribe to such irrefutable fact. To subscribe to it is to think and act to reinforce this spiritualization process in every instance: Bangladesh, dereliction, Playboy party, tax policies,

bugging, satellite spying, gross national pollution, Forest Lawn, genocide, planned parenthood, vegetarianism, Lib, etc.

Notwithstanding all conceivable differences between problems in
size, impact, pervasiveness, structure, background, or reference, they
are fundamentally the same: the processing of physical mass-energy
into the transphysical, spirit. This applies to the virus, the algae, the
spider, the eagle, and man. Short of such understanding, we are cut
off from reality, and although we may be strenuously dedicated, chin-
deep in practical matters, we are brutally cheating ourselves. The
linkage by which the physical becomes the transphysical is the history of the world itself. The need to identify this linkage intel-
lectually has been part and parcel of man's struggle with himself and
with the world. The impetus for the search goes beyond the thirst for
knowledge and beyond the opportunism of instrumentalization. The
central reason, conscious or not, has been the attempt to subdue the
existential anguish of the species. We do not as yet, as common man,
recognize the depth of such anguish. Our fragmentary efforts de-
nounce the callousness we apply in comprehending ourselves.

The paradox of the spirit is that to fully realize itself the whole of
the physical cosmos has to be processed and sublimated. Short of
such metamorphosis, the spirit is but a fragment of its potential self.
Therefore, the presence of anguish and, on the faking side, the culti-
vation of skepticism or cynicism as a manageable shield against it.
Short of solid congruence with the truth that man *is* the actual development, witnessed by every one of us, of matter becoming spirit (and
how sanguine such becoming is), the future is dim, highly hypothetical, and the anguish unabatable. All the pragmatism that practical man can muster cannot even come close to the pragmatism implicit in the consciousness of this etherealization process and its
driving force. It is, one must repeat, the pragmatism of the life of the
earth, the whole four billion years of it.

If this earth experience does not present us with a readable methodology, skeletal as it may be, then nothing else really can, certainly
not the inventive power of our young minds. In fact, the absence of
methodology would mean that nothing really matters, neither pain
nor joy, and the living world would be simple causelessness, blind
and furiously deterministic. That such methodology does exist and
that its mandatory demands might put our souls out of balance is
only testimony to the debilitating confusion of our present history.

To soften the preemptive tone of such methodology is to misread nature and its rigor and take refuge once more in unreal guidance systems, free enterprise being one. It is true that once the methodology is accepted, we can attempt and possibly succeed in coordinating the details: social, cultural, economic, political, administrative, productive, etc., because then their converging nature would be ascertained and an appropriate course of action could be determined. But if fear and conceptual segregation push logic into a corner, acquiescence will cut off our capacity to move. Such a position is not only reprehensible, it is also destructive as it breaks down the connection between the individual and the matrix of his being through incongruence within himself and incongruence with the world from which he originates. Diffidence or indifference toward an idea that affirms the convergence of needs and aims, of consciousness and congruence, of ideal and real, of physical and metaphysical, can be rationalized and eventually dispelled only if impatience and self-pity, conceit and arrogance do not sever the threads of continuity in the process of the logic of one's own making in deference to the iron logic of evolving reality.

The methodology I am speaking of is expressed in these statements:

1) Consequent to the fortuitous or divine triggering of life, the universe of mass-energy is in the process of etherealizing itself into spirit.

2) Intrinsic to this metamorphosis of mass-energy into spirit is the ever-increasing complexity of the systems carrying on the transformation, primary among them, man.

3) The sine qua non spatial mechanism of putting more into less, allowing for the incremental growth of complexity, is the miniaturization process.

4) On this earth, the most comprehensive structure embodying the becoming of etherealization is the city, the invention and creation of homo sapiens.

5) Thus, the city, this etherealization machine, is rigorously governed by the physioenergetic rules of complexity-miniaturization.

6) Among the many options offered to contemporary man, the complex-miniaturized city is the least optional inasmuch as it is mandatory for the spirit of the earth.

7)   The city is a social, cultural, economic, moral, and political imperative and, under the current demographic pressure, it is also a survival necessity.

8)   This gives the lie to most of our priorities and demythologizes practical man (as his paradigms are bankrupt) if it is true that real man is the man of the spirit.

Generally, the following paradigm can be stated:

A)   In any given system, the liveliest (duration) quantum is also the most complex.

B)   In any given system, the most complex quantum is also the most miniaturized.

For a mechanistic universe, the complexity-miniaturization (duration) paradigm would stand for the what, the why, and the how. For a nonmechanistic universe, the complexity-miniaturization (duration) paradigm stands as a necessary but not sufficient condition. That is to say, it stands for a mandatory how. For both of them the paradigm is a *must* toward a higher order of things. This higher order of things includes the eradication of poverty, coercion, disease, intolerance, bigotry, hatred, segregation, etc. To connect the condition of man to the implications of this paradigm, I make the following comparisons. By these I am also denouncing the make-believe of our daily life, its pretense of self-determination, and at the same time pointing out how much this pretension costs each one of us regardless of color, location, nation, political environment, etc.

1. a)   If a tyrant forbids me to visit a friend, I say that he deprives me of my rights.

   b)   If twenty miles of traffic congestion and frustration, the cost of which I bear, separates us and deprives me of my friend, I say that's life, but I still am a free man.

2. a)   If big brother says my children are not good enough for good schooling, I say I am the slave of a monster.

   b)   If the city is such that a good school is too distant and too costly for my children to attend, I say that's life in a free society.

3. a)   If a dictator orders me to buy a car to fill the coffers of corporation X, I say my freedom is impaired.

   b)   If I find out that my survival is conditioned by the purchase of an automobile, I say that is part of life, even though I am a free man.

4. a)   If a bad genie orders me around in circles every morning and evening for perhaps fifteen miles before getting to my work or home, I say I am prisoner of a cruel God.

   b)   If that is what I do morning and evening three hundred days per year to get to work and back, I say that that is the life of a free man, after all.

5. a)   If a mobster compels me to buy his expensive garbage collection service, I say he blackmails me through my health.

   b)   If the tax collector gets from me the same extortionary price for garbage removal, I say that is life, though I am a free man.

6. a)   If the oligarchy refuses me health care, I die in sorrow and pain, an indictment of the cruelty of man toward man.

   b)   If it is simply in the nature of things that I cannot afford hospitalization and care, I say that I lived and died free.

7. a)   If a bureaucrat forbids me to attend events and performances and cuts me off from the cultural-social cornucopia, I say it must be a nightmare.

   b)   If, though the cornucopia is said to be there, I cannot find ways and means of getting at it, I say that is my luck, a free man, hard luck.

8. a)   If the government tells me magazines and journals will be turned off, I say my right of free speech is trod upon.

   b)   If the mailing cost, out of demented priorities and logistics, kills the press, I say there are things even a free man must do without.

9. a)   If a wicked witch orders me to crank out tons of soot each year by burning barrels of black tar, I say life is insane.

   b)   If that is what I produce in pollution while going about the business of survival, I say that is part of the existential picture.

10. a)   If the maniac up there makes me roll carpets of cement and asphalt over houses and gardens, towns and fields, I say madness is controlling my life.

    b)   If that is what I do because, consciously and willfully, I place the things I cherish and need farther and farther away, farther and farther apart, and I must get to them somehow, I say that this is the assertion of my rugged individualism.

11. a) If, in general, the totalitarian who orders me around isolates me from things, institutions, and persons I desire and need, and if, in addition, the few things I can do have a price tag which makes my action unacceptable to the earth (such as the burning of the fossil fuels at exponential rates for demented reasons), I say I am prisoner of an evil order.

b) If, in general, I find that an identical isolation and deprivation is inherent and contextual to the environment I am in, I say that it is my existential situation.

One might forgive such twisted reasoning as there is a trace of truth in the fact that willful evil is worse than faceless, unplanned cruelty, yet the only evil that can and must be accepted is the evil of fate, that which weighs on each of us and cannot be warped by the destiny we battle for. When fate is of our own making, it is not fate anymore, it is coercion, punishment, deprivation, and the curtailment of self-determination. It becomes too absurd for words and deeds when the proposition that these and all similar conditions can be rectified by the reordering of our physical environment. It is almost automatically branded as antidemocratic. The environment is a structure of finite character with definite demands as to its performance. Therefore, with the logic of a chicken, the rugged individualist, rather than putting an ear to the beat of an alternative unknown (as frightening as the sky caving in), prefers to remain ostentatiously "free," knowing inside how deceptive his pretension is and how costly to himself and society is this purely nominal freedom.

This conscious or unconscious hypocrisy cannot be sustained forever. In fact, things have been giving way badly enough and for a sufficient time now to make such posture a crime against humanity. The exodus into suburbia, this withdrawal of society from itself, is a gigantic step backward into isolation and segregation unless it is followed by a forceful reversal and the return of society to truly lovable cityscapes. Busing, the anguish it causes, and the marketing of the issue for political profiteering are but a by-product of the drama pitting nominal freedom against pragmatic coercion with neither side giving a second thought to the fact that given the urban-suburban structure of today, the war is lost before the battles are fought, lost by both sides. The whole ship, blacks, whites, yellows, greens, grays, is sailing away from home into no-man's-land, into the pollution of entropy, away from the spirit.

To object to the preceding with the contention that the conditions considered here are confined to the North American continent and Europe is to fail to understand that those are the models the whole of mankind wants or will want to emulate. The folly of such a dream must haunt our waking hours and make us do a 180° turn, from explosion to implosion, from entropy-pollution to asentropy-life. Taking the city as the environment toward which the bulk of the earth's population gravitates, and calling arcology the environmental, ecological architecture which intentionally applies the complexity-miniaturization paradigm (methodology of evolution), one can state the following arcological commitment:

The arcological commitment is not indispensable for:

1) The alleviation of the ecological crisis, although it is that.
2) The redimensioning of our use of land, air, water, although it is that.
3) The reduction of the pollution caused by technological societies, although it is that.
4) The perception of the nature of waste, affluence, opulence, although it is that.
5) A reasonable sheltering of man as his number moves toward eight billion or more, although it is that.
6) Resolving the problem of energy depletion, distribution, consumption, although it is that.
7) Resolving the problem of segregation of people, things, activities, although it is that.
8) Responding to the increasing encroachment of remoteness by way of gigantic services and their bureaucracies, although it is that.
9) A renewed trust in the future of life in general and man in particular, although it is that.

Most generally, the arcological commitment is not indispensable because it is the best instrument for survival, although it is that.

All these are remedial reasons, important for man but only instrumental to the specific humaneness sought by him. They are manutentive and restorative. They are not specifically creative. By their implementation, the refund of health to man and earth will never be a substitute for grace, but only a threshold to id.

The arcological commitment is indispensable because it advocates a physical system that consents to the high compression of things, energies, logistics, information, and performances. It fosters the thinking, doing, living, learning, playing in human, urban settings that are the essential, critical, vibrant phenomenon of life at its most lively and compassionate, the state of grace (esthetogenesis) possible for a socially and individually healthy man on an ecologically healthy earth.

Prefuture and Its Perils
(Oversimplification)

═══════════

SYNOPSIS: The anticipatory act is planning. If man gives up anticipation he endorses the notion of fate (or providence). The planning
of the technologist rivets its attention on the anticipation of determinism. The planning of the compassionate man focuses its attention
on the anticipation of transcendence.

We, homo sapiens, have used only a fraction of the possible life trajectory in this solar system; according to some calculations, less than $\frac{1}{2200}$ of it. We can be seen as the latest product of a long past (several billion years), a past which in its totality is nothing but the beginning point of an immense perspective losing itself in the darkness of times and spaces to be. The more we become conscious of our potential evolutionary position, that most of reality (2,200 times the past) has yet to realize itself, the more we find ourselves forced into living in and off the future. It is not only the question of what tomorrow or the day after tomorrow will bring, but of how our present is molded by that which does not yet exist.

We foretaste the future in every act composing our lives: the meal we will consume, the journey we will take . . . We plan these events and we sense them before, at times years before, they become the present. This foretaste is often better than the real thing. The present becomes, thus, the prefuture and this prefuture is the context in which we act, whenever we act as self-conscious creatures. In fact, one can say that while the plant and the animal live in the present, man lives in the prefuture. This is so because planning, which is part of the future frame, is performed genetically in the vegetal and animal kingdom; it is performed genetically and culturally by man. It is this cultural frame that projects the universe of man into the future. To "live for today because that is the only thing we have" is renunciation of the human character, and true senselessness.

More comprehensively, one can say that for the mineral world past and future are one, as the rationality of its existence is given, unchangeable, a priori, and things work out according to the law of CONSERVATION OF ENERGY. For the vegetal and animal world the present is all that matters because that is where the action is and has been made possible by life's past inventions. There, life is a process of CONCENTRATION OF ENERGY. For the human world the past is the launching pad for prefuture performances according to man's planning and according to the laws of INCREMENTATION OF ENERGY.

To clarify these assertions, I might observe that the geological stuff in its cosmic bulk obeys a set of deterministic laws. By being under such discipline it has no options but to be what it is and to do so eternally. The cosmic process is thus defined a priori in agreement with the peculiarities of matter-energy.

For the living world there is a durational engrossment and an accumulative bulk of its by-products. Even physically, this bulk might take on astronomical dimensions. The world of fossils is there to document it. This biobulk, accumulated from the beginning of life on the planet by the turnover of the biological mass, has indeed achieved enormous proportions. It could probably constitute a satellite the size of a moon (or many!?).

Of this mass, a quintessence is preserved and present within the mass-energy cycle of any and every instant of the planet. The complexity of the living phenomenon is, in fact, the exact equivalent (in psychomental terms) of the biobulk of history. As an instant compendium of the immense biopsychological chain of the living, it balances in durational terms that part of the physical cosmos it has uncovered, manipulated, and complexified up to the present instant. In addition, and as a physical counterpart of such complexity, is the miniaturization process by which quasi-identical quanta of performance find paths of realization within ever-smaller fractions of matter-energy, space, and time. This concentration of energy, as if around magnetic centers to which biological creatures can be compared, achieves a new quality in the human world, in agreement with its own created law of the incrementation of spirit.

Recapitulating the whole process, it is as if a God would gather tenuously related matter in his hands and by powerfully compressing it would distill its quintessence, the spirit, and through billions of times-years, increase drop by drop the content of the vats of life within which the spirit itself proposes new structures and new organizations. Structures and organizations are the matrix all along the evolutionary path, and the newest stage is always a synopsis of the spirit of all the preceding, carrying in comparatively smaller bulks more vitality, more thrust, and a more subtle etherealized message, the becoming of spirit itself.

To ask what this has to do with the predicaments of man is life questioning the connection between a loaf of bread on the table and the wheat of the field. The bread in such process is only an early station on the road from matter to spirit.

Science is the device by which intelligent life constructs itself along the evolutionary path. The danger in this process of higher and higher synthesis is that applied science is the oversimplifier that breaks down achieved synopsis into analyzable fragments, an act that cannot but leave them dispirited unless the information acquired by the analytical process originates a fuller synthesis (synopsis). Indeed, the cycle opened by analysis is per se an unwinding of life. There is such a thing as the analytical glare which induces blindness, and often the prized analytical quest is not really used as a research instrument but as an armored vehicle, a self-propelled ivory tower.

The distinction between the becoming of life and the processes of technology is frequently not made. We tend to take the fruits of analysis in the raw and with applied science produce oversimplified answers to our many problems, real and imaginary.

The change syndrome that this oversimplification induces in all facets of the social structure puts even more emphasis on the quick rotation of things and the process of obsolescence that accompanies such rotation. In this way, we put ourselves in the position of a listener having only one audition for every musical composition. This has two consequences: 1) The composer sees no reason to be seriously committed to quality; and 2) As it is quite impossible to perceive in the first audition the message of the music, since the message comes through only with familiarization with the piece, allowing the mind to distinguish between soul and extravagance, we remain perceptionally and emotionally separated from the object of our attention, a case where oversimplification enters the soul and stills its pleas.

But oversimplification characterizes planning. We are thus confronted with the dilemma of planning by necessity and thus running the risk of living an oversimple prefuture.

The technology of nature and its planning differs from the technology of man and his planning, as the first is incapable of abstraction. It is indeed experimental and nonanalytical (it is nonplanning, infinitely older than the mind, proportionately wiser but not proportionately more compassionate). By contrast, the planning of the mind deals with symbols and conceptual elements. It is capable of defining the future only by the force of its abstraction.

What we demand from the technological process is concentration on one task at a time and peeling everything away from the given problem until the naked black or white dilemma is unraveled at the core. This allows a good degree of efficiency but puts coarseness into the solution. Some instances:

The bone: Extreme hunger makes one seek the marrow of a found bone. Survival makes the handling of the stone that will crush the bone into a narrowly single-minded tour de force, a contest between the hardness of the bone and the fury of one's hunger. None of the subtle pleasures of the table are present.

The icebox: Life arrested is decomposition-prone. We conglomerate the many unwelcome facets of decomposition in the simple and schematic solution of refrigeration, of keeping the breakdown within the not-too-toxic, not-too-noxious area, so the produce remains stable and edible. We all do this, all of us Westerners.

The gun: Dislike for the adversary is simplified in the impulse to crush his image. Thus, one concentrates one's fury into a steel-encased slug of lead, one's simplified dislike, which can be propelled to crush the adversary.

The My Lai killer puts to rest anything that moves . . . pigs, babies, mothers, and old people. The killer has become technology-triumphant, a robotized psyche.

We always delegate to technological proficiency a narrow band of a rounded reality. In so doing, we exonerate the technological act from the duration-living frame. As a substitute, we use a metronomic time beat, the ticker of the teletype instead of the voice of a person, the abrasiveness of the power-sander instead of the caressing of the craftsman's handstroke. It is quite evident that this oversimplification is essential and necessary for the sake of performance in every instrumental field: flying, printing, constructing, etc. At the same time, this protohuman character of oversimplification imperils life in the act of serving it. At every turn, technology is per se a decomposer, the bull in the china shop. Because of its amorality, its fracturing sways, the technological act must find atonement in the consciousness of the maker and the user. For its power of decomplexification within the complex living event, the technological act must be kept in a guarded context. For its inability to be a becoming and its ability to produce change, the technological act does not partake of life but only of its instrumentalization. We must beware of the process and its limitations.

We can, for instance, produce and mass-produce plastic plants. We can reproduce any of the many stages in their growth, but we cannot fake growth itself, as there is a whole universe of difference between the technological process of imitating vegetation and the durational becoming of a leaf. In a sense, technology is at best only a faking of becoming; the often innocent fraud is indeed a potential undoer of duration. To observe that the fake flower is not a performing instrument points to the necessity of containing technology in its own legitimate, instrumental world, as the false flower performs a function and does so fraudulently.

The observation of an event of becoming breaks also the past-present-future categories it develops in, because the event itself is an uninterrupted phenomenon coming from the past, acting into the present of which it is the maker, and working itself into the future. But why is it that process cannot be identified with becoming? It is because process is manipulation by outer imposition. Indeed, it is difficult to find its originating thrust, as the causes are not ends in themselves but are functions of something else (this characterizes instrumentality). And it is because becoming is growth. It originates inwardly. For becoming, there is a magnet stationed at the center of the phenomenon, a magnet attuned to other magnets, themselves at the core of their own phenomena. Thus, process is an outer manipulation of matter-energy. Becoming is growth from within nourishing itself with matter-energy.

When biology turns to technology, it gains in sharpness and loses in depth, it gains in specialization (analytical fruitfulness) and increases in manipulative power. But it opens the chasms of a lost innocence around life itself. Only a biotechnique inflamed with the spirit of man has the power of discrimination between good and evil and the welcome ability to carry on its tasks of life instrumentalization.

Experimentation (as experience) in biotechnology might reconcile man to the ways of nature and the ways of complexity. It might give him the means to act in the prefuture without making the juncture of the present become the living simulation of a reality that will never articulate itself in flesh and blood but only in gray phantoms.